THE BEAD DIRECTORY

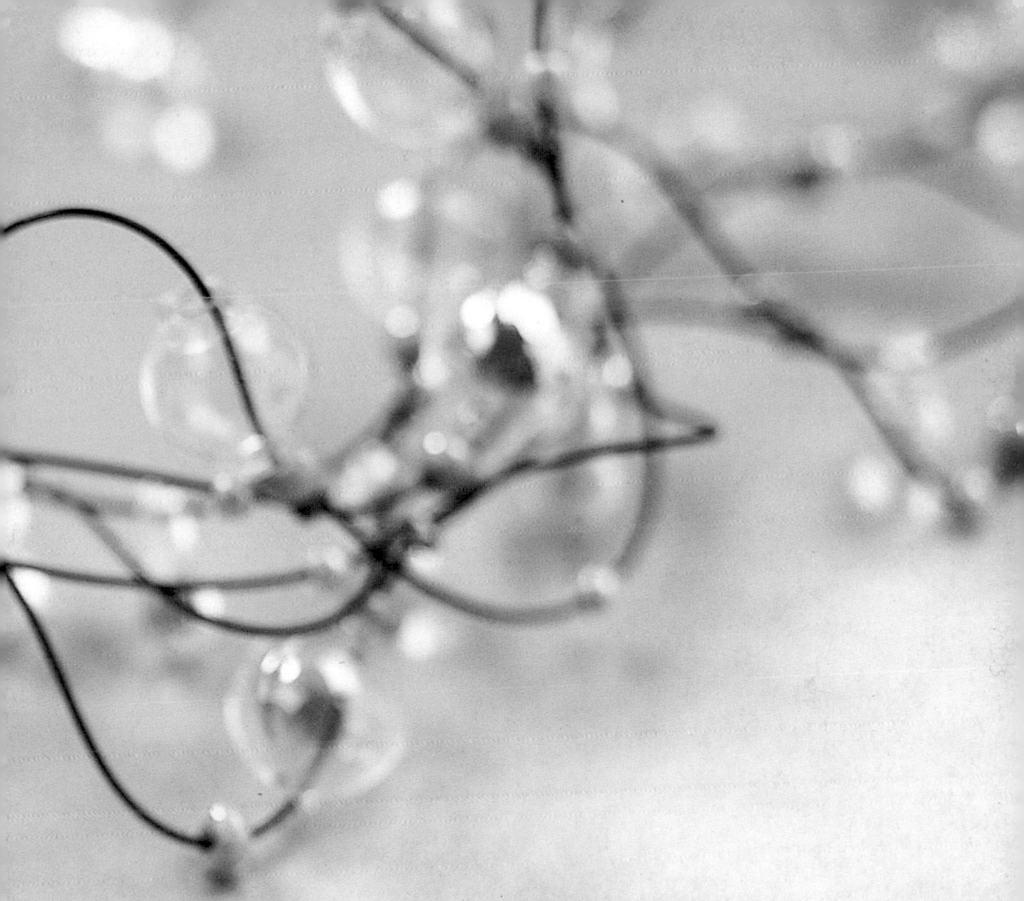

THE BEADDIRECTORY

THE COMPLETE GUIDE TO CHOOSING AND USING MORE THAN 600 BEAUTIFUL BEADS

ELISE MANN

A QUARTO BOOK

Published in North America by

INTERWEAVE PRESS

Interweave Press LLC
201 East Fourth Street
Loveland, CO 80537-5655, USA
www.interweave.com

Library of Congress Cataloging-in-Publication Data
Mann, Elise.
The bead directory: the complete guide to choosing and using more than 600 beautiful beads / Elise Mann, author.
p. cm.
Includes index.
ISBN 1-59668-002-4
1. Beadwork. 2. Beads. I. Title.
TT860.M295 2006
745.58'2--dc22
2005024503

QUAR.BSBI

Conceived, designed, and produced by
Quarto Publishing plc
The Old Brewery
6 Blundell Street
London N7 9BH

Project Editors Susie May, Karen Koll
Art Editor Anna Knight
Assistant Art Director Penny Cobb
Designer Louise Clements
Copy Editor Christine Vaughan
Proofreader Claire Waite Brown
Photographer Martin Norris
Illustrator Kuo Kang Chen
Indexer Pamela Ellis
Art Director Moira Clinch
Publisher Paul Carslake

Manufactured by Universal Graphics, Singapore
Printed by Midas Printing International Limited, China

10 9 8 7 6 5 4 3 2 1

Contents

Foreword 6
How to use this book 8

BEAD DIRECTORY 10

Chapter 1 12 Glass

Chapter 2 66 Crystal

Chapter 3 80 Semiprecious

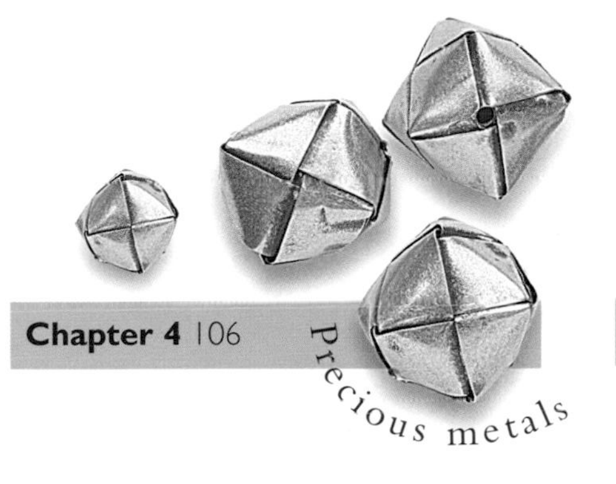

Chapter 4 106 Precious metals

Chapter 5 134 Base metals

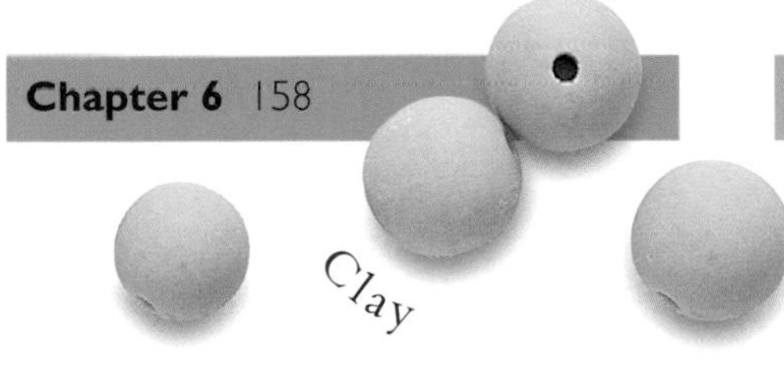

Chapter 6 158 Clay

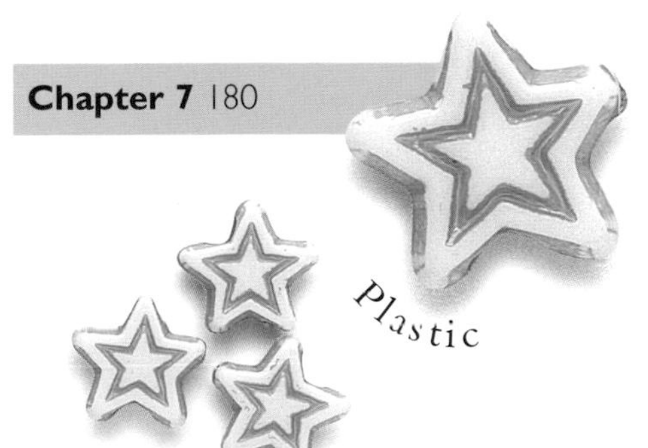

Chapter 7 180 Plastic

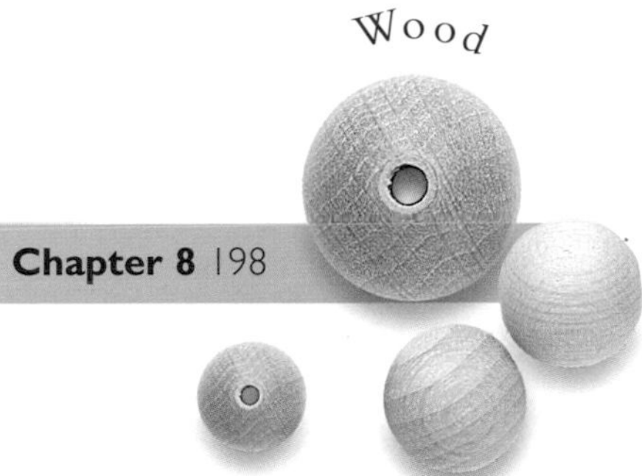

Chapter 8 198 Wood

Chapter 9 210 Other natural materials

Chapter 10 230 Other materials

Chapter 11 236 Findings

How to buy beads 248

Index 252

Sources and credits 256

Foreword

What exactly is a bead? The consensus among beadworkers seems to be that a bead is "any item with a hole in it, worn purely for decorative purposes."

This excludes buttons when they are used to fasten things but includes them when they are sewn on for visual effect only and can also include items such as sequins and even washers and lock-nuts. This book, however, covers only those items that are sold as beads, to limit the types just a little.

At the time of writing, the earliest known beads (as defined above) are probably the drilled shells found in the Blombos Cave, east of Cape Town, and dated to about 75,000 years ago. These show signs of wear, indicating that they were once strung and worn, probably as adornment. Beads have a very long history!

What is it that attracts so many of us to beads? In modern times, the huge variety of colors and shapes available allows the beadworker to produce any style of jewelry: these

versatile little objects can awaken creativity and express individuality. The following pages aim to inspire bead artists, from beginners to professionals, by illustrating this variety and versatility.

This book is intended to help you choose beads that are easily available in stores and by mail order and gives you lots of information about them. A few designer, handmade beads are also included: these are usually found at specialist suppliers or can be bought direct from the artist.

Throughout the book, spherical beads are referred to as "round" and cylindrical beads as "tubes" because that is how most people seem to think of them. For the mix-and-match sets, the examples shown include other beads, in suitable colors, from elsewhere in the book: in many cases, different shaped beads in the same colors would work equally well. Some unlikely looking combinations have also been deliberately included with the intention of sparking some ideas.

How to use this book

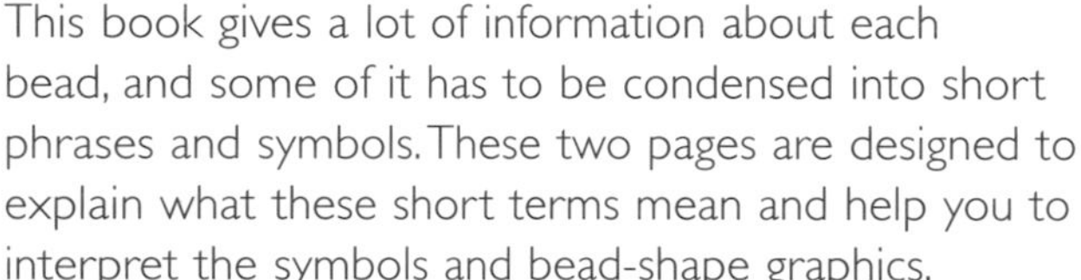

This book gives a lot of information about each bead, and some of it has to be condensed into short phrases and symbols. These two pages are designed to explain what these short terms mean and help you to interpret the symbols and bead-shape graphics.

Chapter name: *The material of each bead in the section*

Number and bead name: *The number indicates the bead's position within the book*

HOW THE BOOK IS ORGANIZED

The beads are arranged in chapters according to material and within the chapters by shape, starting with round beads and moving on through ovals, tubes, and so on, with the most irregular or unusual shapes (such as animal beads) at the end of each chapter.

Bead shape: *When strung, and hole direction*

Bead shape: *Looking straight at hole, and hole position*

2 **Relative weight for size:** *On a scale of 1–5. 1 is very light, 5 very heavy.*

3 **Relative cost:** *1 is the cheapest, 5 the most expensive*

60 **Ruler:** *How many beads on a thread 10 inches (25cm) long*

- Glass
- Crystal
- Semiprecious
- Precious metals
- Base metals
- Clay
- Plastic
- Wood
- Other natural materials
- Other materials
- Findings

18 **Glass**

5 ROUND CAT'S EYE

This glass has a property called chatoyancy, which causes it to reflect light in an unusual way: in this case a band of light, rather like the pupil of a cat's eye, shows around the middle of the bead. The band shows up most clearly on deep colors and rounded shapes, but pale and flatter cat's eye beads are also available.

3 3 32

Hole: *Small*
Stringing: *Fine tiger tail or medium thread*
Weight: *0.8g*
Other sizes: *2mm, 4mm, 6mm, 10mm*
Color range: *Medium*
Length: *8mm*
Width: *8mm*
Depth: *8mm*

Actual size

Mix and match 406 369

6 PEARL

The pearl coating on glass beads is usually of a higher quality than that on plastic pearls, but if it is not, it may rub or peel off if scratched. Glass pearls are available in more colors and shapes than real pearls, but of course they do not have quite the same feel and luster.

3 3 32

Hole: *Small*
Stringing: *Fine tiger tail or medium thread*
Weight: *0.4g*
Other sizes: *Many*
Color range: *Medium*
Length: *8mm*
Width: *8mm*
Depth: *8mm*

Actual size

Mix and match 593 463

7 LUSTER COATED

Opaque luster coatings on glass usually show two or more deep colors, and seem to glow softly when light falls on them. They are unlikely to rub or flake off. The base bead is often black glass. If a whole strand is too intense, the simplest solution is to add colorless glass to pick up and transmit some of the colors.

3 3 28

Hole: *Medium*
Stringing: *Medium tiger tail or heavy thread*
Weight: *1.2g*
Other sizes: *4mm, 6mm, 8mm*
Color range: *Medium*
Length: *9mm*
Width: *10mm*
Depth: *10mm*

Actual size

Mix and match 77 373

Bead data

Bead images: *A close-up of bead and a scatter shot showing several of the same beads from different angles—either one shows the bead at actual size*

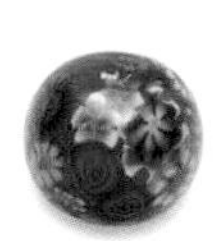

Hole: *Small*
Stringing: *Fine tiger tail or medium thread*
Weight: *0.3g*
Other sizes: *4mm, 8mm, 10mm*
Color range: *Large*
Length: *5.5mm*
Width: *6mm*
Depth: *6mm*

Text: *Information about the bead*

Glass 19

8 DRUK
Druk beads are made in the Czech Republic. They are pressed glass, but no seam lines show, and they are optically perfectly round due to thorough finishing. Druk beads come in many varieties including this satin finish, which reflects very little light in comparison with a plain glass.

Hole: *Small*
Stringing: *Fine tiger tail or medium thread*
Weight: *0.3g*
Other sizes: *4mm, 8mm, 10mm*
Color range: *Large*
Length: *5.5mm*
Width: *6mm*
Depth: *6mm*

Actual size

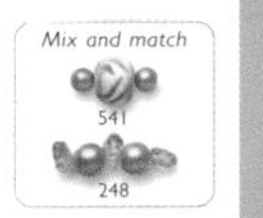

9 SPIRAL SPOTS
Basically red glass, the detailed round pattern on the side of these beads is achieved by touching the end of a heated, patterned cane of glass on to the bead while it is still molten, then pulling the cane away so that a little of the end is left there. There is no coating or paint involved.

Hole: *Medium*
Stringing: *Medium tiger tail or heavy thread*
Weight: *1.6g*
Other sizes: *None*
Color range: *Mixed*
Length: *10mm*
Width: *10mm*
Depth: *10mm*

Actual size

10 GLAZED SPECKLES
The speckles and base color on this bead are a glaze coating, as is used on ceramics. Although the glaze is fired, it could still chip off especially at the holes, and because the bead has been dipped in the thick liquid glaze the coating could be a little uneven, giving a slightly off-round look.

Hole: *Medium*
Stringing: *Medium tiger tail or heavy thread*
Weight: *1.0g*
Other sizes: *None*
Color range: *Medium*
Length: *10mm*
Width: *10mm*
Depth: *10mm*

Actual size

Mix and match 514 492
3 2 25

Mix-and-match panel: *Showing other beads from the book that combine well with this bead*

THE MEASUREMENTS EXPLAINED

Hole:
Small: *Less than 0.5mm*
Medium: *0.5–1.5mm*
Large: *1.5–2.5mm*
Very large: *2.5–3.5mm*
Extra large: *More than 3.5mm*

Stringing:
Suggested suitable stringing materials for the beads:
Fine thread: *Strong fine thread such as Nymo (up to D)*
Medium thread: *Nylon or silk beading thread up to size 4*
Heavy thread: *Nylon or silk beading thread up to size 8*
Fine tiger tail: *Tiger tail beading wire such as Beadalon or Accu-flex 0.01 inch (0.3mm) or less*
Medium tiger tail: *Between 0.01 inch (0.3mm) and 0.02 inch (0.5mm)*
Heavy tiger tail: *Thicker than 0.02 inch (0.5mm)*
Cord: *0.08 inch (2mm) or thicker cord or leather thong*

Weight:
In grams, to nearest 0.1g

Other sizes:
Lengths of other sizes available. "Many" means the range is very large or the sizes are variable

Color range:
None: *This color only*
Small: *One or two other colors*
Medium: *Three to six colors*
Large: *Seven to 20 other colors*
Very large: *21 to 100 colors*
Extremely large: *More than 100 other colors*

Length:
Measurement from one end of the hole to the other, in mm, to nearest 0.5mm

Width:
Measured at the widest part of the bead at right angles to the hole, to nearest 0.5mm

Depth:
Measured at right angles to the width and length, to nearest 0.5mm

FOLD-OUT FLAP

Opposite page 254, you'll find a handy fold-out flap, which you can have open while you refer to the "directory" pages. The flap provides an instant explanation for the symbols used throughout the book.

THE BEAD DIRECTORY

The following pages will lead you through many of the most common and some of the more unusual shapes, sizes, colors, and materials available to us as bead users today.

CHAPTER 1

Glass

There are probably more different beads made of glass than of any other material, allowing for the huge range of colors and shapes that can be made from this very versatile substance.

Glass beads are made in several ways, both by machine and by hand. In all cases the glass must be heated to the melting point, shaped, and then cooled slowly so that it "anneals," which means that the stresses are allowed to even out before the glass sets completely. Glass that is not annealed properly breaks suddenly, and for no apparent reason, sometimes months after it is finished.

Handmade glass beads are often flameworked, which means that they are made individually by melting rods of colored glass in a high-temperature torch flame, usually by wrapping them around a rod (called a mandrel). Some, known as fused glass, are made in a kiln; others by removing molten glass from a furnace and molding or otherwise shaping it.

Glass is cool to the touch when not being worn against the skin, is fairly heavy for its size, and clinks sharply when knocked together, or tapped against the teeth—all these facts can be used to distinguish it from other materials, especially plastic.

Tiny glass seed and bugle beads can be combined to make elaborate three-dimensional pieces, such as this decorative pot, which take advantage of the material's brilliance.

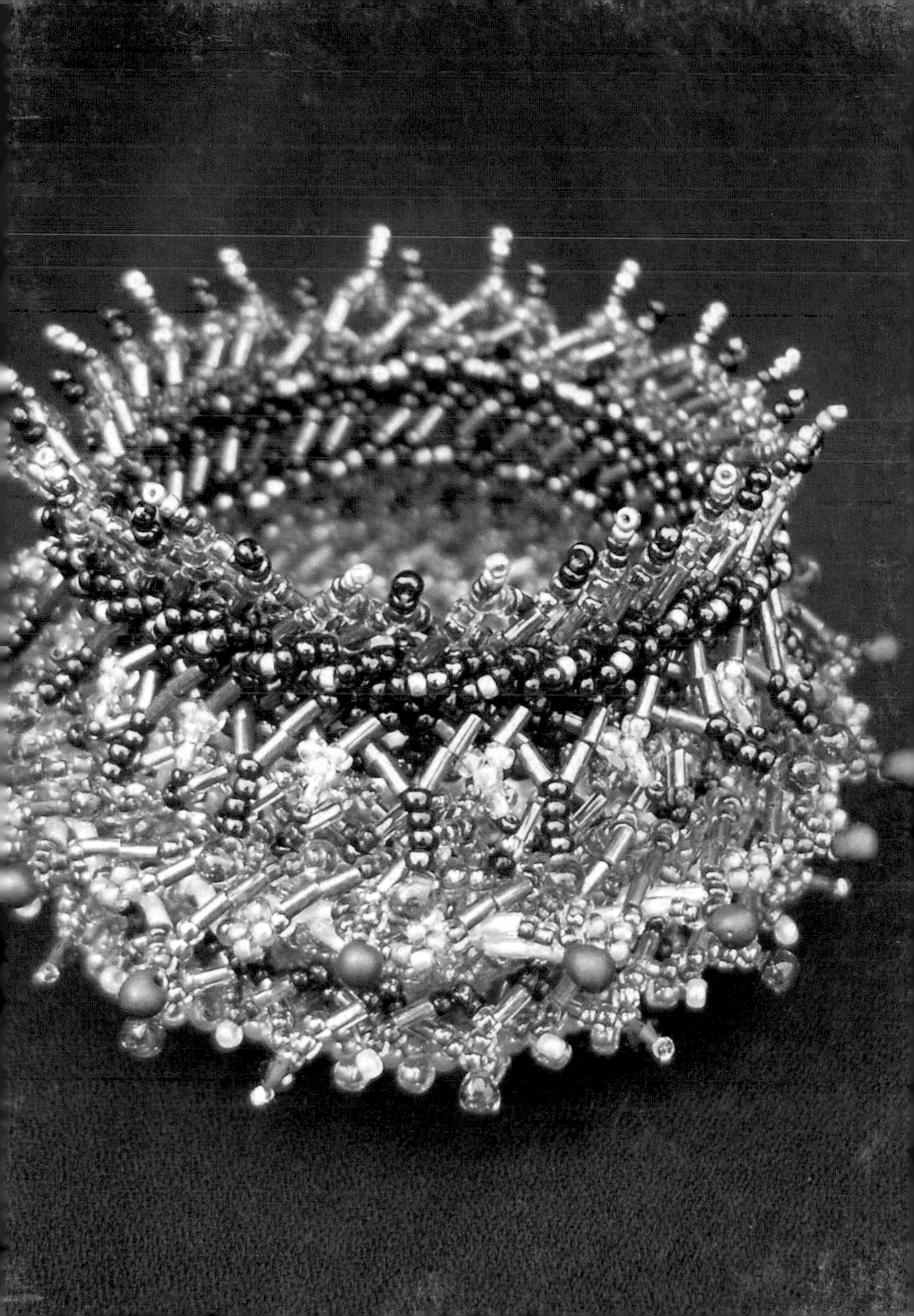

118

SEED BEADS

These beads are so called because of their small size. Not perfectly round, they are usually wider than they are long. They may be sold by weight or by the tube. The most commonly used size, as given in the data below, is known as 11s or 11°s, but they range from the very fine 24°s to the larger 5°s.

Hole: *Medium*
Stringing: *Fine thread*
Weight: *0.006g*
Other sizes: *Many, 1mm to 3.5mm*
Color range: *Very large*
Length: *1.7mm*
Width: *2.2mm*
Depth: *2.2mm*

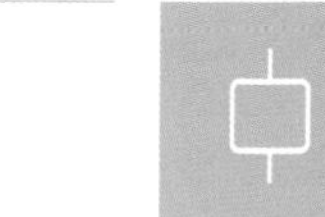

2 TUBE BEADS

At first glance these look very much like seed beads (1), but they are actually cylindrical in shape, with a larger hole, and are much more even. They are also almost the same in width as length, so they are close to square in cross section. They are available in a vast range of colors in the standard size (the larger size comes in fewer colors).

Hole: *Medium*
Stringing: *Fine or medium thread*
Weight: *0.005g*
Other sizes: *3mm*
Color range: *Extremely large*

Length: *1.5mm*
Width: *1.6mm*
Depth: *1.6mm*

17

3 BUGLES

Most of the bugle beads easily available are sized to match the most common seed beads (1), 11°s, in width. These come in various lengths and are sometimes referred to as the number of 11°s they are long. The shortest are roughly the same length as their width but have flatter ends than seed beads.

Hole: *Small*
Stringing: *Fine thread*
Weight: *0.1g*
Other sizes: *Many, 2mm and upward*
Color range: *Large*

Length: *12mm*
Width: *2.2mm*
Depth: *2.2mm*

4 PLAIN ROUND

The plain round glass bead may be the most common bead available today—most companies who make glass beads produce them in a large range of sizes, colors, and coatings, as well as in different types of glass. Pictured below are plain clear (translucent) colored, opaque colored, opal (partly translucent), and coated.

Hole: *Medium*
Stringing: *Fine tiger tail or medium thread*
Weight: *0.2g*
Other sizes: *Many*
Color range: *Large*

Length: *4mm*
Width: *4mm*
Depth: *4mm*

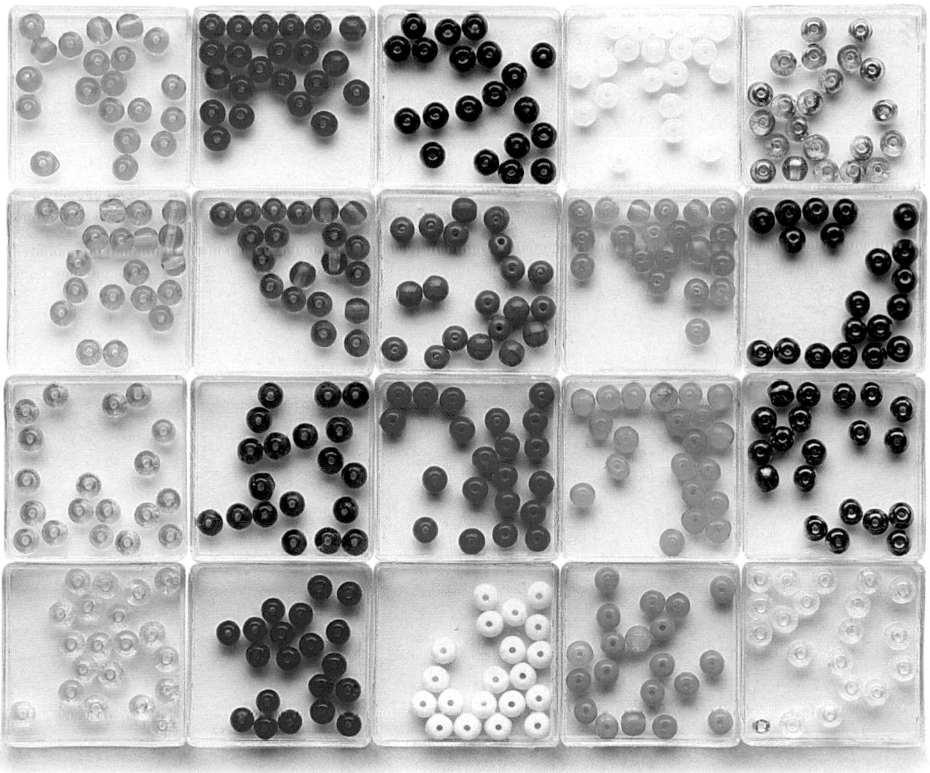

50

5 ROUND CAT'S EYE

This glass has a property called chatoyancy, which causes it to reflect light in an unusual way: in this case a band of light, rather like the pupil of a cat's eye, shows around the middle of the bead. The band shows up most clearly on deep colors and rounded shapes, but pale and flatter cat's eye beads are also available.

Hole: *Small*
Stringing: *Fine tiger tail or medium thread*
Weight: *0.8g*
Other sizes: *2mm, 4mm, 6mm, 10mm*
Color range: *Medium*

Length: *8mm*
Width: *8mm*
Depth: *8mm*

Actual size

Mix and match
406
369

3
3
32

6 PEARL

The pearl coating on glass beads is usually of a higher quality than that on plastic pearls, but if it is not, it may rub or peel off if scratched. Glass pearls are available in more colors and shapes than real pearls, but of course they do not have quite the same feel and luster.

Hole: *Small*
Stringing: *Fine tiger tail or medium thread*
Weight: *0.4g*
Other sizes: *Many*
Color range: *Medium*

Length: *8mm*
Width: *8mm*
Depth: *8mm*

Actual size

Mix and match
593
463

3
3
32

7 LUSTER COATED

Opaque luster coatings on glass usually show two or more deep colors and seem to glow softly when light falls on them. They are unlikely to rub or flake off. The base bead is often black glass. If a whole strand is too intense, the simplest solution is to add colorless glass to pick up and transmit some of the colors.

Hole: *Medium*
Stringing: *Medium tiger tail or heavy thread*
Weight: *1.2g*
Other sizes: *4mm, 6mm, 8mm*

Color range: *Medium*
Length: *9mm*
Width: *10mm*
Depth: *10mm*

Actual size

Mix and match
77
373

3
3
28

8 DRUK

Druk beads are made in the Czech Republic. They are pressed glass, but no seam lines show, and they are optically perfectly round due to thorough finishing. Druk beads come in many varieties including this satin finish, which reflects very little light in comparison with a plain glass.

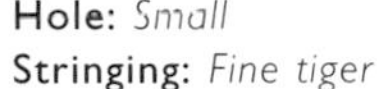

Hole: *Small*
Stringing: *Fine tiger tail or medium thread*
Weight: *0.3g*
Other sizes: *4mm, 8mm, 10mm*
Color range: *Large*

Length: *5.5mm*
Width: *6mm*
Depth: *6mm*

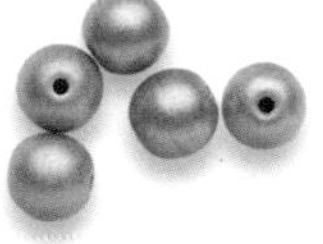

Actual size

9 SPIRAL SPOTS

Basically red glass, the detailed round pattern on the side of these beads is achieved by touching the end of a heated, patterned cane of glass on to the bead while it is still molten, then pulling the cane away so that a little of the end is left there. There is no coating or paint involved.

Hole: *Medium*
Stringing: *Medium tiger tail or heavy thread*
Weight: *1.6g*
Other sizes: *None*
Color range: *Mixed*

Length: *10mm*
Width: *10mm*
Depth: *10mm*

Actual size

10 GLAZED SPECKLES

The speckles and base color on this bead are a glaze coating, as is used on ceramics. Although the glaze is fired, it could still chip off especially at the holes, and because the bead has been dipped in the thick liquid glaze the coating could be a little uneven, giving a slightly off-round look.

Hole: *Medium*
Stringing: *Medium tiger tail or heavy thread*
Weight: *1.0g*
Other sizes: *None*
Color range: *Medium*

Length: *10mm*
Width: *10mm*
Depth: *10mm*

Actual size

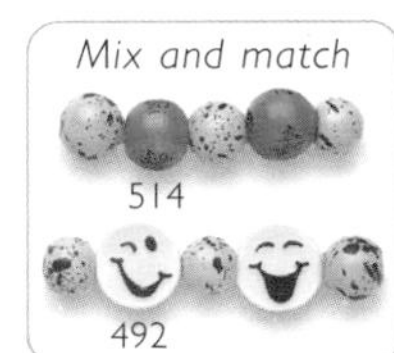

11 GYPSY RINGS

This translucent red glass has been gilded in fine lines, then painted, all by hand. The colors are then fired on for permanency, leaving them very slightly raised on the surface. The result is beautifully delicate, and each one is slightly different, making a string of these look less deliberate and more relaxed than identical beads would.

Hole: *Medium*
Stringing: *Medium tiger tail or heavy thread*
Weight: *3.2g*
Other sizes: *None*
Color range: *None*

Length: *13mm*
Width: *14mm*
Depth: *14mm*

Actual size

Mix and match

12 MATTE SWIRL FLOWERS

The pattern on the black glass is part of the glass, made either with canes (see 9) or using the tip of a fine rod of glass, called a stringer, to draw with melted glass into the main bead. The finished bead has been etched or tumbled to give a matte surface.

Hole: *Medium*
Stringing: *Medium tiger tail or heavy thread*
Weight: *2.5g*
Other sizes: *6mm, 8mm, 10mm*
Color range: *Medium*

Length: *12mm*
Width: *13mm*
Depth: *14mm*

Actual size

Mix and match

13 COLOR LINED

The slight irregularities show that this bead was handmade. A tube of red glass was covered with a thick layer of clear, and the lines added with the tip of a stringer of goldstone glass that has copper in it. This is sometimes done to make the beads less expensive because the clear glass is cheaper to use.

Hole: *Medium*
Stringing: *Medium tiger tail or heavy thread*
Weight: *1.9g*
Other sizes: *8mm, 14mm*
Color range: *Medium*

Length: *10mm*
Width: *12mm*
Depth: *12mm*

Actual size

Mix and match

14 DICHROIC

Dichroic glass has a very bright coating that appears to be a different color depending both on whether light is going through it or reflecting and on the angle of the light. The dichroic glass on this bead has been applied to the outside of an opaque black bead.

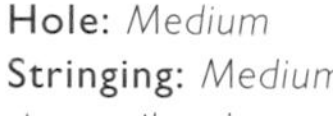

Hole: *Medium*
Stringing: *Medium tiger tail or heavy thread*
Weight: *2.8g*
Other sizes: *6mm, 8mm*
Color range: *Medium*

Length: *12mm*
Width: *13mm*
Depth: *13mm*

Actual size

Mix and match

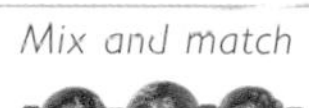

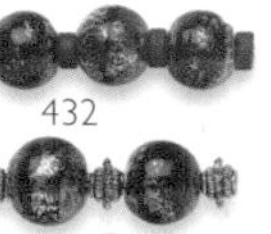

3
5
21

15 CRACKLE

If it is heated or cooled too fast, most glass breaks. This has apparently been taken advantage of here: the inside of the beads have been made to shatter, while the outside and the hole have been reheated and cooled slowly, so they are solid and smooth. The tiny cracks reflect the light in different directions.

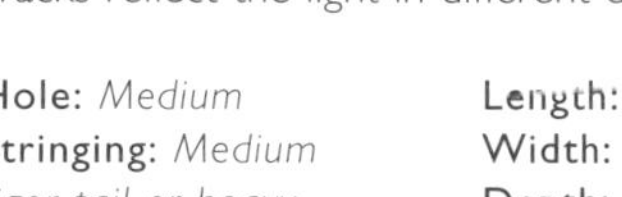

Hole: *Medium*
Stringing: *Medium tiger tail or heavy thread*
Weight: *0.7g*
Other sizes: *None*
Color range: *Medium*

Length: *8mm*
Width: *8mm*
Depth: *8mm*

Actual size

32

16 PAINTED BAND

A solid band of opaque color has been painted on to the midline of these clear colorless beads and splashes of other colors, some of which are translucent, added on top. Although this is a fired coating, it does rub and chip quite easily, so jewelry made with these should be treated with care.

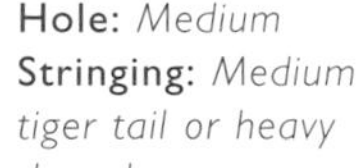

Hole: *Medium*
Stringing: *Medium tiger tail or heavy thread*
Weight: *0.7g*
Other sizes: *None*
Color range: *Medium*

Length: *8mm*
Width: *9mm*
Depth: *9mm*

Actual size

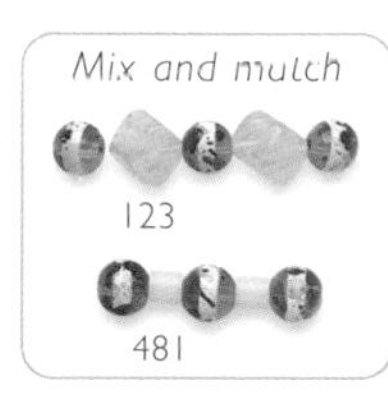

32

32

17 SWIRL PRESSED

The middle line clearly shows that these beads were pressed in a mold rather than made in the flame. An opaque pearly glass, possibly including mica, is lightly swirled with a clear glass and an opaque glass in similar colors to give a textured effect, but the bead is perfectly smooth.

Hole: *Small*
Stringing: *Fine tiger tail or medium thread*
Weight: *0.6g*
Other sizes: *8mm*
Color range: *Medium*

Length: *8mm*
Width: *8mm*
Depth: *8mm*

Actual size

Mix and match
351
88

2

50

18 EYE BEAD

Eye beads were traditionally used as protective charms. Simple eyes are made by putting a dot of white glass on to the molten base bead with a hot stringer, topped by a second, smaller dot of black glass. The bead is then heated in the flame until the dots flatten out and the bead is round again.

Hole: *Small*
Stringing: *Fine tiger tail or medium thread*
Weight: *0.2g*
Other sizes: *None*
Color range: *Mixed*

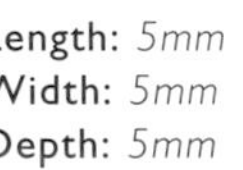

Length: *5mm*
Width: *5mm*
Depth: *5mm*

Actual size

Mix and match
363
503

34

19 DESERT SUN GOLD

This effect is achieved using a two-layer coating. The shiny gold is exposed in the cracks of the matte top coat, which has been used because it shrinks as it dries, like mud under a hot sun. Although it looks fragile, the coating does not seem to rub or flake and is difficult to scratch.

Hole: *Small*
Stringing: *Fine tiger tail or medium thread*
Weight: *0.6g*
Other sizes: *4mm, 6mm*
Color range: *Medium*

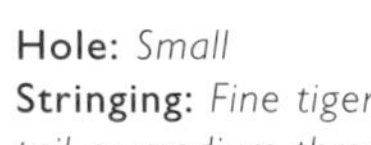

Length: *7.5mm*
Width: *8mm*
Depth: *8mm*

Actual size

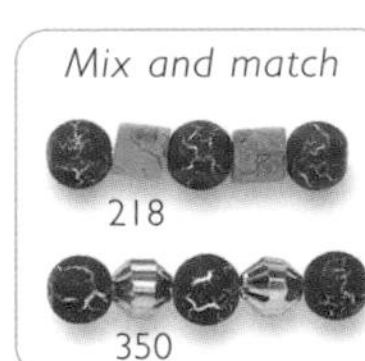
Mix and match
218
350

20 SIDE COATING

The patch of coating shows only from one side of the bead, so a string of these will each have a different amount of the reflective area showing. The white glass is opalescent, meaning it is not quite opaque. A similar patch on a translucent bead would be visible from both sides, shining through the color as well as reflecting.

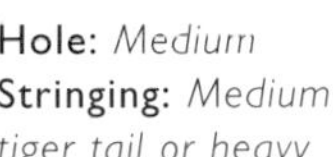

Hole: *Medium*
Stringing: *Medium tiger tail or heavy thread*
Weight: *0.7g*
Other sizes: *4mm, 6mm, 10mm*

Color range: *Medium*
Length: *7.5mm*
Width: *8mm*
Depth: *8mm*

Actual size

Mix and match

44

266

3

3

34

21 ROUNDED MURRINI

Murrini are slices of glass canes, made of smaller rods that have been fused together in a kiln; the rods are stacked in order to create the design. They are often used to decorate beads, but in this case a thick slice of the cane has been formed into each of these round beads, with the patterned ends showing front and back.

Hole: *Small*
Stringing: *Fine tiger tail or medium thread*
Weight: *0.7g*
Other sizes: *None*
Color range: *Medium*

Length: *8mm*
Width: *8mm*
Depth: *8mm*

Actual size

Mix and match

139

361

3

3

32

22 CRYSTAL SPECKS

The tiny pointed-back crystal pieces have been pressed into these beads while the glass was still soft. Unfortunately some are not held in well and come out easily, leaving little dips in the bead, especially if they catch on clothing. It may be worth rubbing hard to remove any loose stones and gluing them back before use.

Hole: *Small*
Stringing: *Fine tiger tail or medium thread*
Weight: *0.8g*
Other sizes: *None*
Color range: *Medium*

Length: *8.5mm*
Width: *8.5mm*
Depth: *8.5mm*

Actual size

Mix and match

260

500

3

3

30

5

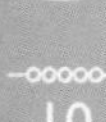

23 CARVED GLASS

A layer of red glass is carved back with engraving tools to produce a raised red design against an inner layer of white glass. This is called cameo glass. If these beads were solid glass they would be very heavy, but the white layer is quite thin so the piece is hollow and slightly translucent.

Hole: *Large*
Stringing: *Heavy thread or fine cord*
Weight: *8.5g*
Other sizes: *20mm*
Color range: *Medium*

Length: *25mm*
Width: *26mm*
Depth: *26mm*

Actual size

Mix and match

571

268

3

3

18

24 FACETED CLEAR

This clear, colorless, uncoated, glass bead has many tiny crisply cut facets that help to reflect and transmit the light in as many directions as possible but is not as bright as coated, cut glass such as 69 or the beads in the crystal chapter. This makes it more subtle and possibly more versatile.

Hole: *Medium*
Stringing: *Medium tiger tail or heavy thread*
Weight: *3.8g*
Other sizes: *4mm, 6mm, 8mm, 10mm, 12mm*

Color range: *Large*
Length: *14mm*
Width: *14mm*
Depth: *14mm*

Actual size

Mix and match

188

268

3

3

25 FACETED CAT'S EYE

The same type of cat's eye glass as 5, these are faceted to give a rather different look. Instead of a band of light, one row of the facets seems to glow, changing tones as the beads move. This also makes the facets more striking without the need for a coating.

Hole: *Medium*
Stringing: *Medium tiger tail or heavy thread*
Weight: *0.6g*
Other sizes: *6mm*
Color range: *Medium*

Length: *8mm*
Width: *8mm*
Depth: *8mm*

Actual size

Mix and match

158

252

26 FOIL LINED

To make this bead, a tube of glass was created in the flame and covered with a layer of silver leaf (a very fine silver foil). A layer of clear glass went on top, with some tiny fragments of colored glass (called frit) sprinkled on the outside. A final thicker layer of clear glass finished the bead.

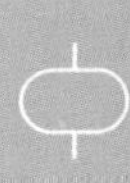

28

Hole: *Large*
Stringing: *Medium tiger tail or heavy thread*
Weight: *1.4g*
Other sizes: *None*
Color range: *Medium*

Length: *9mm*
Width: *11mm*
Depth: *11mm*

Actual size

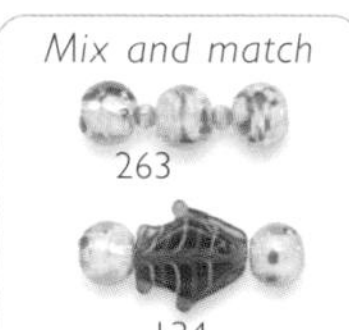

27 SEASHORE MEMORIES

Handmade by a bead artist (Gallow Glass) using a torch technique called flamework, these capture memories of a summer by the seashore. The opaque colors are carefully chosen, built up, and manipulated together to give the wonderful patterns, then a layer of clear glass completes the design.

Actual size

15

Hole: *Large*
Stringing: *Heavy thread or fine cord*
Weight: *7.4g*
Other sizes: *None*
Color range: *None*

Length: *17mm*
Width: *18mm*
Depth: *18mm*

28 FLOATING STARS

This bead designer/maker (Jazzy Lily) has created a tube of glass with a pattern made by swirling colors together, then added the "floating" stars by etching them from a sheet of clear dichroic glass and wrapping that face up around the base tube. More clear glass over the top puts the stars in the middle of the layers.

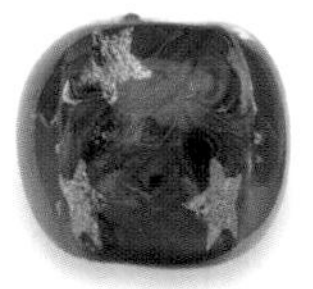

Actual size

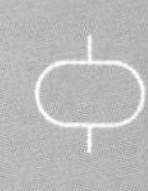

18

Hole: *Large*
Stringing: *Heavy thread or fine cord*
Weight: *6.2g*
Other sizes: *None*
Color range: *None*

Length: *14mm*
Width: *18mm*
Depth: *18mm*

16

29 NARROWBOAT FLOWERS

This Gallow Glass design is inspired by narrowboat art often seen on the canals in Britain. The bright colors are added to the black base bead where they are needed, and then pulled into the required shapes with fine-pointed metal tools to simulate the brushstrokes of this type of art.

Actual size

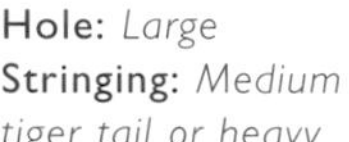

Hole: *Large*
Stringing: *Medium tiger tail or heavy thread*
Weight: *7.2g*
Other sizes: *10mm*
Color range: *None*

Length: *16mm*
Width: *16.5mm*
Depth: *16.5mm*

Mix and match

362
538

25

30 VENETIAN STYLE

Now made in several countries, these are typical of a style once made only in Venice. The band and fine lines are goldstone glass that has copper in it for the metallic look, and the other dots and swirls are added with glass rods or stringers and flattened with pressure rather than heat, which would flatten them into the main bead.

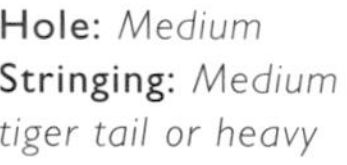

Hole: *Medium*
Stringing: *Medium tiger tail or heavy thread*
Weight: *2.1g*
Other sizes: *8mm*
Color range: *Medium*

Length: *10mm*
Width: *13mm*
Depth: *13mm*

Actual size

Mix and match

375
207

12

31 PULLED-DOT FLOWERS

On to a deep amber base bead, rings of white dots of opaque glass have been almost covered with dots of translucent pink, then pulled together with a metal tool to meet in the middle and make a flower. The yellow center is added and the whole thing heated until it is once again smooth, with no raised areas.

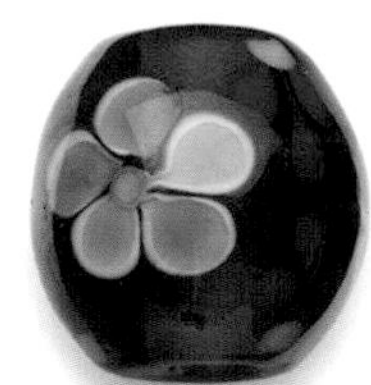
Actual size

Hole: *Large*
Stringing: *Heavy thread or fine cord*
Weight: *13.9g*
Other sizes: *None*
Color range: *Medium*

Length: *21mm*
Width: *21mm*
Depth: *21mm*

Mix and match

175

343

32 INSIDE HEARTS

A turquoise base bead has been topped with white and pink dots, as for the previous bead, but these have been pulled into a series of heart shapes around the middle of the bead. After the other decoration has been added, a thick layer of clear glass makes the hearts appear to float in the middle of the bead.

Actual size

Hole: *Large*
Stringing: *Heavy thread or fine cord*
Weight: *13.9g*
Other sizes: *None*
Color range: *None*

Length: *20mm*
Width: *21mm*
Depth: *21mm*

33 OPAQUE MELON

This shape is often called a melon because its rounded ridges look rather like some types of that fruit (or perhaps like a pumpkin). The bead is made as a sphere, then pressed with a straight-edged tool to make the dips. Plain opaque beads are useful with focal beads because they do not detract from the special piece.

Hole: *Medium*
Stringing: *Medium tiger tail or heavy thread*
Weight: *1.1g*
Other sizes: *6mm, 8mm*

Color range: *Medium*
Length: *10mm*
Width: *10mm*
Depth: *10mm*

Actual size

25

34 FEATHERED MELON

To create this bead, a round bead was made with stripes of different colors going around it. A fine tool was then dragged through the glass, alternately up and down the bead, to pull the lines into a feather pattern (a technique also used in cake decoration). After heating to smooth, the dips were pressed in as for 33.

Actual size

Hole: *Large*
Stringing: *Heavy thread or fine cord*
Weight: *14.8g*
Other sizes: *None*
Color range: *None*

Length: *21mm*
Width: *21mm*
Depth: *21mm*

35 TWISTED WINGS

The extensions on this have been created by pulling out glass from a molten base bead, then using flat pincers to create winglike ridges that are then twisted in the middle with tweezers. Because these wings are quite thin the beads are a little fragile and should be treated with care, especially if used with heavier items.

Hole: *Medium*
Stringing: *Medium tiger tail or heavy thread*
Weight: *1.0g*
Other sizes: *None*
Color range: *Mixed*

Length: *10mm*
Width: *10mm*
Depth: *10mm*

Actual size

36 BRIGHT SPIKES

The spikes standing out from these beads are made in much the same way as the eyes on 18 but with larger dots of glass and without allowing the glass to get hot enough to melt back into the round base bead. The spikes look fragile but are actually quite sturdy because they are thick and very solidly attached.

Hole: *Medium*
Stringing: *Medium tiger tail or heavy thread*
Weight: *2.0g*
Other sizes: *12mm*
Color range: *Mixed*

Length: *10mm*
Width: *14mm*
Depth: *14mm*

Actual size

37 RINGED DOTS

A more flattened round, these markings are made by the designer Jazzy Lily in a similar way to the spikes on 36 but the layers of dots have been melted back into the shape and the last translucent color then pressed into the middle of each to make it more dominant.

Hole: *Medium*
Stringing: *Medium tiger tail or heavy thread*
Weight: *3.1g*
Other sizes: *None*
Color range: *None*

Length: *10mm*
Width: *15mm*
Depth: *15mm*

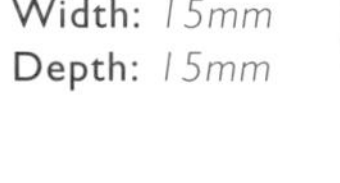

Actual size

38 HOLLOW CANE

A simple hollow glass rod was made with stripes of opaque glass laid along its length. More clear glass was layered over the top, and the whole tube then pulled to thin it down. When complete and cooled, this basic hollow cane was chopped up into short lengths and remelted just enough to round the ends.

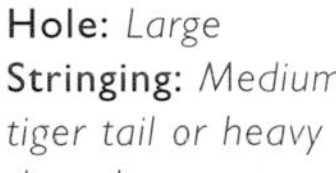

Hole: *Large*
Stringing: *Medium tiger tail or heavy thread*
Weight: *1.7g*
Other sizes: *None*
Color range: *Small*

Length: *9mm*
Width: *11mm*
Depth: *10mm*

Actual size

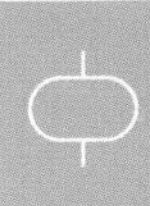

39 DICHROIC SPACER

A narrow strip of dichroic glass was wound in a spiral around a mandrel (metal rod used in flamework) to make this simple spacer bead. The underlying black glass (which has the dichroic coating) can be seen as a line down one side, where the winding finished, and in the edges of the spiral seen at the ends.

Hole: *Medium*
Stringing: *Medium tiger tail or heavy thread*
Weight: *0.9g*
Other sizes: *13mm*
Color range: *Medium*

Length: *7.5mm*
Width: *9.5mm*
Depth: *9.5mm*

Actual size

40 CROW

This traditional shape is known as a Crow bead and is very similar to a Pony bead. These have a confetti-patterned coating, in other words, a speckled pattern that is not permanent. Beads with non-permanent coatings are better used in decorative projects rather than in jewelry where they will be rubbed or on clothing that has to be washed.

Hole: *Large*
Stringing: *heavy thread or fine cord*
Weight: *0.7g*
Other sizes: *None*
Color range: *Medium*

Length: *7mm*
Width: *9mm*
Depth: *9mm*

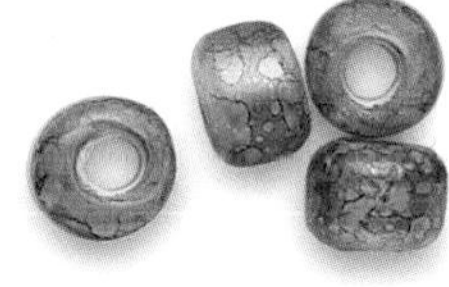

Actual size

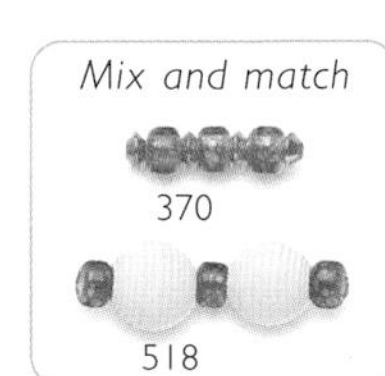

2

2

42

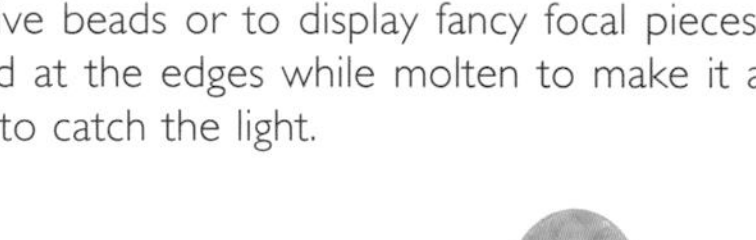

41 BUMPY SPACER

Flattened round beads like this are often used as spacers to give more length when using expensive beads or to display fancy focal pieces. This one has been pinched at the edges while molten to make it a little more interesting and to catch the light.

Hole: *Medium*
Stringing: *Medium tiger tail or heavy thread*
Weight: *0.5g*
Other sizes: *8mm*
Color range: *Medium*

Length: *6mm*
Width: *8.5mm*
Depth: *8.5mm*

Actual size

2

2

45

42 FLOWER SPACER

Another spacer bead, this one molded with an obvious seam line around the middle. The ridging, rather like that on melon beads such as 33, makes it seem flowerlike from some angles. Traditional enough in design for almost any classic piece, the simple shape is also suitable for modern jewelry.

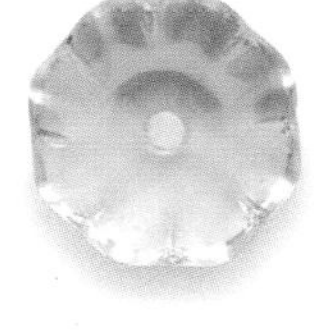

Hole: *Medium*
Stringing: *Medium tiger tail or heavy thread*
Weight: *0.6g*
Other sizes: *None*
Color range: *Medium*

Length: *5.5mm*
Width: *9mm*
Depth: *9mm*

Actual size

3

4

63

43 FLOWER CANE

This is a slice of a hollow cane made with a simple design around the hole and pressed in at the sides to make a flower shape. The slices are heated to remove sharp edges. Because these look best from the side and are uninteresting when strung together they should be used on the ends of pieces or hung from an ice pick bail such as 627.

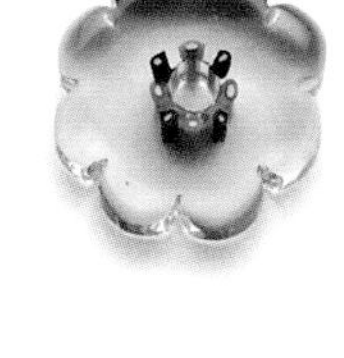

Hole: *Large*
Stringing: *Medium tiger tail or heavy thread*
Weight: *0.8g*
Other sizes: *Variable*
Color range: *Mixed*

Length: *4mm*
Width: *11mm*
Depth: *11mm*

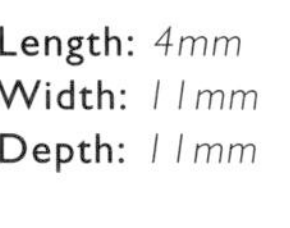

Actual size

44 COATED COIN

Because the glass is translucent the AB (aurora borealis) coating on one side of this coin shape shows through to the other side slightly. Coin beads with a hole across the diameter are useful in place of round (spherical) beads, providing a round profile and length without adding the depth and weight of a similar size sphere.

Hole: *Medium*
Stringing: *Medium tiger tail or heavy thread*
Weight: *0.6g*
Other sizes: *7mm, 15mm*
Color range: *Medium*
Length: *10mm*
Width: *10mm*
Depth: *3.5mm*

Actual size

Mix and match
441
135

45 CARNIVAL DRUM

Molded with a drum shape and deep flower pattern, this bead has a translucent multicolor coating over a translucent core and is known as carnival glass. The seam is very heavy but not very obvious in wear because it is around the edge where it will not easily be noticed. Larger carnival glass items are very collectable.

Hole: *Medium*
Stringing: *Medium tiger tail or heavy thread*
Weight: *1.7g*
Other sizes: *None*
Color range: *Medium*
Length: *14mm*
Width: *14mm*
Depth: *5.5mm*

Actual size

Mix and match
157
505

46 COMPLEX EYE

If simple eye beads are said to have protective properties, this one must be even better. A round bead has been flattened and the symbol built up with lines and dots, from black and white stringers, to make a somewhat Egyptian-looking eye shape, with more dots added at the edges of the bead.

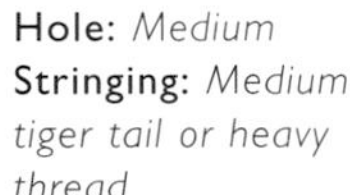

Hole: *Medium*
Stringing: *Medium tiger tail or heavy thread*
Weight: *1.2g*
Other sizes: *None*
Color range: *Small*
Length: *10mm*
Width: *12mm*
Depth: *9mm*

Actual size

Mix and match
83
487

47 DESIGNER CUSHION

A tube of clear dichroic glass over a colored core gives this design by Jazzy Lily its center. A thick layer of clear glass has then been flattened to make a cushionlike shape and a raised line of toning color added to the outside and twisted together in the middle.

4

5

15

Hole: *Large*
Stringing: *Heavy thread or fine cord*
Weight: *7.1g*
Other sizes: *None*
Color range: *None*

Length: *17mm*
Width: *20mm*
Depth: *16mm*

Actual size

Mix and match
544
277

48 PRESSED SPIRAL

Another pressed glass bead, this time with a spiral pattern. The matte effect is achieved by either etching or tumbling to remove the usual shine of glass. The shape and pattern are reminiscent of a seashell, and glass that has been swept about in the sea also tends to have this frosted surface.

2

3

20

Hole: *Medium*
Stringing: *Fine tiger tail or medium thread*
Weight: *0.9g*
Other sizes: *None*
Color range: *Medium*

Length: *13mm*
Width: *11mm*
Depth: *4mm*

Actual size

Mix and match
206
109

49 WRAPPED

A flameworked bead is made by melting the tip of a rod of glass in the torch flame and wrapping it around a metal rod (mandrel) that has been coated with something to allow the bead to be removed later. The glass is usually then heated some more to melt it into the shape required but these have been left at the first stage.

2

3

36

Hole: *Medium*
Stringing: *Medium tiger tail or heavy thread*
Weight: *0.5g*
Other sizes: *None*
Color range: *Small*

Length: *7mm*
Width: *11mm*
Depth: *11mm*

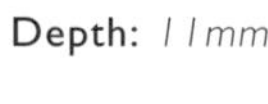

Actual size

Mix and match
21
214

50 CUT HOGAN

These little cut-glass pieces are very commonly used as spacers where a bit of sparkle is required. They are also useful when the other beads in a piece have a large hole because they can fit into it and prevent too much movement on the thread. They will also help secure a large-holed bead on a head pin (629).

Hole: *Medium*
Stringing: *Fine tiger tail or medium thread*
Weight: *0.1g*
Other sizes: *None*
Color range: *Medium*

Length: *3mm*
Width: *5mm*
Depth: *5mm*

Actual size

51 OIL SLICK RING

Depending on the size of the hole and the shape of the next item along, ring beads can fit between beads or overlap the ends slightly for a different look. These have a coating called "oil slick" because in the right light it makes a rainbow like oil on water.

Hole: *Large*
Stringing: *Medium tiger tail or heavy thread*
Weight: *0.2g*
Other sizes: *None*
Color range: *Mixed*

Length: *3mm*
Width: *7mm*
Depth: *7mm*

Actual size

52 FACETED TUBE

Short round tubes, either faceted like these or with flat sides, are another useful spacer shape. If used on their own, they do tend to gap a little on the thread so put beads between them. If the other beads are round, and fit into the ends of the tube, the piece will move and hang well.

Hole: *Large*
Stringing: *Medium tiger tail or heavy thread*
Weight: *0.2g*
Other sizes: *None*
Color range: *Medium*

Length: *4mm*
Width: *5.5mm*
Depth: *5.5mm*

Actual size

2 2 63

53 DISK SPACER

These almost flat disks are also used as spacers but do work quite well on their own. A whole strand of them looks like a flexible, ridged tube, somehow both ancient and futuristic, which can be good as sides to a necklace with a large, dominant center piece. Try two sizes of disks alternately for another look.

Hole: *Medium*
Stringing: *Medium tiger tail or heavy thread*
Weight: *0.5g*
Other sizes: *6mm, 8mm*
Color range: *Large*
Length: *4mm*
Width: *10mm*
Depth: *10mm*

Actual size

54 DISK SPIRAL

The spiral on the side of these disk beads will be seen if the next bead along is small or if the bead is used at the end of a piece. They could also be fixed flat on to beadwork or clothing with the thread coming up through the hole, through an additional small bead, and then back down.

Hole: *Medium*
Stringing: *Medium tiger tail or heavy thread*
Weight: *1.2g*
Other sizes: *None*
Color range: *Large*
Length: *5.5mm*
Width: *13mm*
Depth: *13mm*

Actual size

3 2 45

55 SIMPLE DONUT

A very ancient shape of bead, these could be used as spacers in a large piece or to weight the end of a lariat strand. Loops of pretty thread or tiny beads from both sides would hold these in the middle of a bracelet or necklace, or you could suspend them from earrings (but beware of the weight).

Hole: *Large*
Stringing: *Heavy thread or fine cord*
Weight: *4.7g*
Other sizes: *None*
Color range: *Medium*
Length: *6mm*
Width: *12.5mm*
Depth: *12.5mm*

Actual size

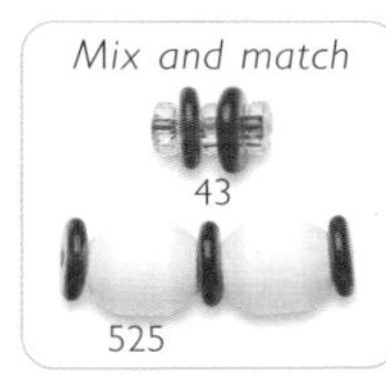

4 3 42

56 MILLEFIORI DONUT

This is effectively a slice of a cane, but that cane has been made up of hundreds of other flower-patterned canes of glass, each made separately, then stretched, cut, and stacked to make these lovely, translucent shapes. These could be linked together with wire or used as suggested for 55.

Actual size

Hole: *Large*
Stringing: *Heavy thread or fine cord*
Weight: *6.0g*
Other sizes: *None*
Color range: *Medium*

Length: *5mm*
Width: *30mm*
Depth: *30mm*

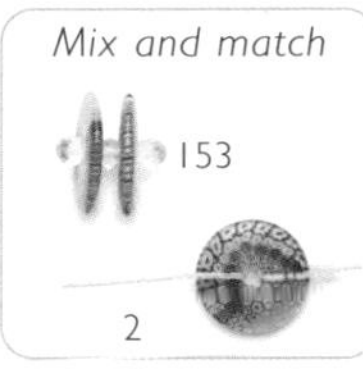

50

57 WHEEL

Unlike the previous bead, this donut or wheel has a thick patterned edge, and it is this that is designed to be seen. The heart shapes around the rim are made from layered dots of color that have been melted into the shape, then dragged with a pointed tool into the final pattern.

Actual size

Hole: *Large*
Stringing: *Heavy thread or fine cord*
Weight: *14.2g*
Other sizes: *None*
Color range: *None*

Length: *11.5mm*
Width: *27mm*
Depth: *27mm*

5

22

58 SPIKED WHEEL

Rather like 36 in construction, this ring-shaped bead has five spikes around the edge only and is designed for use as a fancy spacer. It could perhaps be used to add bright colors here and there in a mainly metallic or natural material piece or as the focal point in a strand of small beads.

Hole: *Large*
Stringing: *Heavy thread or fine cord*
Weight: *1.9g*
Other sizes: *None*
Color range: *Mixed*

Length: *6mm*
Width: *15mm*
Depth: *15mm*

Actual size

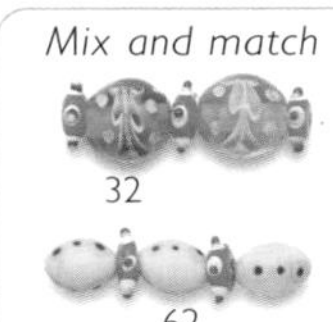

42

59 MOONSTONE FLAT OVAL

2

2

24

This flat, translucent oval is made of what is sometimes called moonstone glass because of its similarity to the gemstone. It also has colors in common with white opals. Flattened ovals are very comfortable to wear because they lie neatly and are not too thick, with no edges to catch on clothing.

Hole: *Medium*
Stringing: *Fine tiger tail or medium thread*
Weight: *0.7g*
Other sizes: *None*
Color range: *None*

Length: *10.5mm*
Width: *8.5mm*
Depth: *5mm*

Actual size

60 CROSSED LINES FLAT OVAL

2

3

25

Another pressed-glass shape with an imprinted pattern and an obvious seam. The pattern shows up well because the opaque glass makes the dips shadowed, while the shine catches highlights on the raised areas, all of which lifts these from being very dull beads to subtly attractive ones.

Hole: *Medium*
Stringing: *Fine tiger tail or medium thread*
Weight: *0.5g*
Other sizes: *None*
Color range: *Medium*

Length: *10mm*
Width: *7.5mm*
Depth: *4.5mm*

Actual size

61 TWISTED FLAT OVAL

2

2

42

These are oval disk beads but twisted and with a luster coating. This rather unusual shape will fit into itself if used in a strand, making an interesting textured tube, but take care not to string them too tightly if used in this way because they can be rather stiff and hang oddly.

Hole: *Medium*
Stringing: *Medium tiger tail or heavy thread*
Weight: *0.8g*
Other sizes: *None*
Color range: *Large*

Length: *6mm*
Width: *12mm*
Depth: *9mm*

Actual size

62 DOTTED OVAL

A common bead shape, this can be called an oval, melon (but see 33), or football (rugby or American), depending on where it is bought or who describes it. These have three eye-dots, with unusual reddish-brown pupils on each side and are etched or tumbled to have a matte finish.

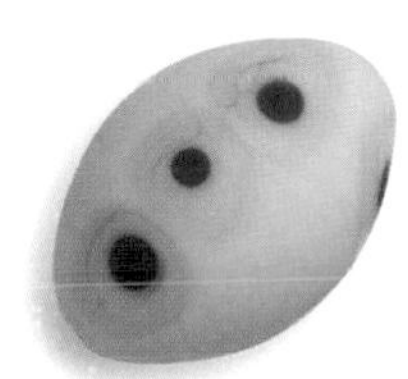

Hole: *Medium*
Stringing: *Medium tiger tail or heavy thread*
Weight: *4.2g*
Other sizes: *None*
Color range: *None*

Length: *19mm*
Width: *13mm*
Depth: *13mm*

Actual size

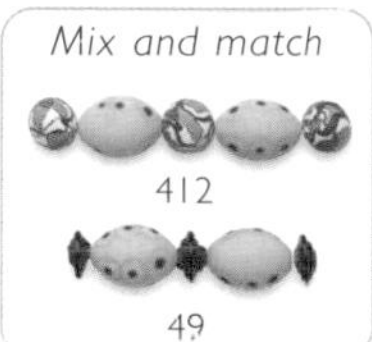

63 OVAL SWIRLS

The same shape as 62 but with the more common shiny glass surface, the pattern on these beads is made by using two colors of glass together and mixing the results enough to get a swirl but not sufficiently to make an in-between color. Pleasingly, no two of these will ever be exactly alike.

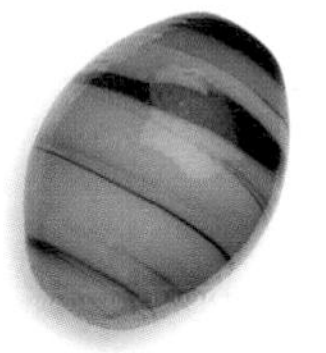

Hole: *Medium*
Stringing: *Medium tiger tail or heavy thread*
Weight: *3.4g*
Other sizes: *None*
Color range: *Medium*

Length: *16mm*
Width: *12.5mm*
Depth: *12.5mm*

Actual size

64 OVAL DICHROIC

The narrow strip of dichroic coated black glass used to make this bead has been wrapped around and around the mandrel, probably over a thin base bead, to make this long oval shape. The black edges of the glass can be seen as a spiral line from one end to the other.

Actual size

Hole: *Medium*
Stringing: *Medium tiger tail or heavy thread*
Weight: *2.3g*
Other sizes: *None*
Color range: *Medium*

Length: *22.5mm*
Width: *9mm*
Depth: *9mm*

2

3

20

65 WHITE LINED OVAL

There is a tube of opaque white glass in the middle of the translucent main color of this bead, with matching dots on the outside. Lining colored glass with white to strengthen the color is an ancient technique still in use today. Seed beads with a white interior like this are known as whitehearts.

Hole: *Medium*
Stringing: *Medium tiger tail or heavy thread*
Weight: *1.5g*
Other sizes: *None*
Color range: *Medium*

Length: *13mm*
Width: *10mm*
Depth: *10mm*

Actual size

Mix and match

476

12

2

2

36

66 FRESHWATER GLASS PEARLS

Freshwater pearls are usually at least slightly uneven and these glass pearls simulate this by having ridges on the underlying glass shape, which is then given the pearl coating. They are not a bad substitute, but similar real pearls are not all that expensive so do compare the look and feel before deciding.

Hole: *Small*
Stringing: *Fine tiger tail or medium thread*
Weight: *0.2g*
Other sizes: *None*
Color range: *Small*

Length: *7mm*
Width: *4mm*
Depth: *4mm*

Actual size

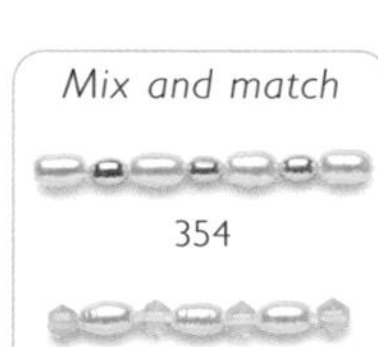

Mix and match

354

82

2

3

21

67 CHEVRONS

The patterned canes used for these beads were probably made by gathering a quantity of colored glass and pressing it into a star-shaped mold; this would then have been repeated for more layers before the results were drawn out into a long tube, then cut and ground away at an angle at the ends, showing the pattern.

Hole: *Large*
Stringing: *Medium tiger tail or heavy thread*
Weight: *1.4g*
Other sizes: *Variable*
Color range: *Medium*

Length: *12mm*
Width: *9mm*
Depth: *9mm*

Actual size

Mix and match

346

46

68 COMBED OVALS

The feather pattern on these long ovals is achieved by adding rings of glass, heating until they are incorporated in the main bead, and then pulling through the lines with a metal tool. Blue and white glass is very classical, and the decoration is also an old technique, so these are similar to some very ancient beads.

Actual size

Hole: *Large*
Stringing: *Heavy thread or fine cord*
Weight: *2.1g*
Other sizes: *None*
Color range: *Medium*

Length: *20mm*
Width: *10mm*
Depth: *10mm*

Mix and match

386

20

13

69 FACETED OVAL

These are just cut glass with a limited number of facets but made bright and very sparkly with an AB coating to reflect the light. If the coating was on both sides, the bead would not allow much light through and could look metallic so only one side is covered.

Hole: *Medium*
Stringing: *Medium tiger tail or heavy thread*
Weight: *1.1g*
Other sizes: *10mm, 14mm*
Color range: *Large*

Length: *12mm*
Width: *9mm*
Depth: *9mm*

Actual size

Mix and match

574

197

21

70 GOLDEN DETAILS

Good-quality pressed glass with an almost invisible seam, the bead here has been coated with a gold paint or glaze that has then been wiped off the surface before it dried so that it only remains in the impressed pattern. The color could be scratched out, but the bead is quite durable.

Hole: *Medium*
Stringing: *Medium tiger tail or heavy thread*
Weight: *0.8g*
Other sizes: *None*
Color range: *None*

Length: *12.5mm*
Width: *7mm*
Depth: *7mm*

Actual size

Mix and match

8

539

20

3 3 20

71 BLUE LINED RIDGES

The seams in this pressed glass bead are untrimmed, but because the whole shape is ridged they are not really noticeable in use. The blue glass in the center is rather irregular, and the clear glass on top of it has small random air bubbles in a lot of cases.

Hole: *Medium*
Stringing: *Medium tiger tail or heavy thread*
Weight: *2.2g*
Other sizes: *None*
Color range: *Small*

Length: *13mm*
Width: *13mm*
Depth: *13mm*

Actual size

Mix and match
336
264

3 4 14

72 STRAWBERRY QUARTZ

Very clear, crisply faceted glass with many flecks of pink inside it, these are sold as strawberry quartz but are actually not made from a semiprecious stone. Some special glass such as goldstone is traditionally included with semiprecious stones as it is cut and drilled in the same way, but this is not the case here.

Hole: *Medium*
Stringing: *Medium tiger tail or heavy thread*
Weight: *3.7g*
Other sizes: *12mm*
Color range: *None*

Length: *18mm*
Width: *12mm*
Depth: *12mm*

Actual size

Mix and match
293
191

3 4 12

73 BICONE

The bicone shape is so called because it is two cones end to end (tip to tip and the shape would be a spindle). Interesting for standard threading, bicones are also used when the design requires rows of beads that seem to interlock or patterns of four beads in a ring because the shapes fit together with very small gaps.

Actual size

Hole: *Medium*
Stringing: *Medium tiger tail or heavy thread*
Weight: *4.4g*
Other sizes: *None*
Color range: *None*

Length: *21mm*
Width: *14mm*
Depth: *14mm*

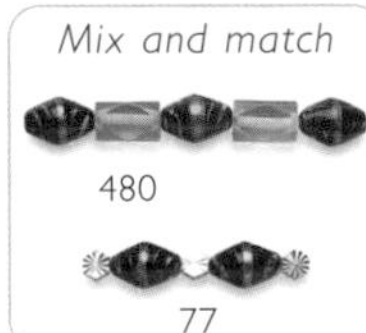
Mix and match
480
77

74 BIG BICONE

This is the largest bead in this book by a very long way, and it is also very heavy. Excellent as a focal bead, more than three in a necklace would probably be uncomfortable to wear. It could be used as part of home decor, for example, as a light pull, or as decoration on a curtain tie-back.

50% of actual size

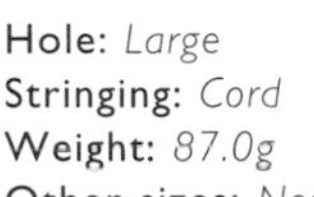

Hole: *Large*
Stringing: *Cord*
Weight: *87.0g*
Other sizes: *None*
Color range: *None*

Length: *92mm*
Width: *28mm*
Depth: *28mm*

Mix and match

491

517

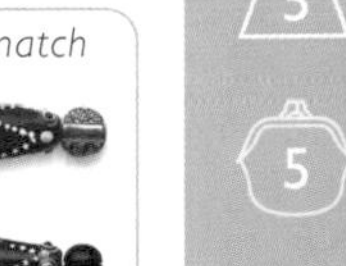

75 DOUBLE TUBE

To create this rather unusual shape, a clear tube of glass has been surrounded with a shorter layer, which has not been heated enough to blend in, with slices of decorative cane between the two. The white in the center, around the hole, is bead release, used to prevent the glass from sticking to the mandrel when the bead is made.

Actual size

Hole: *Large*
Stringing: *Cord*
Weight: *16.6g*
Other sizes: *None*
Color range: *None*

Length: *27mm*
Width: *20mm*
Depth: *20mm*

Mix and match

337

567

76 VASE

This shape reminds me of an ancient vase seen in a museum. A ring of glass has been added to each end of a round bead; the decoration has been added with glass threads that have been left standing up on the surface rather than melted into the base bead.

Actual size

Hole: *Large*
Stringing: *Cord*
Weight: *13.6g*
Other sizes: *None*
Color range: *None*

Length: *25mm*
Width: *22mm*
Depth: *22mm*

Mix and match

216

366

77 CATHEDRAL

Known as cathedral beads, and made in the Czech Republic, these have stepped ends with a metallic coating. The faceted ring around the middle gives the color of the glass more intensity: light is reflected through the facets from inside the metal coating as well as in the usual way, giving extra tones.

Hole: *Medium*
Stringing: *Medium tiger tail or heavy thread*
Weight: *0.7g*
Other sizes: *None*
Color range: *Medium*

Length: *10mm*
Width: *8mm*
Depth: *8mm*

Actual size

Mix and match

191

93

78 FACETED BAND

Like 77, the central band on this bead is faceted, but the ends are ridged in a twisted pattern and not coated. The beauty of this bead comes partly from the small amount of a second color included roughly in the middle of the main hue before the glass was shaped.

Hole: *Medium*
Stringing: *Medium tiger tail or heavy thread*
Weight: *0.7g*
Other sizes: *None*
Color range: *Medium*

Length: *10mm*
Width: *8mm*
Depth: *8mm*

Actual size

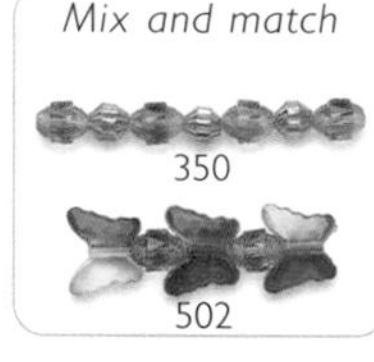

79 FACETED OVAL

The few facets on this oval shape make it almost a shallow bicone. Glass is colored by adding different minerals, and this kind of deep red was traditionally achieved using gold, making it the most expensive color. Modern science has found other ways to make red glass, but the old method is still in use for some pieces.

Hole: *Medium*
Stringing: *Medium tiger tail or heavy thread*
Weight: *0.5g*
Other sizes: *12mm, 15mm*

Color range: *Large*
Length: *9mm*
Width: *6.5mm*
Depth: *6.5mm*

Actual size

80 FACETED BICONES

Faceted glass bicones are often seen as substitutes for the more expensive crystal versions but are lovely in themselves. As mentioned in 73, bicones fit together well to make patterns, and they are particularly attractive in right-angle weave or tip to tip in a circle with small beads between the outer points making a star or flower.

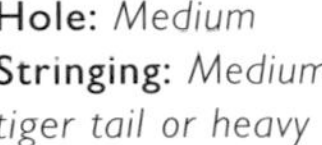

Hole: *Medium*
Stringing: *Medium tiger tail or heavy thread*
Weight: *0.5g*
Other sizes: *4mm, 6mm, 10mm*

Color range: *Large*
Length: *8mm*
Width: *8mm*
Depth: *8mm*

Actual size

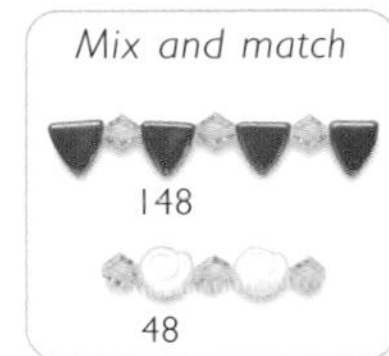

81 SQUARE BICONE

Not really a bicone, this bead is more like two slightly rounded pyramids base to base. They do however fit together in a very similar way to bicones and so are useful for the same stitches and patterns. These have a very slight luster coating that brings out the subtle colors.

Hole: *Medium*
Stringing: *Medium tiger tail or heavy thread*
Weight: *0.2g*
Other sizes: *None*
Color range: *Medium*

Length: *6mm*
Width: *5mm*
Depth: *5mm*

Actual size

82 PRESSED BICONES

These little pressed-glass bicones can be used in much the same way as 80, but they do not sparkle or catch the light nearly as much as the faceted version. They are an inexpensive substitute for practice, for backgrounds where a large number of beads are required, or for use alongside more exciting beads.

Hole: *Medium*
Stringing: *Medium tiger tail or heavy thread*
Weight: *0.1g*
Other sizes: *None*
Color range: *Medium*

Length: *4mm*
Width: *4mm*
Depth: *4mm*

Actual size

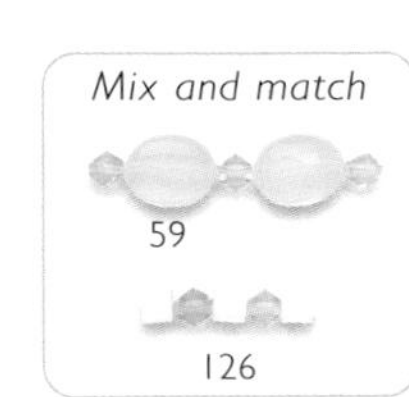

83 ANCIENT GEM SHAPE

The shallow points on the front and back of these beads, along with the pressed facets, give an impression of gemstones cut in an ancient fashion. The luster coating adds to this effect, and a string of these, perhaps with some antiqued traditional shapes of metallic beads, would be very appealing.

Hole: *Medium*
Stringing: *Medium tiger tail or heavy thread*
Weight: *0.5g*
Other sizes: *None*
Color range: *Medium*

Length: *8mm*
Width: *8mm*
Depth: *6.5mm*

Actual size

Mix and match

487

125

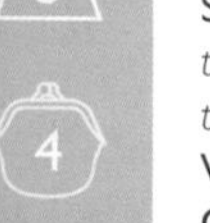

84 FLAT BLOCK

Two colors of glass pressed into a square thick tile, this bead has silver leaf in the center around the hole. The silver has split apart a little when the bead was molded, giving a pleasing crackled effect. These work well in jewelry intended to be substantial but not thick, such as bracelets that may have to fit under jacket sleeves.

Hole: *Medium*
Stringing: *Medium tiger tail or heavy thread*
Weight: *2.3g*
Other sizes: *None*
Color range: *Small*

Length: *13mm*
Width: *13mm*
Depth: *6mm*

Actual size

Mix and match

389

327

85 FAN

Actual size

Art deco lovers should appreciate this fan-patterned molded square tile, gilded in the dips, and made even more interesting by having the hole diagonally from corner to corner. The deep blue and gold combination would also work well in designs inspired by older art, such as ancient Egyptian pieces.

Hole: *Medium*
Stringing: *Medium tiger tail or heavy thread*
Weight: *1.5g*
Other sizes: *None*
Color range: *Medium*

Length: *17mm*
Width: *17mm*
Depth: *4mm*

Mix and match

143

399

86 DROP TWIST

Simple drops of glass have been flattened and twisted to make this shape. These could be used with a triangle bail (626) or strung together in a long strand. They will hang better with small beads between them because otherwise each one will interfere with the movement of the next, which could spoil the way the piece lies.

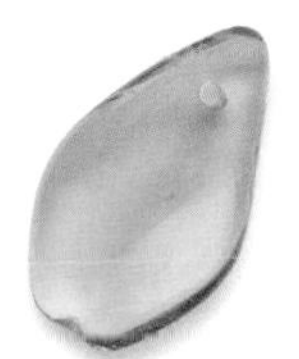

Hole: *Medium*
Stringing: *Medium tiger tail or heavy thread*
Weight: *0.8g*
Other sizes: *None*
Color range: *Medium*

Length: *3mm*
Width: *16mm*
Depth: *10mm*

Actual size

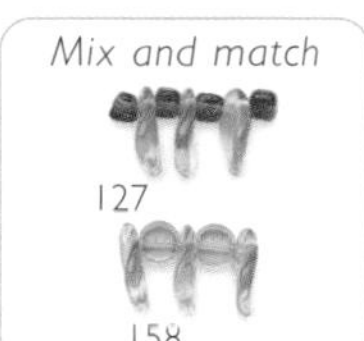
Mix and match

84

87 CROSS WITH HEART

The seams on this pressed shape are rather too obvious in the corners where the arms meet, but this is a fun shape with the added detail of the little heart in the middle. Good for dangling on a head pin (629), from a simple strand of beads, or as earrings, keeping the heart vertical.

Hole: *Medium*
Stringing: *Medium tiger tail or heavy thread*
Weight: *1.4g*
Other sizes: *None*
Color range: *Medium*

Length: *14mm*
Width: *14mm*
Depth: *9mm*

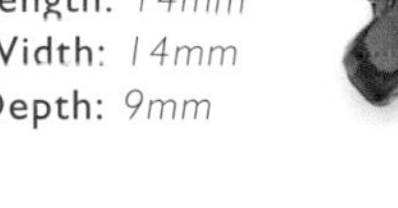

Actual size

Mix and match

18

88 BANANA

A wonderfully silly bead made to look like a banana. I have also seen glass beads in the shape of oranges, apples, pears, and a bunch of grapes. A fruit salad jewelry set would be great fun. If used as the main bead in a strand, put smaller items between these to allow them to hang neatly.

Hole: *Medium*
Stringing: *Medium tiger tail or heavy thread*
Weight: *0.9g*
Other sizes: *None*
Color range: *None*

Length: *5mm*
Width: *17.5mm*
Depth: *5mm*

Actual size

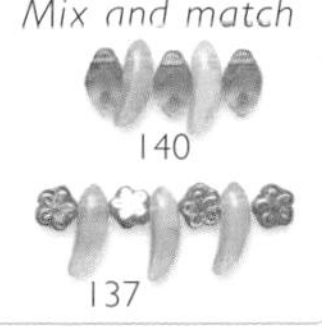
Mix and match

50

89 DAGGERS

2
3
50

A flat, flared shape, this looks like the blade of a dagger. A short strand of these tied into a circle makes a flower or star shape, and if threaded on their own they will roughly alternate up and down from the thread to give themselves space, so add small beads between them if they are to lie flat.

Hole: *Small*
Stringing: *Fine tiger tail or medium thread*
Weight: *0.3g*
Other sizes: *None*
Color range: *Large*

Length: *5mm*
Width: *15.5mm*
Depth: *3mm*

Actual size

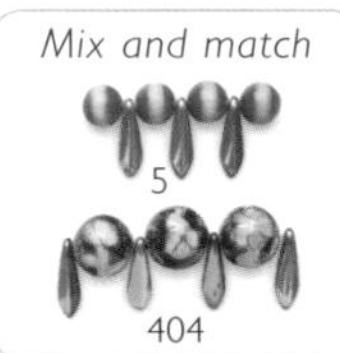

Mix and match
5
404

90 MAGATAMA

1
2
72

Think of these as large seed beads (1) with an off-center hole or as very small top-drilled drops. Used in bead embroidery, making beaded creatures, and as spacers, they also look agreeable on their own in a strand where they will push each other into all directions rather than hanging neatly.

Hole: *Medium*
Stringing: *Fine tiger tail or medium thread*
Weight: *0.1g*
Other sizes: *None*
Color range: *Large*

Length: *3.5mm*
Width: *5mm*
Depth: *5mm*

Actual size

Mix and match
214
3

91 FACETED DROP

28

A classical, narrow-faceted drop, these have the hole across the narrow end so that they will dangle down from their strand. To hang a number of these without them turning over, allow for the size of the widest part along the strand and fill in with small beads or a tube bead, in this case at least 6mm long.

Actual size

Hole: *Small*
Stringing: *Fine tiger tail or medium thread*
Weight: *1.1g*
Other sizes: *None*
Color range: *Medium*

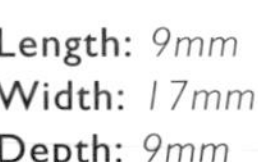

Length: *9mm*
Width: *17mm*
Depth: *9mm*

Mix and match
350
152

92 ROUNDED FACETED DROP

As well as being a much fatter drop than 91, these also have their holes along the length of the shape rather than along the top. To dangle these, use a head pin (629). The facets are not sharply cut, and do not extend to the tips of the shape, so the bead is more rounded.

Hole: *Medium*
Stringing: *Medium tiger tail or heavy thread*
Weight: *1.6g*
Other sizes: *12mm*
Color range: *Medium*

Length: *12.5mm*
Width: *10mm*
Depth: *10mm*

Actual size

20

93 TRUNCATED DROP

This drop is cut crisply, quite like 91, but it has a hole along its length, and the tips at both ends are flat, so the final result is more like 92. The lack of sharp tips can be a definite advantage in a necklace, or other jewelry worn next to the skin.

Hole: *Medium*
Stringing: *Medium tiger tail or heavy thread*

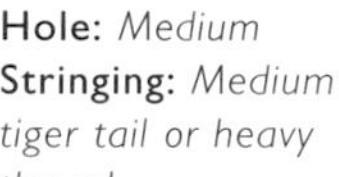

Weight: *0.5g*
Other sizes: *12mm, 15mm*
Color range: *Medium*

Length: *10mm*
Width: *7mm*
Depth: *7mm*

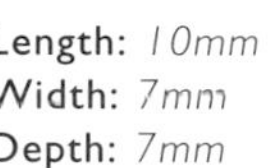

Actual size

3

25

94 FROSTED DROP

A longish drop, this has been etched or tumbled to create a matte surface, which on clear glass gives a frosted look. These beads need cleaning inside before use because the bead release left in the hole is loose and powdery, and will come out because the stringing material moves in the beads during wear.

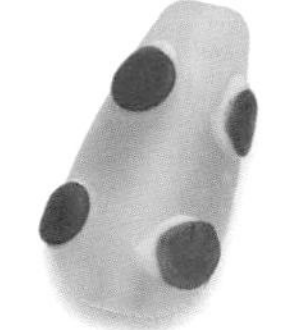

Actual size

Hole: *Large*
Stringing: *Heavy thread or fine cord*
Weight: *3.3g*
Other sizes: *None*
Color range: *Small*

Length: *21mm*
Width: *12mm*
Depth: *12mm*

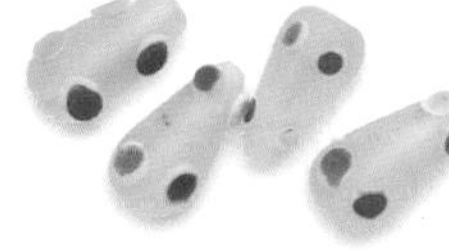

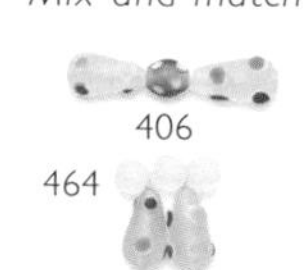

3

12

95 OPAQUE DROP

Basically a simple opaque glass drop, these are made more exciting with a spiral of goldstone glass that contains minute copper flakes to give the metallic shine. This would be applied as a raised thread of glass on the outside of the base bead, and then the whole piece would be reheated to work it into an even shape.

Hole: *Medium*
Stringing: *Medium tiger tail or heavy thread*
Weight: *1.2g*
Other sizes: *None*
Color range: *Medium*

Length: *13mm*
Width: *9mm*
Depth: *9mm*

Actual size

Mix and match
30
365

16

96 LINED DROP

Based on a tube of blue glass with a thick clear layer, these beads are made special by the inclusion of gold leaf (very thin foil) around the tube at the widest point of the finished drop. Gold foil is less commonly used these days than silver, due to price, but this is a classical technique.

Hole: *Medium*
Stringing: *Medium tiger tail or heavy thread*
Weight: *0.4g*
Other sizes: *None*
Color range: *Medium*

Length: *16mm*
Width: *10mm*
Depth: *10mm*

Actual size

Mix and match
44
335

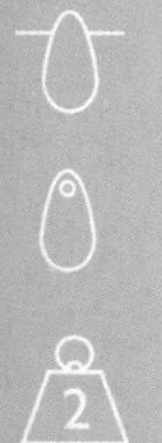
42

97 TEARDROP

The opal look of this drop is not a coating; it is in the glass itself, which, although clear and colorless, gives beautiful subtle tints as the light hits it and picks up the tones of any adjacent beads. This, together with their simple shape, makes them suitable for use in almost any beading project.

Hole: *Small*
Stringing: *Fine tiger tail or medium thread*
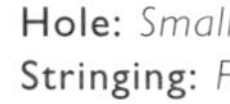
Weight: *0.4g*
Other sizes: *None*
Color range: *None*

Length: *6mm*
Width: *10mm*
Depth: *6mm*

Actual size

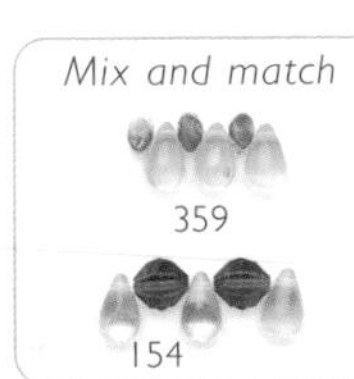
Mix and match
359
154

98 PEARL DROP

The peachy color of this glass pearl is similar to some of the best natural colored pearls, but many unnatural colors are also available. Very smooth, even drops like this would be rare in the natural world, too. None of this makes these any less useful for jewelry where soft tones are required.

Hole: *Small*
Stringing: *Fine tiger tail or medium thread*
Weight: *1.2g*
Other sizes: *20mm*
Color range: *Medium*

Length: *15mm*
Width: *8mm*
Depth: *8mm*

Actual size

Mix and match

177

349

99 LUSTER DROPS

This long, thin drop shape with a deep, soft luster coating would be suitable strung along the length of a piece or dangled, using a head pin (629), from the main strand or at the bottom of an earring. They would also be lovely at the end of almost any kind of fringe.

Actual size

Hole: *Medium*
Stringing: *Medium tiger tail or heavy thread*
Weight: *4.6g*
Other sizes: *None*
Color range: *Medium*

Length: *20mm*
Width: *15mm*
Depth: *15mm*

Mix and match

108

7

100 CLEAR DROP

The clarity of the glass used for these amazing drops is very impressive, and there are no seam lines or other imperfections. One could believe that they were polished blue-flecked quartz if it were not for the odd large air bubble (quartz rarely has bubbles much larger than the head of a pin).

Hole: *Medium*
Stringing: *Medium tiger tail or heavy thread*
Weight: *6.0g*
Other sizes: *None*
Color range: *None*

Length: *3mm*
Width: *8mm*
Depth: *8mm*

Actual size

Mix and match

5

310

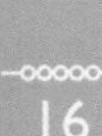

101 PYRAMID

With its square base and triangular sides, this shape can be used in many ways. Two used with flat ends together makes almost a cube, which will fit into others of the same kind in much the same way as 81. Arranged point to point a second effect is attained and a third when strung point to base.

Actual size

Hole: *Medium*
Stringing: *Medium tiger tail or heavy thread*
Weight: *2.0g*
Other sizes: *None*
Color range: *Medium*

Length: *16mm*
Width: *11mm*
Depth: *11mm*

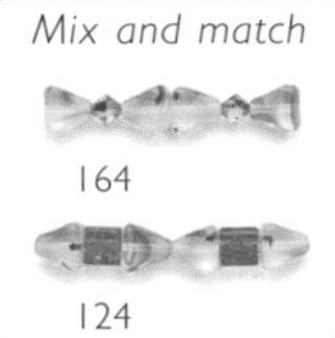

Mix and match

164

124

10

102 FUSED TRIANGLE

The dichroic glass used in these beads was cut from a sheet with the pattern already on it, and clear glass cut to the same shape but a little larger was put over the top. These were put into a kiln and fused together, with a separator between the layers so that a hole was formed across the wide end.

Hole: *Large*
Stringing: *Fine cord*
Weight: *9.3g*
Other sizes: *None*
Color range: *None*

Length: *25mm*
Width: *40mm*
Depth: *8mm*

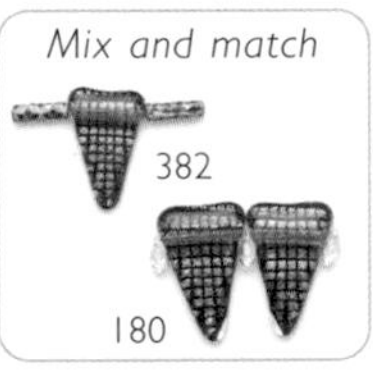

Mix and match

382

180

Actual size

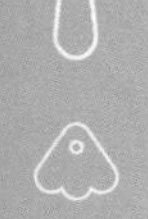

84

103 DUCK FOOT

Sold as a duck foot, this shape could also be considered to be a section of a flower, feathers, or a small wing. Cute to use when making beaded animals, as a decoration at the edge of the neckline or along a hem on clothing, or as a separator in jewelry.

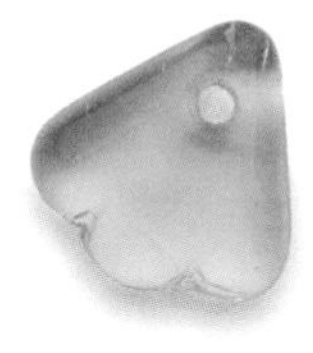

Hole: *Small*
Stringing: *Fine tiger tail or medium thread*
Weight: *0.2g*
Other sizes: *None*
Color range: *Medium*

Length: *3mm*
Width: *7mm*
Depth: *7mm*

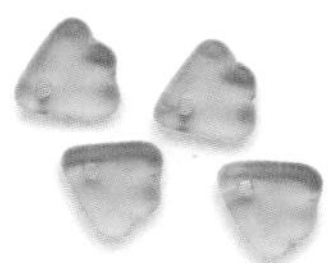

Actual size

Mix and match

283

155

104 ROUNDED TRIANGLE

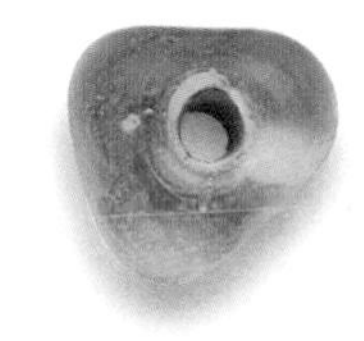

Lined with colored glass, but mainly clear, these are a little irregular and have rounded corners. When strung together, they look even more irregular, in fact rather like random tumble-polished gemstones. They could be used as separators in pieces intended to look as though they date from early times.

Hole: *Medium*
Stringing: *Medium tiger tail or heavy thread*
Weight: *0.4g*
Other sizes: *None*
Color range: *Medium*

Length: *5mm*
Width: *8mm*
Depth: *8mm*

Actual size

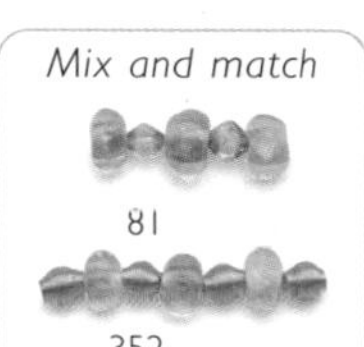

Mix and match
81
352

105 MODERN TRIANGLE

Fundamentally similar in shape to 104, these are pressed into an accurate triangle with sharper points, although they are still rounded a little to make them comfortable to use and wear. The flat shape makes them useful for bead embroidery, or they could be hung from a triangle bail (626) to give a pointed end to a slightly futuristic piece.

Hole: *Small*
Stringing: *Fine tiger tail or medium thread*
Weight: *0.5g*
Other sizes: *None*
Color range: *Medium*

Length: *4mm*
Width: *10mm*
Depth: *10mm*

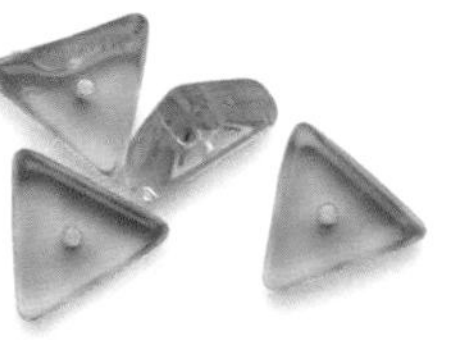

Actual size

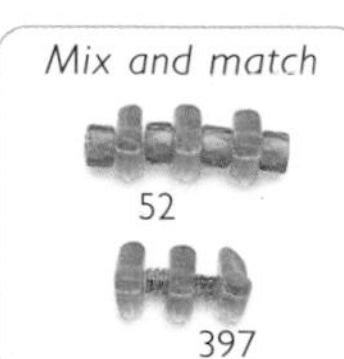

Mix and match
52
397

106 FUSED MOSAIC

These beads are made in a kiln, like 102, using three layers: a backing of black glass; a middle layer consisting of a random mosaic of fragments of dichroic coatings on either black glass (used face up) or clear glass (used face down); and a third layer of clear glass laid over the top.

Actual size

Hole: *Large*
Stringing: *Fine cord*
Weight: *30g*
Other sizes: *None*
Color range: *None*

Length: *30mm*
Width: *70mm*
Depth: *8mm*

Mix and match
265
14

5
5
17

107 TWO-HOLE FUSED

Between the dichroic glass at the back of this piece and the top clear layer, the maker has included a fragment of thin brass in the shape of a leafy twig. Tiny air bubbles, trapped around the brass as the glass fuses, add to the design. Double holes allow these to be used to connect two strands of beads.

Mix and match

69 373

Hole: *Large*
Stringing: *Heavy thread or fine cord*
Weight: *9.9g*
Other sizes: *None*
Color range: *None*

Length: *15mm*
Width: *49mm*
Depth: *8mm*

Actual size

3
3
32

108 SQUARE CUSHION

Roughly the shape of a stuffed pillow or cushion with flat ends, these have a gentle luster. These beads are quite flat, but gently rounded, so they are useful as a subtle spacer. A whole string would be easy and comfortable to wear with a certain amount of movement in the beads, so they could also be used as a main bead.

Hole: *Medium*
Stringing: *Medium tiger tail or heavy thread*
Weight: *0.6g*
Other sizes: *None*
Color range: *Medium*

Length: *8mm*
Width: *8mm*
Depth: *5mm*

Actual size

Mix and match

201

123

3
3
21

109 ROUNDED TABLET

The flat faces of these tablet beads reflect light, but the rounded edges make them more comfortable to wear than sharply rectangular tablets. These thin pieces will have very little movement if strung together, so separate them with a small bead to allow the piece to bend and drape pleasingly.

Hole: *Small*
Stringing: *Fine tiger tail or medium thread*
Weight: *0.7g*
Other sizes: *None*
Color range: *Medium*

Length: *12mm*
Width: *8.5mm*
Depth: *4mm*

Actual size

Mix and match

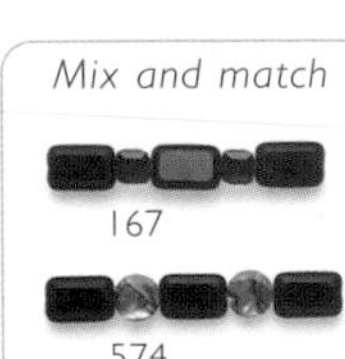

167

574

110 MILLEFIORI TILE

Thick slices of glass canes have been melted and squashed on to a base bead, then the whole piece was pressed into this tablet shape. They are very attractive, but the shape is another that will need to be separated by small spacers, or the piece will not be able to flex easily.

Actual size

Hole: *Medium*
Stringing: *Medium tiger tail or heavy thread*
Weight: *1.9g*
Other sizes: *None*
Color range: *Medium*

Length: *16mm*
Width: *10mm*
Depth: *6mm*

16

111 SQUARED OVAL

Silver foil lined with two colors of glass, this bead was probably made as an oval shape, then flattened on four sides using a marver (a flat piece of pressed carbon or metal used to shape flameworked beads). Thread the beads with the same colors together or to create a very different look, with all the beads arranged the same way.

Hole: *Medium*
Stringing: *Medium tiger tail or heavy thread*
Weight: *1.7g*
Other sizes: *None*
Color range: *Medium*

Length: *16mm*
Width: *8mm*
Depth: *8mm*

Actual size

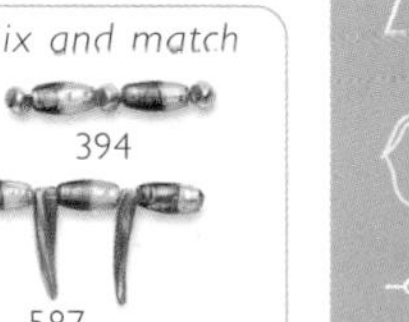

16

112 HEXAGON TUBE

Although they look similar to 111, except that there are six sides, these tubes were made in a mold. Seams can just be seen at two of the edges on each bead. The shape allows the glass to reflect a little more light than a plain round tube would.

Hole: *Medium*
Stringing: *Medium tiger tail or heavy thread*
Weight: *0.9g*
Other sizes: *None*
Color range: *Medium*

Length: *11.5mm*
Width: *7mm*
Depth: *7mm*

Actual size

22

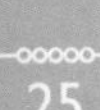

25

113 DICHROIC TUBE

A strip of dichroic glass has been rolled around a mandrel to make this simple tube, then pinched and twisted with tweezers to decorate it. This dichroic does not have clear glass over the top as some other pieces do (for example 106 and 116), so the effect is slightly dulled.

Hole: *Medium*
Stringing: *Medium tiger tail or heavy thread*
Weight: *1.7g*
Other sizes: *6mm, 8mm*
Color range: *Medium*

Length: *10mm*
Width: *10mm*
Depth: *10mm*

Actual size

9

114 ASYMMETRIC TUBE

The white center of this bead is bead release, which could be at least partially cleaned out. There is something rather novel about the thick bands of decoration on one end only. These would make interesting ends for a lariat-style necklace or could be dangled in the middle of a Y-shape.

Actual size

Hole: *Large*
Stringing: *Cord*
Weight: *8.9g*
Other sizes: *None*
Color range: *None*

Length: *30mm*
Width: *17mm*
Depth: *17mm*

9

115 FLOWERED TUBE

A flower garden all on their own, just a few of these beads could make a very plain piece eye-catching. The flowers all have white dot rings as the backgrounds, with color added on top and the dots then pulled in to make the petal shapes. The flowers done first are flatter because they have begun to melt in.

Actual size

Hole: *Large*
Stringing: *Cord*
Weight: *13.0g*
Other sizes: *None*
Color range: *None*

Length: *30mm*
Width: *16mm*
Depth: *16mm*

116 RIDGED TUBE

A designer piece by Jazzy Lily, these have dichroic glass wrapped around a lavender-colored tube in the center, with a thick layer of clear glass over the top. This top layer changes the look of the dichroic glass (compare it with 39 or 113), and the ridges change the way the light is reflected.

Actual size

Hole: *Large*
Stringing: *Cord*
Weight: *8.6g*
Other sizes: *None*
Color range: *None*

Length: *22mm*
Width: *17mm*
Depth: *17mm*

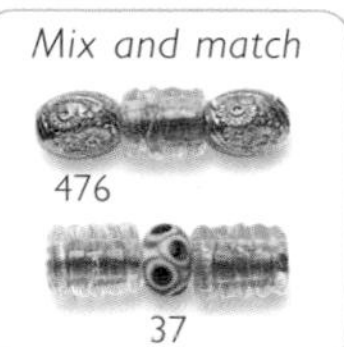

Mix and match

476

37

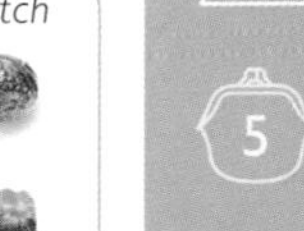

12

117 SPECTRA TUBE

The main metallic coating on this tube bead has a matte surface, but the strands of the same color swirled randomly over the top of this are shiny, so they catch the light and show up against the background. Several other shapes are made with this type of decoration, some with the strands and background in different colors.

Hole: *Medium*
Stringing: *Medium tiger tail or heavy thread*
Weight: *1.4g*
Other sizes: *5mm*
Color range: *Mixed*

Length: *20mm*
Width: *6mm*
Depth: *6mm*

Actual size

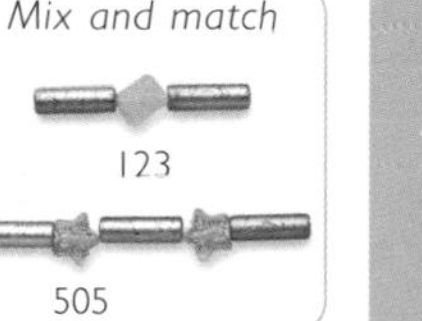

Mix and match

123

505

3

13

118 GYPSY TUBE

Opaque black glass has been painted with colors and gilded in fine lines and dots to make this complex pattern. The bead is so regular that it must be molded, but the decoration has been applied by hand, and there are slight irregularities that add to the beauty of a strand of these beads.

Hole: *Medium*
Stringing: *Medium tiger tail or heavy thread*
Weight: *3.1g*
Other sizes: *None*
Color range: *Medium*

Length: *20mm*
Width: *9mm*
Depth: *9mm*

Actual size

Mix and match

369

406

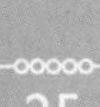

119 SPECKLED TUBE

This glass may be intended to simulate tortoise shell or just the texture of an animal's fur. It was probably made by creating the base tube of amber-colored glass, rolling it over a sprinkle of black glass fragments (called frit), and then heating until the fragments have melted into the main shape.

Hole: *Medium*
Stringing: *Medium tiger tail or heavy thread*
Weight: *1.2g*
Other sizes: *None*
Color range: *None*
Length: *10mm*
Width: *9mm*
Depth: *9mm*

Actual size

120 DICHROIC STRIPE

A strip of clear dichroic glass, with the coating on the outside, has been wrapped around a mandrel to make the basic tube, then a fine stripe of dichroic on black has been added on top in a wave pattern. The bead must then have been reheated and rolled to incorporate this decoration into the tube shape.

Hole: *Medium*
Stringing: *Medium tiger tail or heavy thread*
Weight: *1.1g*
Other sizes: *None*
Color range: *Medium*
Length: *14mm*
Width: *7mm*
Depth: *7mm*

Actual size

121 TRIANGLE TUBE

A three-sided tube sits on one side when worn, so a point is always facing out. The decoration is fumed, which means that while the glass thread squiggles were still molten, a fragment of gold was held in the hottest part of the flame so that it vaporized, and this vapor was deposited on to the sticky glass.

Hole: *Medium*
Stringing: *Medium tiger tail or heavy thread*
Weight: *2.4g*
Other sizes: *None*
Color range: *Medium*
Length: *18mm*
Width: *10mm*
Depth: *10mm*

Actual size

122 SQUARE TUBE

A square tube can look too modern for some jewelry pieces, but this one has a desert sun coating (similar to 19, but with a silver base layer instead of the gold), which breaks up the sharp-edged look and makes the bead more versatile. As usual with flat-ended beads, add spacers to help the movement of a strand.

Hole: *Medium*
Stringing: *Medium tiger tail or heavy thread*
Weight: *0.9g*
Other sizes: *6mm*
Color range: *Medium*

Length: *11mm*
Width: *7mm*
Depth: *7mm*

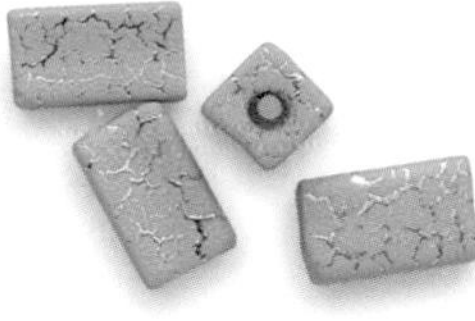

Actual size

Mix and match

210

378

2

23

123 ROSY CUBE

This cube shape is not very sharp and is made more attractive by having the hole diagonally so that more sides are visible in wear and a strand will move well. The disadvantage of this hole direction is that there will always be a corner pressing inward, so avoid using these at the back of a necklace if the front is heavy.

Hole: *Small*
Stringing: *Fine tiger tail or medium thread*
Weight: *1.5g*
Other sizes: *None*
Color range: *Medium*

Length: *12mm*
Width: *12mm*
Depth: *12mm*

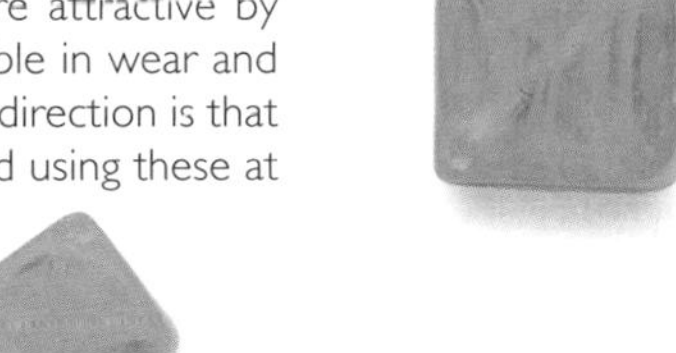

Actual size

Mix and match

169

239

3

21

124 DYED GLASS

These cubes appear to have been dyed after stringing in a tight strand because there was dye on the tied ends of the threading material when they were delivered, and there is no color on the flat hole ends of the bead. The color is consistent and does not rub off easily.

Hole: *Small*
Stringing: *Fine tiger tail or medium thread*
Weight: *0.5g*
Other sizes: *None*
Color range: *Medium*

Length: *6mm*
Width: *6mm*
Depth: *6mm*

Actual size

42

125 SQUARE SEED

Japanese cube beads are pretty regular and can be used where a standard size and shape are required, such as in larger beadweaving projects, peyote, or brick-stitch work. They could be considered to be a type of substantial squared-off seed bead and used in much the same way.

Hole: *Medium*
Stringing: *Fine tiger tail or medium thread*
Weight: *0.1g*
Other sizes: *None*
Color range: *Very large*

Length: *4mm*
Width: *4mm*
Depth: *4mm*

Actual size

Mix and match

1

520

126 SILK SEED

Silk glass is made by whisking the molten glass so that it is full of small bubbles, then pulling out the result so that the bubbles are stretched with it into very fine lines. This gives the look of hundreds of strands of silk all aligned along the rod. In this case, the rod has been made into crisp cubes.

Hole: *Medium*
Stringing: *Fine tiger tail or medium thread*
Weight: *0.2g*
Other sizes: *None*
Color range: *None*

Length: *4mm*
Width: *4mm*
Depth: *4mm*

Actual size

Mix and match

234

577

127 ENGLISH LACE MAKER'S SQUARE CUT

Traditionally used as the decoration on the end of a lace maker's bobbin, called a spangle, these rough cubes are made more or less round, and then pressed on the four sides with textured paddles to flatten them into this shape. They are still made this way in England today.

Hole: *Medium*
Stringing: *Medium tiger tail or heavy thread*
Weight: *0.2g*
Other sizes: *8mm*
Color range: *Medium*

Length: *5mm*
Width: *5mm*
Depth: *5mm*

Actual size

Mix and match

125

508

128 TRUNCATED DIAGONAL CUBE

The points of these cubes are rounded or removed where the hole passes through them, so that the length is slightly less than the squared measurement of the cube might suggest. One side has a reflective AB (aurora borealis) coating, and this will show on different beads along the strand when worn.

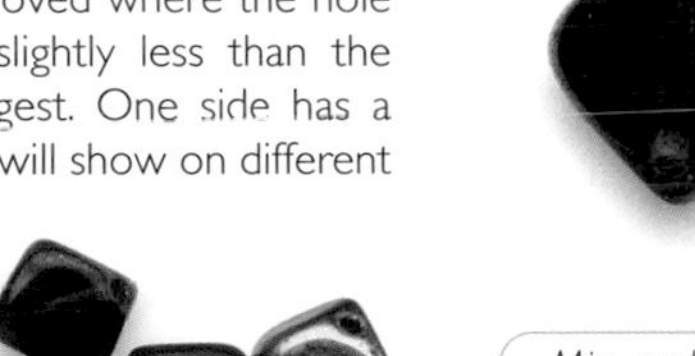

Hole: *Small*
Stringing: *Fine tiger tail or medium thread*
Weight: *0.6g*
Other sizes: *9mm*
Color range: *Large*

Length: *7mm*
Width: *8mm*
Depth: *8mm*

Actual size

129 DICHROIC CHUNK

Somewhere between a cube and a randomly shaped nugget, the dichroic glass on this bead has a thin coating of clear glass over the top to add to its brightness and reflectivity. A strip of dichroic was wrapped around a round bead (the edges can just be seen) and then pressed into this shape.

Actual size

Hole: *Medium*
Stringing: *Medium tiger tail or heavy thread*
Weight: *5.1g*
Other sizes: None
Color range: *Small*

Length: *15mm*
Width: *18mm*
Depth: *17mm*

130 POLYGON

The twelve flat faces of this bead are decorated with slices of cane, which must have been accurately placed and incorporated into the main bead before the final shape was created. The angled edges and points have been emphasized with raised dots. A few of these special but heavy beads would be sufficient in a piece of jewelry.

Actual size

Hole: *Large*
Stringing: *Heavy thread or fine cord*
Weight: *14.6g*
Other sizes: None
Color range: None

Length: *22mm*
Width: *22mm*
Depth: *19mm*

Mix and match

588

75

131 CHINESE FACE

Made to resemble the mask for a Noh play, these flattened ovals have been decorated using stringers of colored glass to make a face on both sides. The eyes and brows are cleverly created by placing two dots of black glass, flattening them, and adding a strip of white glass over the top.

Actual size

Hole: *Large*
Stringing: *Heavy thread or fine cord*
Weight: *4.2g*
Other sizes: *None*
Color range: *None*

Length: *16.5mm*
Width: *18mm*
Depth: *10mm*

Mix and match

381

160

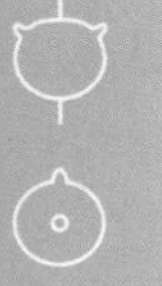

132 OWL HEAD

Glass animals are commonly made in the flame as decorative figures, and some are available as beads. The details extend farther out from the main bead than most embellishments. These parts can be delicate, so designs should avoid other strands that could strike them, and they should be stored carefully.

Actual size

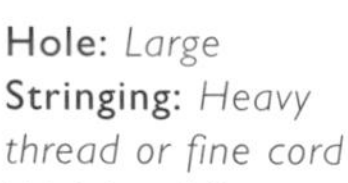

Hole: *Large*
Stringing: *Heavy thread or fine cord*
Weight: *6.8g*
Other sizes: *None*
Color range: *None*

Length: *15mm*
Width: *20mm*
Depth: *20mm*

Mix and match

538

331

133 PRESSED FROG

The mold line on these pressed beads is clearly visible but does not really detract from the charm of these little critters. As well as a fun strand, perhaps with a pond-life theme, the frogs would add an out-of-the-ordinary element to an embroidered or woven watery design.

Hole: *Medium*
Stringing: *Medium tiger tail or heavy thread*
Weight: *1.1g*
Other sizes: *None*
Color range: *Mixed*

Length: *13mm*
Width: *10mm*
Depth: *8mm*

Actual size

Mix and match

141

463

134 DIAMOND FISH

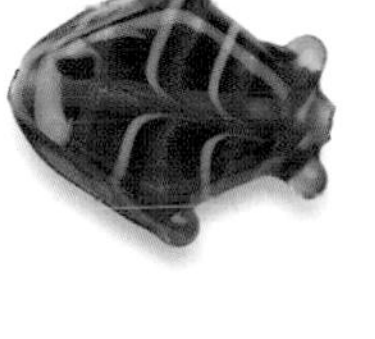

Pressed-glass diamond shapes have been decorated with fine lines of glass pulled into a feathery pattern to suggest scales and tiny dots used for eyes. They have been further embellished in the flame with extra glass added to make fins top and bottom, and a tail, which turns them into these little fancy fish.

Hole: *Medium*
Stringing: *Medium tiger tail or heavy thread*
Weight: *2.2g*
Other sizes: *None*
Color range: *Medium*

Length: *17mm*
Width: *16mm*
Depth: *7mm*

Actual size

135 LUSTER FISH

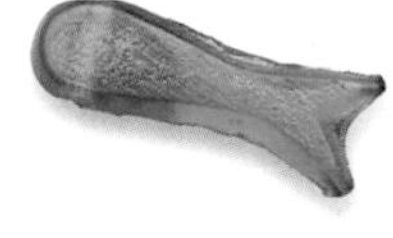

These simply shaped pressed fish with a slight luster coating are spoiled by very obvious seams. Unusually, the hole is across the head, which is about the same width as the tail, meaning that these beads will hang together neatly without any spacers, although the shape of the beads would be more easily seen if spacers were used.

Hole: *Medium*
Stringing: *Medium tiger tail or heavy thread*
Weight: *0.8g*
Other sizes: *None*
Color range: *Mixed*

Length: *8mm*
Width: *20mm*
Depth: *4mm*

Actual size

136 CAT HEAD

The detail on this pressed glass cat head is lovely and is emphasized with gold coloring in the recesses, probably added by dipping the beads and wiping the gold off of the higher points. A whole cat could be made using a few beads for a body, legs, and tail, perhaps on wire so that it could be posed.

Hole: *Small*
Stringing: *Fine tiger tail or medium thread*
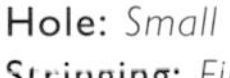
Weight: *1.2g*
Other sizes: *None*
Color range: *Medium*

Length: *13mm*
Width: *11mm*
Depth: *6.5mm*

Actual size

63

137 MIDDLE-HOLE FLOWER

Holes in this position mean that the flower shapes will not be seen if the beads are strung along a strand. These can, however, be attached to a main piece by taking the thread up through the hole, through a small bead to hold it in place, and then back down through the flower. This will hold the shape flat, showing its face.

Hole: *Small*
Stringing: *Fine thread*
Weight: *0.4g*
Other sizes: *None*
Color range: *Medium*

Length: *4mm*
Width: *9mm*
Depth: *9mm*

Actual size

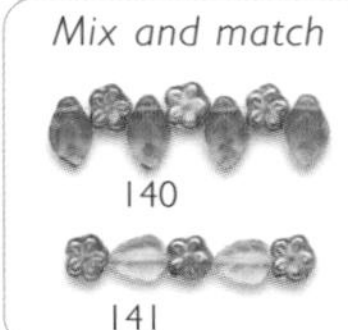

Mix and match

140

141

32

138 SIMPLE FLOWER

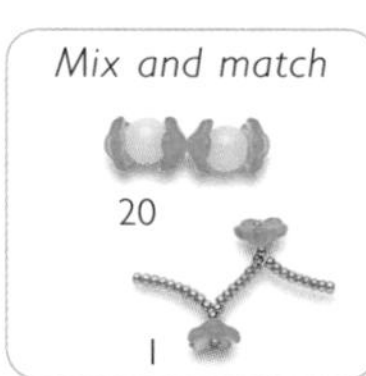

These flowers will show their faces (either the plain or the coated side) along the length of a strand. The pressed shape is indented with petals, but these are more noticeable on the coated side. Several simple strands of these in different colors would make a delightful summery necklace, perhaps with a few leaf shapes added in.

Hole: *Small*
Stringing: *Fine tiger tail or medium thread*
Weight: *0.4g*
Other sizes: *None*
Color range: *Medium*

Length: *8mm*
Width: *8mm*
Depth: *4mm*

Actual size

Mix and match

20

1

36

139 BUTTON FLOWER

The hole on these flowers is across the back rather like a button. This works well on embroideries or added to the top of beadwork. If strung tightly together they make groups showing their faces in different directions but if separated with small beads, they tend to turn over in wear showing the plain backs.

Hole: *Medium*
Stringing: *Fine tiger tail or medium thread*
Weight: *0.3g*
Other sizes: *None*
Color range: *Medium*

Length: *7mm*
Width: *7mm*
Depth: *5.5mm*

Actual size

Mix and match

363

502

140 CROSS-HOLE LEAF

With a hole across the base of each leaf, these hang from their strand easily, although if used together, spacers will be necessary to allow them to move loosely. Use with a triangle bail (626) at the end of any kind of drop, such as an earring or even with 138 to make miniature plants.

Hole: *Small*
Stringing: *Fine thread*
Weight: *0.4g*
Other sizes: *None*
Color range: *Medium*

Length: *7.5mm*
Width: *12.5mm*
Depth: *3mm*

Actual size

Mix and match

377

86

34

141 LONG-HOLE LEAF

Simple to use in a strand, these beads have the hole along their length. If the design requires leaves to hang from a strand, they can be used with head pins (629). There are impressed veins on both sides, but they are shallow and not easy to see.

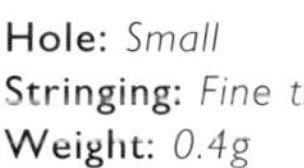

Hole: *Small*
Stringing: *Fine thread*
Weight: *0.4g*
Other sizes: *None*
Color range: *Medium*

Length: *10mm*
Width: *8mm*
Depth: *3mm*

Actual size

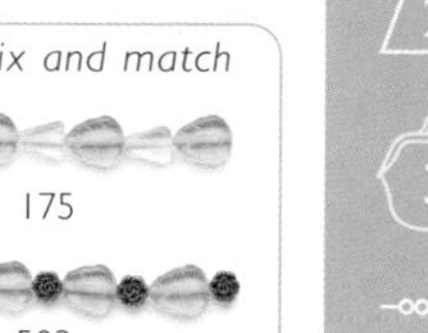

Mix and match

175

503

25

142 THROUGH-HOLE LEAF

These have a hole in the third possible direction for a flat leaf-shaped bead, from front to back at the widest point. The leaves would stick out in random directions from the main strand if used alone or with other beads (perhaps flowers), or they could be hung using an ice pick bail (627).

Hole: *Small*
Stringing: *Fine thread*
Weight: *0.5g*
Other sizes: *None*
Color range: *Medium*

Length: *3.5mm*
Width: *11mm*
Depth: *3.5mm*

Actual size

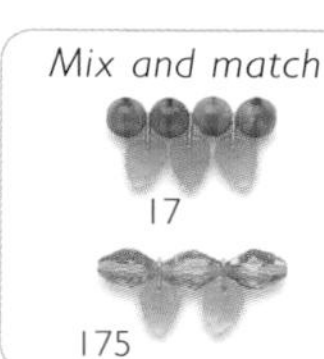

Mix and match

17

175

72

3 3 18

143 TEXTURED HEART

Pressed with a texture on its flat sides and with an AB coating on one of them, this thin frosted heart is pretty and delicate looking. Most standard heart shapes are about as broad at their widest point as they are long; this one is very slightly wider, and the top dip is shallow.

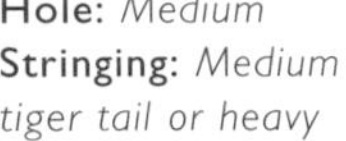

Hole: *Medium*
Stringing: *Medium tiger tail or heavy thread*
Weight: *1.3g*
Other sizes: *None*
Color range: *Medium*

Length: *14mm*
Width: *15mm*
Depth: *4mm*

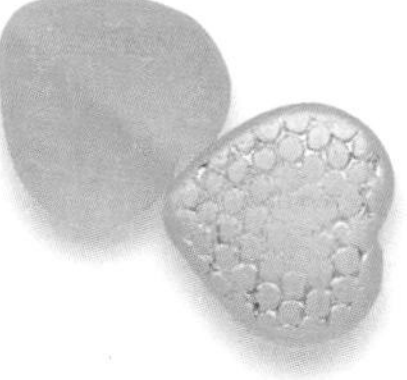

Actual size

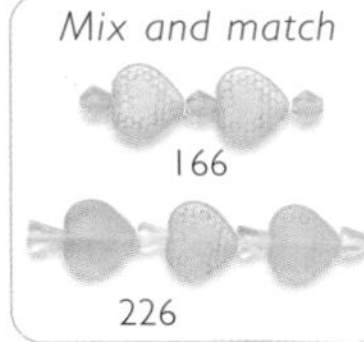

2 3 14

144 LONG HEART

The stretched-out shape of this heart is unusual. The dip between the top bumps is deep so if strung together, these beads will fit into each other slightly diminishing the total length of the strand. Tiny beads between them would solve this and emphasize the shapes.

Hole: *Medium*
Stringing: *Medium tiger tail or heavy thread*
Weight: *0.9g*
Other sizes: *None*
Color range: *Medium*

Length: *18mm*
Width: *11mm*
Depth: *3.5mm*

Actual size

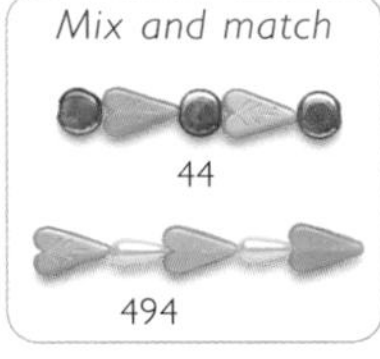

3 3 16

145 PART-FROSTED HEART

The edges of these hearts are rounded and frosted, but the flat front and back are glossy, so that light comes through clearly. The combination of finishes make the heart more attractive visually than either all matte or all shiny glass would be.

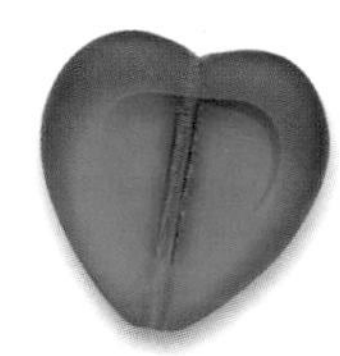

Hole: *Medium*
Stringing: *Medium tiger tail or heavy thread*
Weight: *1.8g*
Other sizes: *None*
Color range: *Medium*

Length: *16mm*
Width: *15mm*
Depth: *5mm*

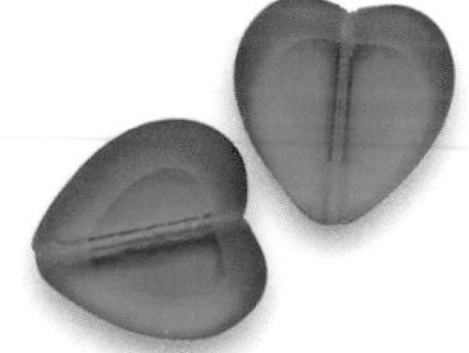

Actual size

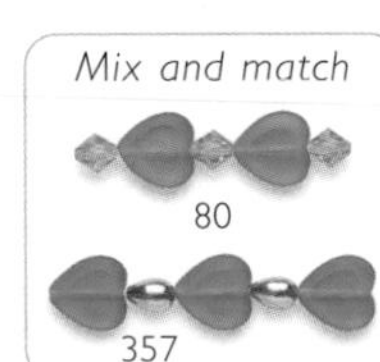

146 ROUNDED HEART

This small rounded heart shape is very comfortable against the skin; one side has an AB coating. A few of these could be added into a simple strand of beads to give it a lift. They would also be good for sewing on to clothing, as earrings, as fringe ends, or even glued on to cards.

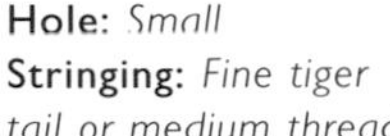

Hole: *Small*
Stringing: *Fine tiger tail or medium thread*
Weight: *0.5g*
Other sizes: *6mm, 8mm*
Color range: *Medium*

Length: *10mm*
Width: *10mm*
Depth: *3.5mm*

Actual size

25

147 TOP-HOLE HEART

Here's another rounded heart shape but with the hole from front to back, so these are not suitable for use along a strand if the shape is to be seen. Use with an ice pick or triangle bail (627 or 626) to hang, or use the method suggested for 137 to attach them to a piece with their face outward.

Hole: *Medium*
Stringing: *Medium tiger tail or heavy thread*
Weight: *1.8g*
Other sizes: *None*
Color range: *Medium*

Length: *5.5mm*
Width: *15.5mm*
Depth: *5mm*

Actual size

45

148 SHIELD

Known as a shield shape these have an all-over dull metallic coating. Because there is more glass below the hole than above it they will mostly hang downward when worn but could flip over to point in either direction on a bracelet or at the sides and back of a necklace.

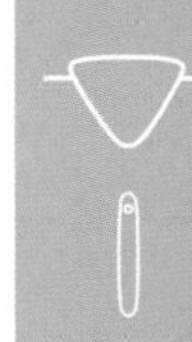

Hole: *Medium*
Stringing: *Medium tiger tail or heavy thread*
Weight: *1.0g*
Other sizes: *None*
Color range: *Medium*

Length: *10mm*
Width: *10mm*
Depth: *10mm*

Actual size

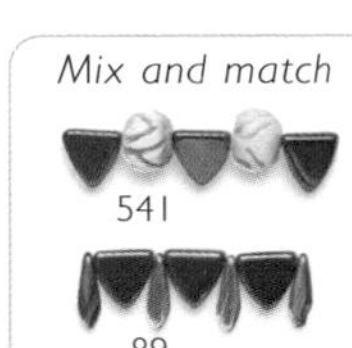

3

25

CHAPTER 2

Crystal

The type of crystal used for the beads in this chapter is a form of glass with a high lead content, which makes it more expensive to produce. When used to make tableware such as drinking glasses and vases, it is usually referred to as lead crystal. Its chemical composition makes the glass optically clearer, and most crystal beads are faceted to take advantage of this property. Different colors are seen even in uncolored crystal beads because the light is refracted at different angles as it enters and leaves the beads through varying thicknesses of glass—the bead splits the white light in the same way a prism does.

An AB (aurora borealis) coating is often applied to one side of a crystal bead, to accentuate the light-scattering properties. This coating looks opaque (that is, light does not come through) and metallic from the side it is covering, but on transparent beads the color and brightness of sparkle shows through strongly when the bead is seen from the other side.

There are several qualities of crystal available—higher grades have a higher lead content; the regularity of the facets also varies. Some of the best crystal beads are hand-faceted.

Natural crystal, sometimes called rock crystal, appears in the semiprecious chapter.

Suspended crystals in a lattice of glass seed beads give this bracelet sparkle and shape. The fastenings are balls of beads with corresponding loops.

25

149 FINE HEXAGON-CUT ROUND

In general, the higher the number of facets on a crystal bead the greater the sparkle. The shape of the facets contributes to the overall shape—to make a more rounded bead many tiny hexagons are used, becoming smaller and more stretched out toward the holes.

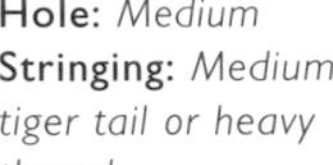

Hole: *Medium*
Stringing: *Medium tiger tail or heavy thread*
Weight: *1.6g*
Other sizes: *6mm, 7mm, 8mm, 12mm, 14mm, 16mm*

Color range: *Large*
Length: *10mm*
Width: *10mm*
Depth: *10mm*

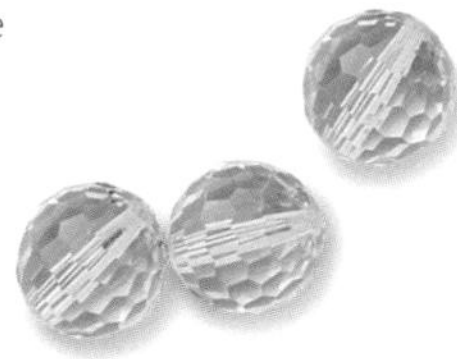

Actual size

Mix and match

290

7

32

150 TRIANGLE-CUT ROUND

These are more angular and thus less rounded than 149 and have fewer facets, but the triangles meeting at the center line reflect light very strongly as do the diamond shapes on the next row, so they appear very bright when worn. This cutting pattern is more modern than the standard hexagon cut.

Hole: *Medium*
Stringing: *Medium tiger tail or heavy thread*
Weight: *0.7g*
Other sizes: *4mm, 6mm, 8mm*

Color range: *Large*
Length: *8mm*
Width: *8mm*
Depth: *8mm*

Actual size

Mix and match

191

168

50

151 HEXAGON-CUT OPAQUE ROUND

These show what is probably the most common cut for a round crystal bead, a double row of hexagons around the center line with stretched hexagons between these and the hole ends. These are opaque black crystal, reflective but not translucent. There is an AB (aurora borealis) coating, which is not at all obvious.

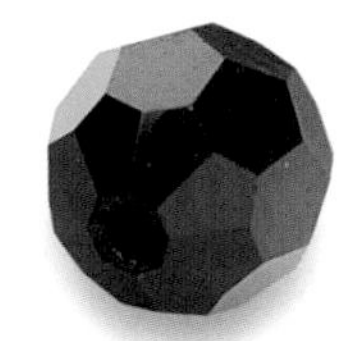

Hole: *Medium*
Stringing: *Medium tiger tail or heavy thread*
Weight: *0.2g*
Other sizes: *13 sizes, 3mm to 20mm*

Color range: *Large*
Length: *5mm*
Width: *5mm*
Depth: *5mm*

Actual size

Mix and match

216

363

152 HEXAGON-CUT ROUND

This is much the same cut as the previous bead but using a lower quality crystal, that is, one with a smaller percentage lead content. The facets are also a little less even (they are visually perfect on 151). These are a little lighter and less light-catching than beads of the same size and cut in first-rate crystal.

Hole: *Medium*
Stringing: *Medium tiger tail or heavy thread*
Weight: *0.3g*
Other sizes: *4mm, 8mm*

Color range: *Large*
Length: *5mm*
Width: *6mm*
Depth: *6mm*

Actual size

Mix and match

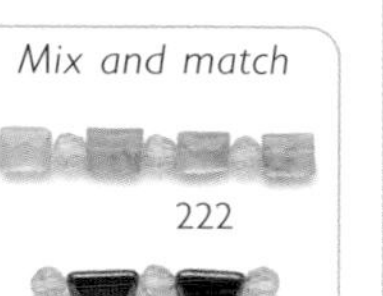

222

148

153 DIAMOND-CUT ROUND

Rounder than the triangle cut, not as round as the fine hexagons, this is a compromise cut, again slightly uneven and made from the lower-grade crystal. Although the sparkle is reduced, if these are used with other crystal beads, the difference between the qualities is generally unnoticeable. Putting both grades into one work may look odd.

Hole: *Medium*
Stringing: *Medium tiger tail or heavy thread*
Weight: *0.6g*
Other sizes: *4mm, 6mm*

Color range: *Large*
Length: *8mm*
Width: *8mm*
Depth: *8mm*

Actual size

Mix and match

208

126

3

4

32

154 RECTANGLE-CUT ROUND

Another of the more modern cuts, these move away from a round shape to have more pointed ends; two rows of rectangles around the center line give a large, bright reflective area despite fewer facets. This color is called black ice to distinguish it from the standard black, which is usually opaque.

Hole: *Medium*
Stringing: *Medium tiger tail or heavy thread*
Weight: *0.6g*
Other sizes: *4mm, 6mm*

Color range: *Large*
Length: *8mm*
Width: *7mm*
Depth: *7mm*

Actual size

Mix and match

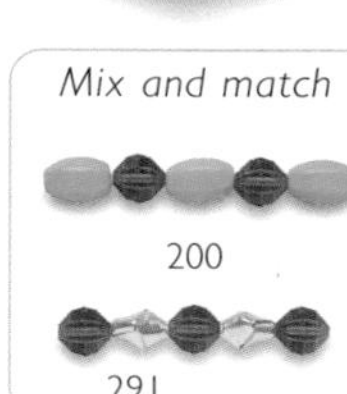

200

291

4

32

155 OFF ROUND

Somewhere between a round and a cushion shape, this has one row of stretched hexagons along the center line rather than two lines of identical shapes meeting or interlinking there (as for all the previous beads in this chapter). This makes the equator ring much more obvious, so the bead looks even less rounded than it actually is.

Hole: *Medium*
Stringing: *Medium tiger tail or heavy thread*
Weight: *0.5g*
Other sizes: *4mm, 5mm, 6mm, 8mm*
Color range: *Large*
Length: *7mm*
Width: *7mm*
Depth: *7mm*

Actual size

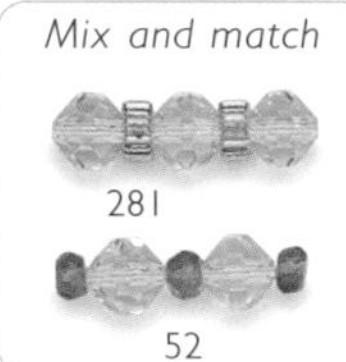

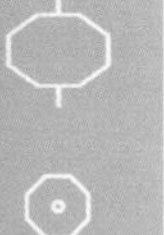

156 DIAMOND-CUT CUSHION

Definitely a cushion shape, rounded but much shorter than it is wide. Two rows of diamond facets make the reflective central line, giving a good sparkle. These are more commonly used between larger or more heavily decorated beads, but the shape is very attractive on its own, perhaps interspersed with the same shape in a different size.

Hole: *Medium*
Stringing: *Medium tiger tail or heavy thread*
Weight: *0.6g*
Other sizes: *8mm*
Color range: *Large*
Length: *5mm*
Width: *8mm*
Depth: *8mm*

Actual size

157 DOMED DISK

Showing one of its flat octagonal faces in use, this shape is domed on both sides by a faceted ring meeting at an unfaceted band with the hole going through it. These beads are particularly useful where a fairly wide round shape is preferred but height is not required, such as on slim bracelets.

Hole: *Medium*
Stringing: *Medium tiger tail or heavy thread*
Weight: *0.3g*
Other sizes: *5mm, 8mm*
Color range: *Large*
Length: *6mm*
Width: *6mm*
Depth: *4.5mm*

Actual size

42

158 FLATTER DISK

This disk has a much larger flat surface than 157. It is almost round due to the number of facets on the edge of the bead, leading to a similar unfaceted band. Useful in the same way as the previous beads but has less sparkle and perhaps a more modern look.

Hole: *Medium*
Stringing: *Medium tiger tail or heavy thread*
Weight: *0.5g*
Other sizes: *6mm, 10mm*
Color range: *Large*

Length: *8mm*
Width: *8mm*
Depth: *4.5mm*

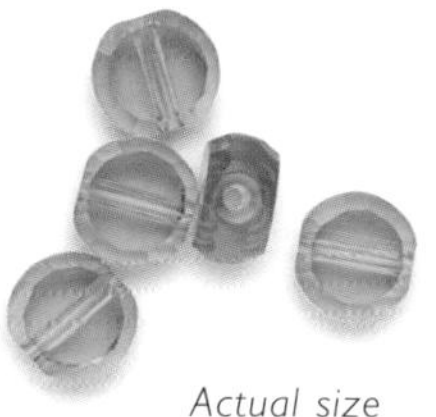

Actual size

2

32a

159 POINTED DISK

The facets on this disk come to a point in the middle, and this, combined with the AB coating on one side, gives this shallow shape a very bright sparkle. Because they are pierced near the thin edge they can be hung using a jump ring or bail (605, 606, 626, or 627) or added to flat work and embroidery.

Hole: *Medium*
Stringing: *Medium tiger tail or heavy thread*
Weight: *0.3g*
Other sizes: *6mm, 12mm*

Color range: *Large*
Length: *4mm*
Width: *8mm*
Depth: *8mm*

Actual size

63

160 WHEEL

Flat on the ends but diamond faceted on the sides, which face outward when this bead is strung. If these are used next to each other, the strand will either gap when curved showing the thread or will be very stiff. To avoid this, use rounded beads in between.

Hole: *Medium*
Stringing: *Medium tiger tail or heavy thread*
Weight: *0.4g*
Other sizes: *6mm*
Color range: *Large*

Length: *4mm*
Width: *8mm*
Depth: *8mm*

Actual size

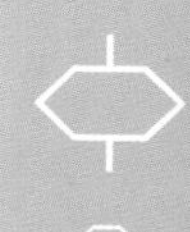

63

84

161 DIPPED WHEEL

The wheel shape has only two rows of facets; its special feature is the rounded dips in the two ends (that is, either side of the hole). These are made to fit over the ends of round beads. Strands made with these shapes interspersed with rounds look very solid but move well. Allow for the overlap when calculating lengths.

Hole: *Medium*
Stringing: *Medium tiger tail or heavy thread*
Weight: *0.4g*
Other sizes: *6mm*
Color range: *Large*
Length: *3mm*
Width: *8mm*
Depth: *8mm*

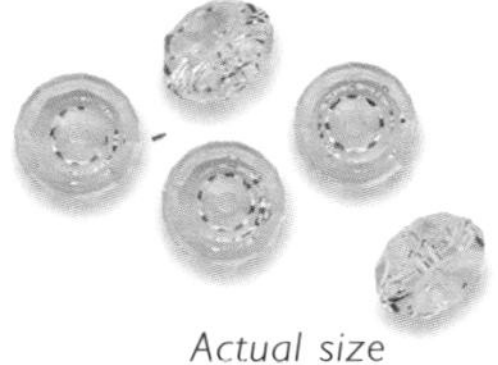
Actual size

Mix and match
187
5

72

162 FACETED DISK

This could be considered a disk with facets or a short, cut bicone (see 164). With just one row of facets on either side of the very sharply cut central line, these are usually used as spacers to add light and movement to a piece, rather than on their own.

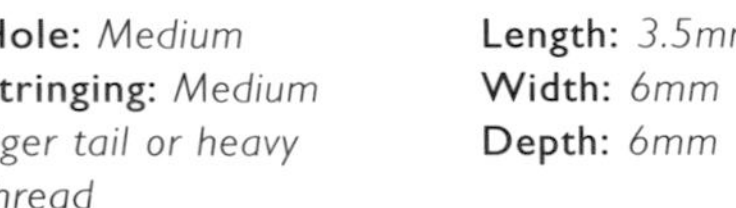

Hole: *Medium*
Stringing: *Medium tiger tail or heavy thread*
Weight: *0.1g*
Other sizes: *8mm*
Color range: *Large*
Length: *3.5mm*
Width: *6mm*
Depth: *6mm*

Actual size

Mix and match
285
83

125

163 FLOWER

These flowers (also called Margaritas) are faceted much as 162 but with a shaped edge and a flatter profile. Used along a strand they are not very impressive (although they can be useful as spacers), but they can be attached flat by bringing thread up through the hole, through a small bead, and then back down and into fabric or other beadwork.

Hole: *Medium*
Stringing: *Medium tiger tail or heavy thread*
Weight: *0.1*
Other sizes: *8mm, 10mm, 12mm, 14mm*
Color range: *Large*
Length: *2mm*
Width: *6mm*
Depth: *6mm*

Actual size

Mix and match
234
166

164 FACETED BICONE

These are AB coated, and probably the most popular crystal bead, sometimes called diamond shape. These beads are very good in strands and for certain bead stitches, such as right-angle weave, because they fit into each other so neatly.

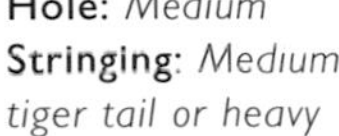

Hole: *Medium*
Stringing: *Medium tiger tail or heavy thread*
Weight: *0.2g*
Other sizes: *3mm, 4mm, 5mm, 7mm, 8mm, 10mm, 12mm*

Color range: *Large*
Length: *6mm*
Width: *6mm*
Depth: *6mm*

Actual size

Mix and match

219

256

42

165 OPAL BICONE

The facets on this version are less precise than those on 164, and the grade of crystal is lower. These are mainly interesting because opal crystal, a less translucent but not totally opaque material, is less commonly used because it lowers the brilliance of the beads, but does not change the reflectivity.

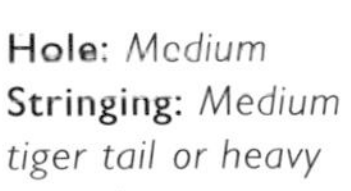

Hole: *Medium*
Stringing: *Medium tiger tail or heavy thread*
Weight: *0.2g*
Other sizes: *4mm, 8mm*

Color range: *Medium*
Length: *6mm*
Width: *6mm*
Depth: *6mm*

Actual size

42

166 ASYMMETRIC BICONE

Examine these beads closely to see that one end (one cone) of this faceted bicone is actually longer than the other. This is not obvious in individual beads, but gives an appealing texture to a strand. They can all be threaded in the same direction or arranged in pairs with the like ends together.

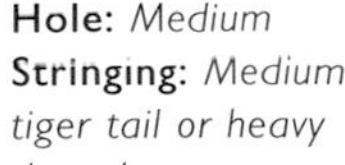

Hole: *Medium*
Stringing: *Medium tiger tail or heavy thread*
Weight: *0.1g*
Other sizes: *8mm, 9mm*

Color range: *Large*
Length: *4.5mm*
Width: *5mm*
Depth: *5mm*

Actual size

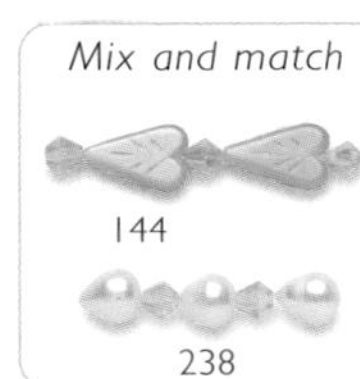

56

42

167 HIGH-CUT CUBE

These have small squares on each face with crisp facets from the edges of the cube to the edges of each square. This shaping avoids a large flat area and therefore the need for spacer beads. Because the light reflects from the inner squares, these beads appear smaller than 169 despite having the same outer measurements.

Hole: *Medium*
Stringing: *Medium tiger tail or heavy thread*
Weight: *0.5g*
Other sizes: *4mm, 8mm, 10mm, 12mm*

Color range: *Large*
Length: *6mm*
Width: *6mm*
Depth: *6mm*

Actual size

Mix and match

314

148

42

168 OPAQUE CUBE

These are the same size and shape as 167 but made of opaque crystal. The two are both shown to illustrate how very different they look. The opaque crystal is just as reflective as the translucent one but appears much less bright because there is no light transmitted or refracted through the bead.

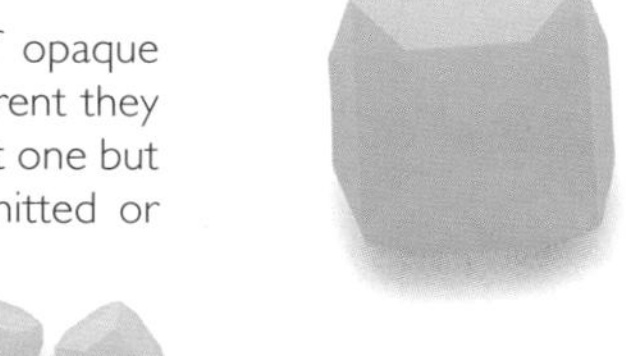

Hole: *Medium*
Stringing: *Medium tiger tail or heavy thread*
Weight: *0.5g*
Other sizes: *4mm, 8mm, 10mm, 12mm*

Color range: *Large*
Length: *6mm*
Width: *6mm*
Depth: *6mm*

Actual size

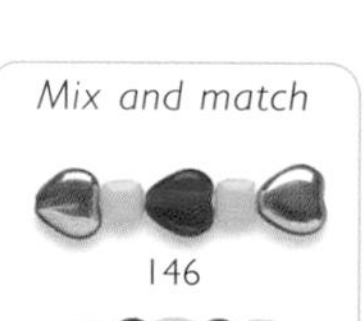

Mix and match

146

406

45

169 FLATTER CUBE

A much simpler cut of cube bead, these just have the edges flattened off at an angle to make the extra facets. They look much chunkier than 167 and will not move well against each other, so rounded spacers will be required to allow a strand of these beads to curve without leaving loose thread and gapping.

Hole: *Medium*
Stringing: *Medium tiger tail or heavy thread*
Weight: *0.4g*
Other sizes: *4mm*
Color range: *Large*

Length: *5.5mm*
Width: *6mm*
Depth: *6mm*

Actual size

Mix and match

212

8

170 DIAGONAL-HOLE CUBE

Although this is a similar cut to 169, much more sparkle is achieved in wearing because one of the points of the cube will always be pointing outward. The two corners with the hole going through them are cut flat. Any jewelry made with these must not be tight because there is also a point facing inward.

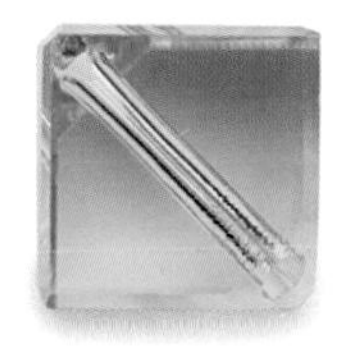

Hole: *Medium*
Stringing: *Medium tiger tail or heavy thread*
Weight: *0.6g*
Other sizes: *4mm, 6mm*

Color range: *Large*
Length: *7.5mm*
Width: *6mm*
Depth: *6mm*

Actual size

171 LONG BICONES

These are similar in cut to the standard bicone shapes such as 164 but far longer in comparison to their width. They make very dramatic slim strands and are suitable for those who find sharper-angled cut-crystal beads a little uncomfortable to wear. The ends are flat but small, so spacers are only necessary if a lot of movement is required.

Hole: *Medium*
Stringing: *Medium tiger tail or heavy thread*
Weight: *0.5g*
Other sizes: *None*
Color range: *Large*

Length: *14.5mm*
Width: *6mm*
Depth: *6mm*

Actual size

172 SMOOTHER LONG BICONE

This bead is made of lower-grade crystal than 171, with the facets less crisp and slightly uneven, but it is still very attractive and impressive in quantity so worth using if several strands of crystal are required. The inferior sparkle and quality of cut are not generally noticeable unless it is used mixed in with better pieces.

Hole: *Medium*
Stringing: *Medium tiger tail or heavy thread*
Weight: *0.1g*
Other sizes: *12mm*
Color range: *Large*

Length: *8mm*
Width: *4mm*
Depth: *4mm*

Actual size

173 FACETED TUBE

A short tube with slightly rounded ends (to allow a strand of these to move against each other well), the sides of this are cut into eight facets. The pictured bead is frosted (although available in translucent and opaque, too), which removes almost all of the sparkle, but light is still refracted through the crystal.

Hole: *Medium*
Stringing: *Medium tiger tail or heavy thread*
Weight: *0.4g*
Other sizes: *None*
Color range: *Large*

Length: *7.5mm*
Width: *4.5mm*
Depth: *4.5mm*

Actual size

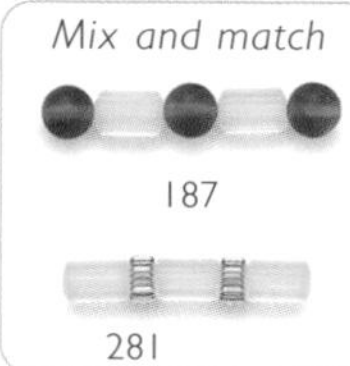

174 SQUARE-CUT OVAL

The ends of this shape are faceted in the same way as the long bicones, with two rows of square facets along the center line, making another classic cut-crystal shape. More or differently shaped facets would make it more rounded, like 175, but possibly the bead would not catch and return as much light.

Hole: *Medium*
Stringing: *Medium tiger tail or heavy thread*
Weight: *0.8g*
Other sizes: *9mm, 15mm*
Color range: *Large*

Length: *12mm*
Width: *8mm*
Depth: *8mm*

Actual size

175 HEXAGON-CUT OVAL

There are 66 facets on each of these beads, giving a rounded look but lots of reflection. An AB coating has been applied to one side only because it would otherwise cover the color, but because the crystal is opaque it cannot be seen through the bead and so shows randomly on a strand.

Hole: *Medium*
Stringing: *Medium tiger tail or heavy thread*
Weight: *1.7g*
Other sizes: *9mm, 12mm*
Color range: *Large*

Length: *15mm*
Width: *10mm*
Depth: *10mm*

Actual size

176 DROP BICONE

Much like 164 but drilled through one end rather than through the middle so that it can be dangled from a strand or used with a triangle bail (626). If strung tightly without spacers, these will point in all directions giving a thick, sparkly look. Stitched to clothing, they stand at an angle.

Hole: *Medium*
Stringing: *Medium tiger tail or heavy thread*
Weight: *0.7g*
Other sizes: *6mm*
Color range: *Large*

Length: *8mm*
Width: *9mm*
Depth: *9mm*

Actual size

Mix and match

93

310

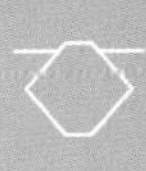

177 ANGLED DROP

This very bright cut with its AB coating would be eye-catching used on a head pin (629) or along a strand. They could be used all in the same direction, perhaps reversing this at the midpoint of a necklace, or used in pairs tip to tip or end to end for a different look.

Hole: *Medium*
Stringing: *Medium tiger tail or heavy thread*
Weight: *0.5g*
Other sizes: *6.5mm, 9mm*
Color range: *Large*

Length: *8mm*
Width: *7mm*
Depth: *7mm*

Actual size

Mix and match

52

219

178 SHORT-ANGLED DROP

Although slightly less flat at one end than 177, these could be used in much the same way. They are lower-quality crystal, though, and the facets are less accurately cut, so the sparkle is far less even allowing for the fact that these do not have an AB coating.

Hole: *Medium*
Stringing: *Medium tiger tail or heavy thread*
Weight: *0.3g*
Other sizes: *None*
Color range: *Large*

Length: *8mm*
Width: *6.5mm*
Depth: *6.5mm*

Actual size

Mix and match

357

7

179 SHARP DROP

These drops are cut so that all the facets come together to a point at the tip. Use spacers if these are to dangle from a strand because they will otherwise twist in all directions, but unlike 176 they are too narrow to make a good mass in that way.

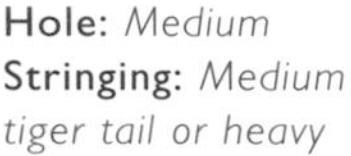

Hole: *Medium*
Stringing: *Medium tiger tail or heavy thread*
Weight: *0.4g*
Other sizes: *13mm, 15mm, 18mm, 22mm, 28mm*

Color range: *Large*
Length: *5.5mm*
Width: *11mm*
Depth: *11mm*

Actual size

Mix and match
375
164

180 ROUNDED DROP

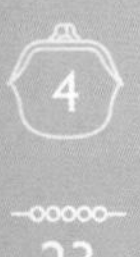

Highly faceted and with an AB coating, these narrow drops are excellent on clothing or embroideries because they are very reflective, not too deep, and have their hole near the tip for easy attachment. Alternatively, they can be strung on a strand with spacers or used with a triangle bail (626) for drop ends.

Hole: *Medium*
Stringing: *Medium tiger tail or heavy thread*
Weight: *0.6g*
Other sizes: *13mm*
Color range: *Large*

Length: *11mm*
Width: *7mm*
Depth: *7mm*

Actual size

Mix and match
151
194

181 LONG DROP

A similar cut to 179 but these are pierced from tip to tip rather than across the top so the facets do not meet in a sharp point. These are also rather wider, so the whole thing appears rounder and less crisp. String along a strand as for 177 or drop on a head pin (629).

Hole: *Medium*
Stringing: *Medium tiger tail or heavy thread*
Weight: *0.7g*
Other sizes: *9mm, 12mm, 13.5mm, 15mm, 18mm*

Color range: *Large*
Length: *10mm*
Width: *8mm*
Depth: *8mm*

Actual size

Mix and match
358

264

182 ALMOST OVAL DROP

These have an extra row of facets toward the top of the drop, so they are more rounded at both ends. In fact the shape is partly disguised by the cut, making them appear almost oval if used individually. They are probably best used as dangles (on a head pin, 629) or grouped together on a strand to emphasize the shape.

Hole: *Medium*
Stringing: *Medium tiger tail or heavy thread*
Weight: *1.2g*
Other sizes: *6mm, 10mm, 11mm*

Color range: *Large*
Length: *12mm*
Width: *8mm*
Depth: *8mm*

Actual size

Mix and match

21

183 MORE ROUNDED DROP

An extra round of facets toward the base of these drops makes them more rounded than 181, and they are also fatter. More faces may mean more colors are shown, but the shallower angles between them often mean that the sparkle is less bright. They can, though, be used in much the same ways.

Hole: *Medium*
Stringing: *Medium tiger tail or heavy thread*
Weight: *0.8g*
Other sizes: *5mm, 9mm*

Color range: *Large*
Length: *7mm*
Width: *10mm*
Depth: *7mm*

Actual size

Mix and match

36

184 HEART

The hole is at the top of these hearts, so they are most useful hung on a triangle bail (626) or on a loop of beads, as a dangle from a strand or the bottom of an earring or lariat. They are also suitable for embroidery, clothing, or even to decorate a very special greetings card.

Hole: *Medium*
Stringing: *Medium tiger tail or heavy thread*
Weight: *0.6g*
Other sizes: *18mm, 28mm*

Color range: *Large*
Length: *5mm*
Width: *10mm*
Depth: *10mm*

Actual size

Mix and match

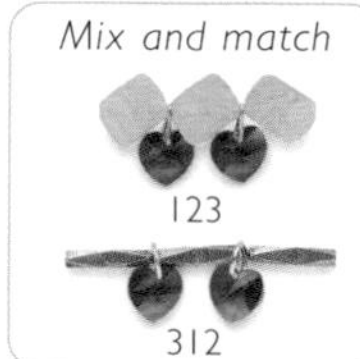

125

CHAPTER 3

Semiprecious

This chapter covers beads made of semiprecious stones, also known as gemstones, plus other materials such as pearls and coral, which are considered semiprecious. Precious stones, such as emeralds, rubies, and diamonds, are not included because they are extremely high in price and so are very rarely drilled for beads (although very low-grade drilled emerald, for example, can be found). Small precious stones are occasionally set into precious metal beads.

Although many of the beads here have a color range of "small" or "none," this refers to the shape in that particular material. Most of the stone shapes are available in a large range of other semiprecious stones.

In general, pearls should not be allowed to rub against each other or other beads, so knots are often used between them. This is not, however, shown in most of the mix-and-match sets, because it is not essential. When calculating how many beads to buy for a strand, make experimental knots with the thread that is to be used and measure them. Add this measurement to the length of the bead, then multiply that total to work out the number of beads required.

Small drops and round silver beads are used to emphasize the shape of these long ovals and to make them hang correctly.

3

3
32

185 ROUND LEOPARD-SKIN JASPER

Almost all semiprecious stones are available as basic round polished beads in various sizes. These can be beautiful on their own, in graduated sets, and with precious metals, and those reputed to have healing properties or to bring good fortune are often found in "power" bracelets along with 186 and 255.

Hole: *Medium*
Stringing: *Medium tiger tail*
Weight: *0.7g*
Other sizes: *Many*
Color range: *None*

Length: *8mm*
Width: *8mm*
Depth: *8mm*

Actual size

Mix and match

550

371

3
3
25

186 THREE-HOLE MOSS AGATE

Three-hole beads are most commonly used in "power" bracelets, with the two ends of the elastic cord pulled out through the hole at right angles to the main drilling and knotted, often with a shaped bead such as 255 as extra decoration. They can also be used at the midpoint of a Y-shaped necklace.

Hole: *Large*
Stringing: *Heavy tiger tail*
Weight: *1.4g*
Other sizes: *8mm*
Color range: *None*

Length: *10mm*
Width: *10mm*
Depth: *10mm*

Actual size

Mix and match

258

179

3

4
42

187 MATTE AMETHYST

A matte finish, where the surface is deliberately left rough or treated to create a frosted look, is less common in semiprecious stones and is usually only used on translucent stones. This finish is much more subtle than the usual high polish, useful in jewelry intended to be low-key rather than eye-catching, and with antiqued metals.

Hole: *Medium*
Stringing: *Medium tiger tail*
Weight: *0.3g*
Other sizes: *8mm*
Color range: *None*

Length: *6mm*
Width: *6mm*
Depth: *6mm*

Actual size

Mix and match

472

391

188 ROUND WHITE FRESHWATER PEARL

A pearl is created when a particle of grit or a fragment of broken shell gets inside an oyster. The reaction of the oyster is to lay down layers of a material called nacre around the irritation, eventually forming a pearl. Nacre is delicate, so good quality pearls are usually separated along a strand by knotting soft thread.

Hole: *Small*
Stringing: *Silk*
Weight: *1.3g*
Other sizes: *Many*
Color range: *Small*

Length: *10mm*
Width: *10mm*
Depth: *10mm*

Actual size

189 ROUND CULTURED PEARL

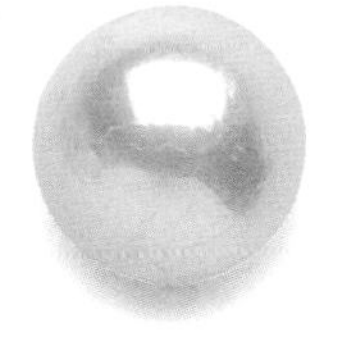

Cultured pearls are just like natural pearls, except that the irritant in the oyster has been inserted intentionally rather than happening naturally. Only about five percent of such "seeded" oysters actually produce a good quality pearl, and of course they take many years to lay down the layers of nacre, so even cultured pearls are never going to be inexpensive.

Hole: *Small*
Stringing: *Silk*
Weight: *0.5g*
Other sizes: *Many*
Color range: *Small*

Length: *7mm*
Width: *7mm*
Depth: *7mm*

Actual size

3

36

190 HEXAGON-CUT ONYX

Faceted semiprecious stone beads are generally far more expensive than uncut beads of similar size and material because even more stone is wasted, and the cutting is almost always done by hand, which is time-consuming. This cut involves rows of uneven hexagons creating an almost round shape.

Hole: *Medium*
Stringing: *Medium tiger tail*
Weight: *0.6g*
Other sizes: *10mm*
Color range: *None*

Length: *8mm*
Width: *7.5mm*
Depth: *7.5mm*

Actual size

3

32

191 TRIANGLE-CUT GARNET

These are flattened rounds with the facets cut as triangles on a translucent stone. Garnet is often very dark, as here, but shows its red color more strongly when faceted as light is refracted through the stone as well as reflected off of the many surfaces. Compare with the opaque stone 190.

Hole: *Medium*
Stringing: *Medium tiger tail*
Weight: *0.5g*
Other sizes: *None*
Color range: *None*

Length: *5mm*
Width: *6mm*
Depth: *6mm*

Actual size

Mix and match
385
313

192 BLACK POTATO PEARL

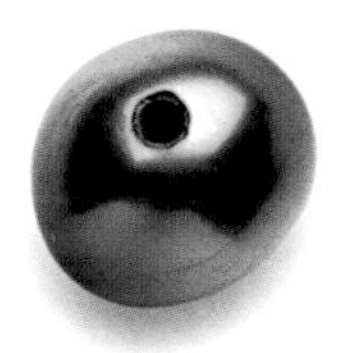

This shape of pearl is sometimes referred to as a potato, which does not seem to do it justice. These are drilled across the center of the shape but along the narrower axis, so a strand of these will be wider but require more beads. This is one of the deepest blacks available in natural pearls.

Hole: *Small*
Stringing: *Silk*
Weight: *0.1g*
Other sizes: *Many*
Color range: *Small*

Length: *4mm*
Width: *5mm*
Depth: *4mm*

Actual size

63

193 METALLIC GRAY FRESHWATER PEARL

This rather irregular shape is common in freshwater pearls, although the deep, almost metallic gray coloring makes these more desirable to some designers. The drill direction is more usual than 192. A lighter gray silk used for knotting would enhance the depth of color of these pearls, but black could emphasize the sheen instead.

Hole: *Small*
Stringing: *Silk*
Weight: *0.2g*
Other sizes: *Many*
Color range: *Small*

Length: *7mm*
Width: *4mm*
Depth: *4mm*

Actual size

36

194 CREAM FRESHWATER PEARL

Freshwater pearls can be as perfect as those from oysters found in the sea but are often ridged or ringed, and some oysters make much more irregular shapes. This creamy color is popular where the more common off-white pearl would be too light to tone with other materials in the jewelry or clothes.

Hole: *Small*
Stringing: *Silk*
Weight: *0.2g*
Other sizes: *Many*
Color range: *Small*

Length: *5mm*
Width: *6mm*
Depth: *5mm*

Actual size

195 GRAY FRESHWATER PEARL

The surface of these light gray pearls is particularly vulnerable to damage, so they should be stored carefully to prevent them from rubbing against each other or anything else. In use, knot between them with soft thread such as silk. Once strung, a box that allows them to lie cushioned in a line or gentle curve would be the best.

Hole: *Small*
Stringing: *Silk*
Weight: *0.7g*
Other sizes: *Many*
Color range: *Small*

Length: *9mm*
Width: *7mm*
Depth: *7mm*

Actual size

Mix and match

287

166

196 OIL SLICK FRESHWATER PEARL

When these pearls catch the light they show bands of color rather like oil on water in the sunlight, and are sometimes called rainbow pearls. The banding is typical of a freshwater pearl, and adds to the changing colors by giving more surfaces for the light to hit.

Hole: *Small*
Stringing: *Silk*
Weight: *0.9g*
Other sizes: *Many*
Color range: *Small*

Length: *10mm*
Width: *8mm*
Depth: *8mm*

Actual size

15

197 LONG OVAL FRESHWATER PEARL

This is probably the color most people think of when they hear the word "pearl." The slightly unusual long oval shape, almost a barrel, is a little less classical than a round pearl, and so could lend itself to eclectic modern pieces where a plain round would seem out of place. It would also work in a simple strand.

Hole: *Small*
Stringing: *Silk*
Weight: *1.0g*
Other sizes: *Many*
Color range: *Small*

Length: *17mm*
Width: *7mm*
Depth: *7mm*

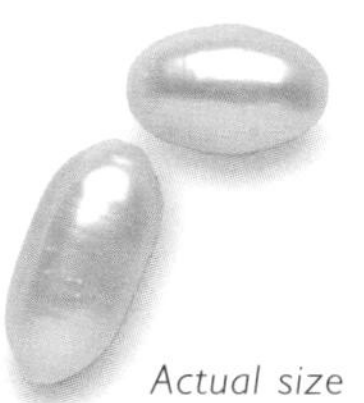
Actual size

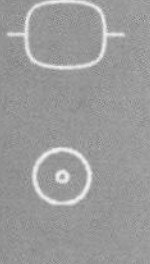

9

198 BARREL AMBER

Amber is one of the most difficult materials to identify correctly because the weight, warmth, and sound are very similar to good plastic simulations. Look for seam lines and discontinuities in any markings, and holes should look drilled. A hot needle pressed into the hole opening (where a mark will not show) gives a characteristic smell quite unlike melting plastic.

Hole: *Large*
Stringing: *Medium tiger tail or heavy thread*
Weight: *16.0g*
Other sizes: *None*

Color range: *None*
Length: *29mm*
Width: *26mm*
Depth: *26mm*

Actual size

42

199 OVAL AVENTURINE

Small, thin oval beads are good in narrow strands with small round beads, and can be very useful as long spacers, especially at the back of a necklace or in multistrand pieces. Aventurine is often simulated in glass, and goldstone (215) is sometimes called aventurine glass due to the specking pattern in both materials.

Hole: *Small*
Stringing: *Fine tiger tail*
Weight: *0.2g*
Other sizes: *None*
Color range: *None*

Length: *6mm*
Width: *4mm*
Depth: *4mm*

Actual size

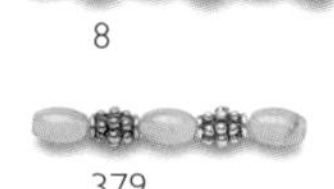

200 HEXAGON OVAL TURQUOISE

Turquoise can be plain, but most have this attractive pattern caused by the veins of the material on which it was formed, which is known as the matrix. This oval shape with its six flattened sides has gently rounded edges, and is seen in some very ancient jewelry, so these are perhaps most suitable for classical pieces.

Hole: *Medium*
Stringing: *Medium tiger tail or heavy thread*
Weight: *1.5g*
Other sizes: *None*
Color range: *None*
Length: *16mm*
Width: *8mm*
Depth: *8mm*

Actual size

201 SIDE-PIERCED RICE GARNET

Very dark red garnet hardly shows its color at all, looking almost black in lower light levels. This side-drilled pointed rice shape is interesting in groups on its own, giving a spiked or toothed look to both sides of the piece, but is also useful as a spacer where a round bead would be too dull.

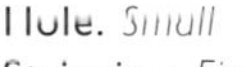

Hole: *Small*
Stringing: *Fine tiger tail*
Weight: *0.2g*
Other sizes: *None*
Color range: *None*
Length: *3.5mm*
Width: *7mm*
Depth: *3.5mm*

Actual size

202 ROUGH OVAL AMBER

Clear amber with only a little mottling looks very different from 198 but is basically the same material. These uneven shapes waste less material than a rounded or even precisely oval bead, so they are less expensive but still look good. Check as for 198 to be sure it is amber and not a simulation.

Hole: *Medium*
Stringing: *Medium tiger tail or heavy thread*
Weight: *0.2g*
Other sizes: *Many*
Color range: *None*
Length: *11mm*
Width: *5mm*
Depth: *5mm*

Actual size

3

4

18

203 FLAT OVAL RHODOCHROSITE

Flat ovals are good for pieces where width is required but depth would be a nuisance, such as in bracelets intended to fit under a cuff. These are made more attractive by the simple cut, a large diamond shape on the front and back with other facets around it.

Hole: *Medium*
Stringing: *Medium tiger tail*
Weight: *1.6g*
Other sizes: *None*
Color range: *None*
Length: *14mm*
Width: *10mm*
Depth: *5mm*

Actual size

Mix and match

385

359

3

4

21

204 SCARAB LAPIS

High-quality lapis lazuli is deep blue, often with gold streaks. Lower grades have some green or white inclusions as do these carved beads. The carving imitates scarab beetles, a fortunate symbol according to the ancient Egyptians. Reconstituted lapis, where chips and powder have been formed into shapes is also available and is much less expensive.

Hole: *Medium*
Stringing: *Medium tiger tail*
Weight: *0.8g*
Other sizes: *Variable*
Color range: *None*
Length: *12mm*
Width: *10mm*
Depth: *5mm*

Actual size

Mix and match

399

441

3

3

20

205 DISK MOTHER-OF-PEARL

Mother-of-pearl is shell from the inside of an oyster or sometimes a similar shell. The layer of pearly material is usually thin, so small, flat shapes are common. Not all of the surface of a mother-of-pearl bead will necessarily have the lustrous coating so check quality before buying.

Hole: *Medium*
Stringing: *Medium tiger tail or heavy thread*
Weight: *0.9g*
Other sizes: *None*
Color range: *None*
Length: *12.5mm*
Width: *4mm*
Depth: *4mm*

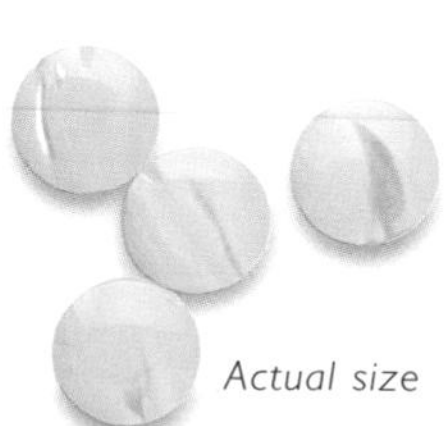

Actual size

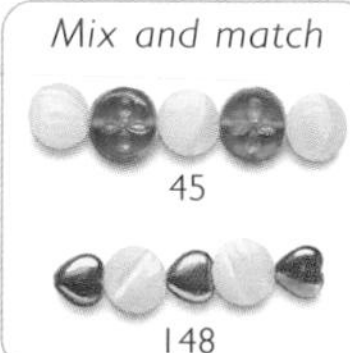

Mix and match

45

148

206 FACETED DISK JADE

Jade comes in many varieties: although much of it is various shades of green, it can be white, gray, yellow, orange, and even violet. Translucence varies, too, from opaque to almost transparent when used thinly. Jade can actually be either of two different minerals, jadeite and nephrite; the difference was not even recognized until around 1863.

Hole: *Medium*
Stringing: *Medium tiger tail*
Weight: *0.8g*
Other sizes: *None*
Color range: *Medium*

Length: *10mm*
Width: *5mm*
Depth: *5mm*

Actual size

207 RONDELLE ROSE QUARTZ

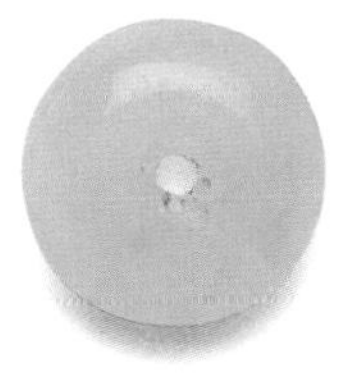

Rondelles, flattened round beads drilled through the middle of the circle rather than across, are usually used as spacers for more elaborate beads as they are sufficiently rounded at the sides to allow movement without taking up much space. Rose quartz is popular in summer designs because it looks light and delicate.

Hole: *Medium*
Stringing: *Medium tiger tail*
Weight: *0.5g*
Other sizes: *Many*
Color range: *None*

Length: *4.5mm*
Width: *8mm*
Depth: *8mm*

Actual size

208 PEACH FRESHWATER PEARL

Another of the wonderful natural colors of pearls, these peachy shades are uncommon and very attractive. When working with these as the main bead, choose neutral or very soft colors to accompany them, for example, cream pearls and colorless crystals. Alternatively, the effect of a few peach pearls in with dark stones such as garnets can be striking.

Hole: *Small*
Stringing: *Silk*
Weight: *0.2g*
Other sizes: *Many*
Color range: *Small*

Length: *4.5mm*
Width: *6mm*
Depth: *6mm*

Actual size

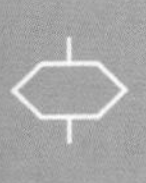

84

209 CUT RONDELLE AMETHYST

These are tiny faceted rondelles of low-grade amethyst; the color is pale and slightly mottled, whereas a higher grade would be stronger and more even. These would work well as spacers, particularly for flat-ended cut stones that need a rounded bead to allow movement or to add small amounts of color to mainly metallic or rock crystal pieces.

Hole: *Small*
Stringing: *Fine tiger tail*
Weight: *0.05g*
Other sizes: *None*
Color range: *None*

Length: *3mm*
Width: *4mm*
Depth: *4mm*

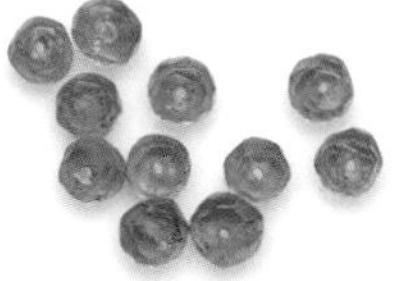

Actual size

Mix and match

582

298

84

210 ROUGH RONDELLE AQUAMARINE

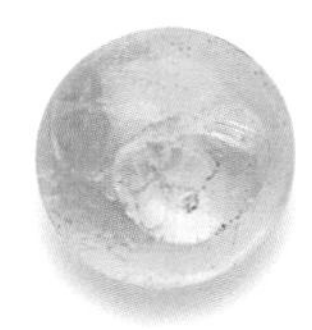

The blue of aquamarine is so delicate that a single bead can look almost colorless, but in a group or with other complementary or toning colors it shows clearly. This shape is a perfect spacer because it takes up little length along the strand but has rounded ends to help with the drape and movement of a piece.

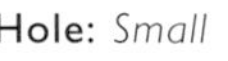

Hole: *Small*
Stringing: *Fine tiger tail*
Weight: *0.1g*
Other sizes: *None*
Color range: *None*

Length: *3mm*
Width: *5mm*
Depth: *5mm*

Actual size

Mix and match

42

281

63

211 BUTTON FRESHWATER PEARL

Pearls with flat backs have grown against the side of the shell rather than in the middle of the oyster itself. These are particularly suitable for use in embroidery: either simply stitch through the hole or come up through it with the needle, add a tiny bead or a knot, and go back down through the pearl.

Hole: *Small*
Stringing: *Silk*
Weight: *0.3g*
Other sizes: *Many*
Color range: *Small*

Length: *4mm*
Width: *7mm*
Depth: *7mm*

Actual size

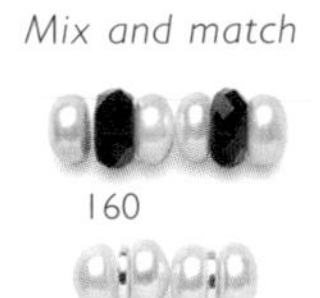

Mix and match

160

285

212 ROUNDED DISK HEMATITE

The sides of these disks are slightly rounded to make them more useful as spacers or on their own because this allows them to move against each other so that a strand can drape well. The deep gray metallic look of hematite is neutral enough to make it go with almost anything, especially other shiny opaque beads.

Hole: *Medium*
Stringing: *Medium tiger tail*
Weight: *0.1g*
Other sizes: *None*
Color range: *None*

Length: *2mm*
Width: *4mm*
Depth: *4mm*

Actual size

Mix and match
379
168

213 DISK PYRITE

A flat disk is less useful as a spacer as it does not contribute to the movement of a piece but is still useful if the other beads in the strand are rounded at the ends. Iron pyrite is also known as fool's gold because in its natural state it forms nuggets that shine and mislead prospectors.

Hole: *Medium*
Stringing: *Medium tiger tail*
Weight: *0.1g*
Other sizes: *None*
Color range: *None*

Length: *2mm*
Width: *4mm*
Depth: *4mm*

Actual size

Mix and match
66
363

214 TUBE GARNET

The ends of these little tubes are rounded making them perfect for use as spacers or strung together. Small insignificant beads with a strong color like this can be used to unify a piece of jewelry by alternating them with a random selection of more eye-catching beads.

Hole: *Small*
Stringing: *Fine tiger tail*
Weight: *0.1g*
Other sizes: *None*
Color range: *None*

Length: *3mm*
Width: *3mm*
Depth: *3mm*

Actual size

Mix and match
457
137

18

215 TUBE GOLDSTONE

Goldstone is not truly a semiprecious material, being glass with tiny copper flecks. Legend has it that a monk spilled a tray of copper shavings into a vat of molten glass and loved the result. It is included with semiprecious stones because it is usually cut and drilled in the same way rather than worked as glass.

Hole: *Medium*
Stringing: *Medium tiger tail*
Weight: *0.5g*
Other sizes: *None*
Color range: *Small*

Length: *14mm*
Width: *4mm*
Depth: *4mm*

Actual size

Mix and match

258

13

21

216 TWISTED TUBE HEMATITE

Hematite probably comes in more shapes and sizes than any other semiprecious stone bead, possibly because it is easy to work. It is also often imitated with a glass that looks and feels very similar and is known as hematine, among other related names. Light catches on the curves and edges of this shape making it rather striking.

Hole: *Medium*
Stringing: *Medium tiger tail*
Weight: *1.7g*
Other sizes: *16mm*
Color range: *None*

Length: *12mm*
Width: *6mm*
Depth: *6mm*

Actual size

Mix and match

574

318

50

217 SQUARE TUBE MALACHITE

Malachite has lines and swirls of many shades of green and is a popular stone for sculpture work as well as for beads. These square tubes would not hang well if strung on their own but would go well with small round beads or in a straight piece requiring little flexibility, such as a fringe.

Hole: *Small*
Stringing: *Fine tiger tail*
Weight: *0.1g*
Other sizes: *None*
Color range: *None*

Length: *5mm*
Width: *3.5mm*
Depth: *3.5mm*

Actual size

Mix and match

265

263

218 ROUGH CRAZY LACE CUBE AGATE

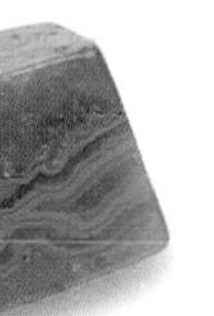

This kind of agate varies in color, so these cubes are all different but look wonderful together. The cubes are not at all even, so they would not be suitable for a woven or particularly geometric piece, and because the sides are flat, rounded spacers will be required to allow a strand to move well.

Hole: *Medium*
Stringing: *Medium tiger tail*
Weight: *0.6g*
Other sizes: *None*
Color range: *Variable*

Length: *6mm*
Width: *6mm*
Depth: *6mm*

Actual size

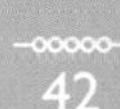

219 CUBE HEMATITE

These cubes are very regular and would work well in large-scale beadweaving and any stitch requiring an even shape but would be very inflexible strung on their own. Magnetic hematite is also available; the beads cling to each other, and strands can be overlapped to hold together avoiding the need for clasps.

Hole: *Medium*
Stringing: *Medium tiger tail*
Weight: *0.3g*
Other sizes: *6mm*
Color range: *None*

Length: *4mm*
Width: *4mm*
Depth: *4mm*

Actual size

220 ANGLED CUBE CARNELIAN

Cubes drilled at an angle will always lie with a point or edge upward, and because there are no flat areas at the ends, a strand of this shape will move and drape well. However, they can be uncomfortable to wear, so do not use these at the back of a heavy necklace or in a tight bracelet.

Hole: *Medium*
Stringing: *Medium tiger tail*
Weight: *0.5g*
Other sizes: *None*
Color range: *None*

Length: *9mm*
Width: *6mm*
Depth: *6mm*

Actual size

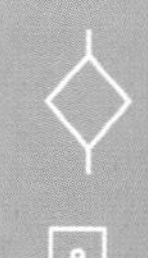

221 FLAT RECTANGLE LABRADORITE

Individual beads made of labradorite can look unimpressive, but a whole strand of them will catch the light in ways reminiscent of chips of opal (actual opal beads are very expensive). The gleam is usually seen on only one part of each bead, so the look changes as the piece moves.

Hole: *Small*
Stringing: *Fine tiger tail*
Weight: *0.2g*
Other sizes: *None*
Color range: *None*

Length: *9mm*
Width: *5mm*
Depth: *3mm*

Actual size

222 CUT RECTANGLE CARNELIAN

These carnelian beads are much more translucent than 220, and advantage of this difference has been taken by cutting the stone so that the facets reflect and refract the transmitted light. They are suitable for use in bracelets because they have a slim profile and so do not catch on clothing.

Hole: *Medium*
Stringing: *Medium tiger tail*
Weight: *0.5g*
Other sizes: *14mm*
Color range: *Variable*

Length: *9mm*
Width: *7mm*
Depth: *5mm*

Actual size

223 SQUARE CUSHION OCEAN JASPER

Jasper is usually thought of as red but appears in many forms (see 230 and 231), including this mix of colors often sold as ocean jasper. The cushion shapes are rounded at the sides, so they move well together and make a magnificent bracelet or choker with no other beads added.

Hole: *Medium*
Stringing: *Medium tiger tail*
Weight: *2.7g*
Other sizes: *None*
Color range: *Variable*

Length: *14mm*
Width: *6mm*
Depth: *6mm*

Actual size

224 FLAT DIAMOND LAPIS

This lapis is of a lower quality than 204 and some inclusions of green and white can be seen. Overall the wonderful strong color typical of this stone is clear, though, and the shape makes a strand that moves and hangs well, is comfortable to wear, and is visually interesting.

Hole: *Medium*
Stringing: *Medium tiger tail*
Weight: *0.7g*
Other sizes: *None*
Color range: *None*

Length: *17mm*
Width: *7mm*
Depth: *4mm*

Actual size

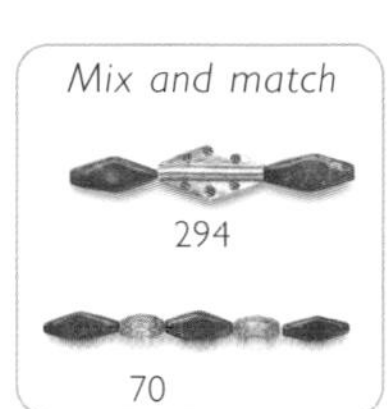

15

225 TWO-HOLE HALF-DISK TIGER EYE

Tiger eye exhibits chatoyancy (see 5) and is naturally this color but is often found dyed. This shape is flat on the back so it lies neatly against the skin in jewelry and has two holes to allow it to join strands of beads while holding them apart. Use beads the same width or smaller than the space between the holes.

Hole: *Medium*
Stringing: *Medium tiger tail*
Weight: *1.2g*
Other sizes: *None*
Color range: *None*

Length: *7mm*
Width: *14mm*
Depth: *6mm*

Actual size

36

226 TRIANGLE ROCK CRYSTAL

Rock crystal is also known as clear quartz and is not related (except in appearance) to the lead crystal glass used in decorative pieces and beads. Because they are drilled point to base these triangles can give different looks by stringing them all in the same direction or in pairs, tip to tip or base to base.

Hole: *Small*
Stringing: *Fine tiger tail*
Weight: *0.2g*
Other sizes: *None*
Color range: *None*

Length: *6mm*
Width: *5.5mm*
Depth: *3mm*

Actual size

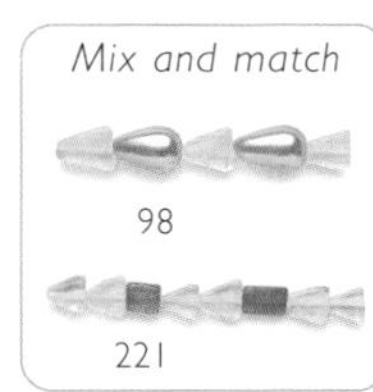

42

23

227 ARROWHEAD HEMATITE

An impressive shape used at the end of a drop or fringe, these are also interesting used all in the same direction along a strand because they fit into each other and move well. A small round or diagonally pierced square will fit into the space between these if they are used flat ends together.

Actual size

Hole: *Medium*
Stringing: *Medium tiger tail*
Weight: *1.7g*
Other sizes: *None*
Color range: *None*

Length: *11mm*
Width: *17mm*
Depth: *3mm*

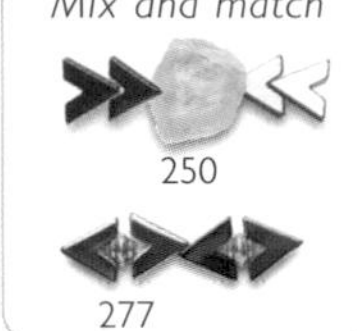

72

228 TRIANGLE DONUT JADE

Traditional donut beads are round, as 229 and 230, but other shapes such as squares and these triangles are also available. Flat triangles can be used with leather, cord, or strands of fine beads looped around one side so that the beads hang down or on two sides so that the beads lie along a strand.

Actual size

Hole: *Extra large*
Stringing: *Heavy tiger tail*
Weight: *3.4g*
Other sizes: *None*
Color range: *Variable*

Length: *3.5mm*
Width: *29mm*
Depth: *29mm*

72

229 DONUT SODALITE

Standard donuts are a common shape for semiprecious stones. They can be strung directly through the hole, showing a thin edge, but are more usually seen with loops on either side or are held flat on a strand by threading through the donut, then through a bead large enough not to slip through, and finally back through the donut.

Actual size

Hole: *Very large*
Stringing: *Heavy tiger tail*
Weight: *2.0g*
Other sizes: *30mm*
Color range: *None*

Length: *3.5mm*
Width: *20mm*
Depth: *20mm*

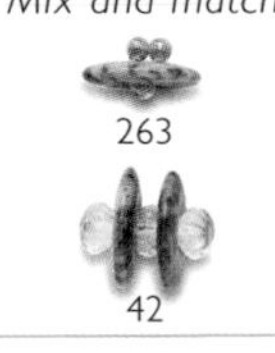

230 DRILLED DONUT LEOPARD-SKIN JASPER

Some donuts are drilled through both sides, as these are. This allows them to be used along a strand, with a small bead in the center to hide the stringing material, if required, or to be put on a head pin (629) so that the open shape can be dangled from a strand, perhaps as part of an earring.

Hole: *Medium*
Stringing: *Medium tiger tail*
Weight: *3.9g*
Other sizes: *None*
Color range: *None*

Length: *25mm*
Width: *25mm*
Depth: *5mm*

Actual size

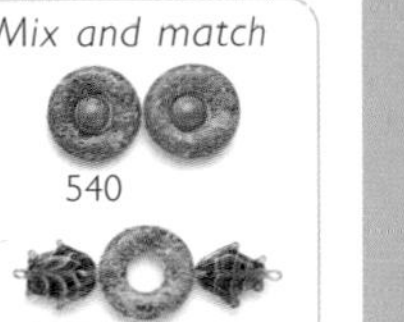

10

231 HALF DONUT JASPER

This shape is known as a half donut, despite having part of the ring all the way around. It is only drilled through the top of the loop so is probably best used on a head pin (629) with a small round bead on the pin to fit into the space, if required.

Hole: *Medium*
Stringing: *Heavy tiger tail*
Weight: *12.7g*
Other sizes: *None*
Color range: *Variable*

Length: *6mm*
Width: *45mm*
Depth: *34mm*

Actual size

4

4

42

232 AXE HEAD AGATE

An axe head or quarter-round shape, these are drilled across the tip and so require spacers between them so they can hang loosely, as does any wide drop. Although many semiprecious stones are technically agates, the name is most often applied to this kind of mixed banded pattern, which is often found dyed, although the natural colors show here.

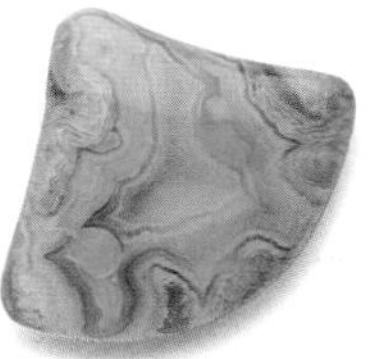

Actual size

Hole: *Medium*
Stringing: *Medium tiger tail*
Weight: *4.5g*
Other sizes: *None*
Color range: *Variable*

Length: *27mm*
Width: *22mm*
Depth: *6mm*

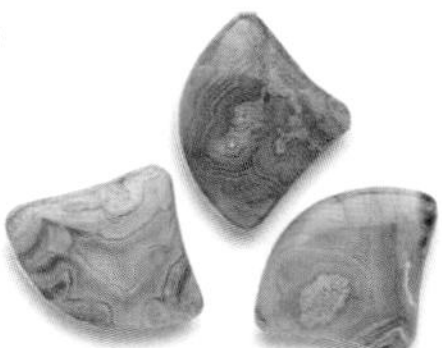

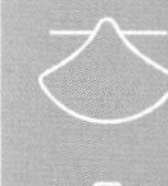

10

233 ROUNDED HEART RODONITE

Somewhat similar to 203, and even with a similar name, this is however a different mineral and the inclusions are usually calcite (white) and pyrite (gray). These softly rounded heart shapes fit slightly into each other if strung together and also look good used individually to show off the shape, perhaps hung downward or stitched to fabric.

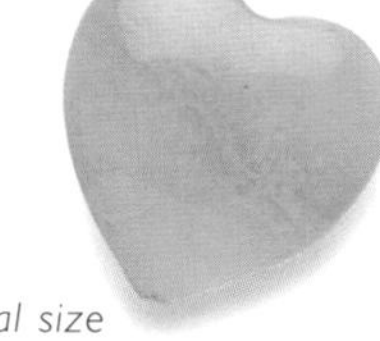

Actual size

Hole: *Medium*
Stringing: *Medium tiger tail*
Weight: *4.7g*
Other sizes: *None*
Color range: *None*

Length: *19mm*
Width: *20mm*
Depth: *8mm*

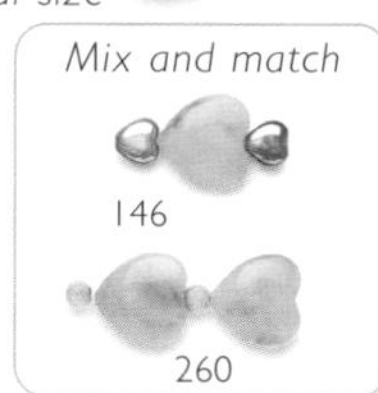

Mix and match

146

260

234 HEART BLUE LACE AGATE

The flat faces of these hearts make them suitable for embroidery as well as jewelry, and the overall shape is excellent at the end of a fringe or earring drop. The pastel blue of this agate, along with its clear bands, makes it popular for summer wear due to its delicate look.

Hole: *Small*
Stringing: *Fine tiger tail*
Weight: *0.2g*
Other sizes: *None*
Color range: *None*

Length: *6mm*
Width: *6mm*
Depth: *3mm*

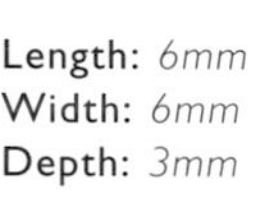

Actual size

Mix and match

298

155

235 FLOWER CHINESE JADE

This is the color that most people associate with jade (but see 206, 228, and 253). These large carved flowers are fortunately not as delicate as they look and can be used either by bringing a loop of thread, wire, or strand of fine beads around through the hole or strung as 236.

Actual size

63

Hole: *Medium*
Stringing: *Medium tiger tail*
Weight: *5.2g*
Other sizes: *15mm*
Color range: *Small*

Length: *4mm*
Width: *30mm*
Depth: *30mm*

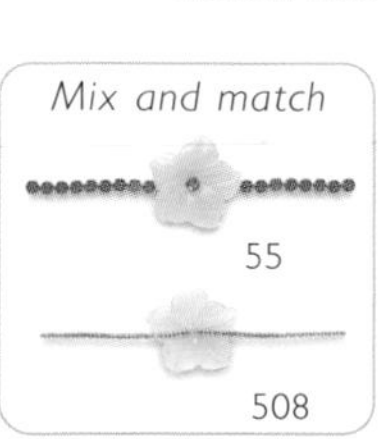

Mix and match

55

508

236 FLOWER CARNELIAN

Small carved flowers are usually used sewn on to cloth or by bringing thread up through to the front of the bead, through a seed bead (see 1) and back down through the flower again. This can be used to particularly good effect if wire is used instead of thread, perhaps on a tiara, so the flower can move on a stem.

Hole: *Small*
Stringing: *Fine tiger tail*
Weight: *0.4g*
Other sizes: *None*
Color range: *Variable*

Length: *4mm*
Width: *8mm*
Depth: *7mm*

Actual size

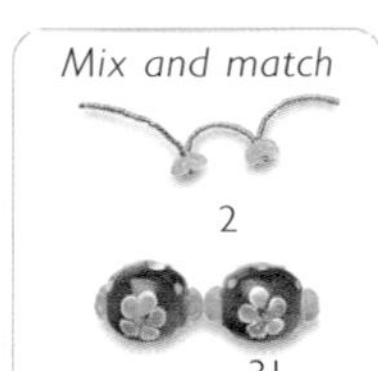

Mix and match

2

31

237 LEAF MOSS AGATE

Moss agate is so called because of its green strands of color in a mainly clear background. If the background is white, it is sometimes called tree agate. The leaf shape is attractive along a strand, at the end of fringes or earring drops, and particularly in association with flower shapes.

Hole: *Medium*
Stringing: *Medium tiger tail*
Weight: *0.6g*
Other sizes: *None*
Color range: *None*

Length: *12mm*
Width: *8mm*
Depth: *4mm*

Actual size

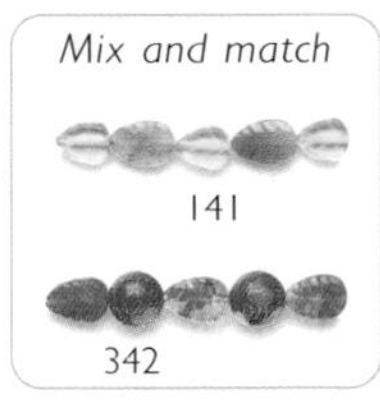

Mix and match

141

342

238 DROP FRESHWATER PEARL

A pleasingly fat drop, this is probably best used as a dangle, as part of an earring, or descending from the main strand of a piece using a head pin (629) or knotting but could also be used all in the same direction on a necklace or with half pointing each way from the midpoint. Slimmer drops are also available.

Hole: *Small*
Stringing: *Silk*
Weight: *0.9g*
Other sizes: *Many*
Color range: *Small*

Length: *10mm*
Width: *9mm*
Depth: *9mm*

Actual size

Mix and match

182

332

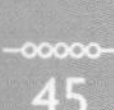
45

239 FACETED DROP AMETHYST

Translucent stones such as amethysts benefit the most from faceting, as both reflected and transmitted light is affected by the angled faces. As with all drops drilled across the top, use spacers at least the size of the widest part of the drop to allow them to hang freely.

Hole: *Small*
Stringing: *Fine tiger tail*
Weight: *0.2g*
Other sizes: *None*
Color range: *None*

Length: *5.5mm*
Width: *9mm*
Depth: *4mm*

Actual size

Mix and match

63

240 DROP GARNET

These little drop shapes may be off-cuts from the creation of more complex garnet beads, tumble polished, and then drilled to make the best use of what otherwise might be waste. These are slim enough to be used without spacers if the design allows for beads pointing in random directions along a strand.

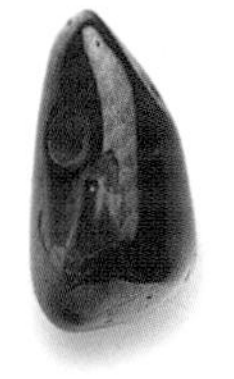

Hole: *Small*
Stringing: *Fine tiger tail*
Weight: *0.3g*
Other sizes: *None*
Color range: *None*

Length: *4mm*
Width: *8mm*
Depth: *8mm*

Actual size

Mix and match

17

241 DROP TOURMALINATED QUARTZ

The dark strands in these clear drops are tourmaline, so this is called tourmalinated quartz. Rock crystal with similar gold-colored strands is called rutilated quartz. Because these drops are drilled along their length they can be used along a strand or dangled on a head pin (629). Try grouping them in pairs tip to tip or end to end.

Hole: *Medium*
Stringing: *Medium tiger tail*
Weight: *0.7g*
Other sizes: *None*
Color range: *None*

Length: *15.5mm*
Width: *6mm*
Depth: *6mm*

Actual size

Mix and match

242 TUMBLED DROPS CITRINE

Rough pieces of citrine have been tumble polished rather than deliberately shaped, but the drilling place and direction has been chosen to make these into drops that sit evenly along a strand. Careful use of spacers will allow them to lie flat, but they are also attractive when used next to each other turning in random directions.

Hole: *Medium*
Stringing: *Medium tiger tail*
Weight: *1.8g*
Other sizes: *Many*
Color range: *None*

Length: *9mm*
Width: *15mm*
Depth: *14mm*

Actual size

Mix and match

202

264

28

243 RANDOM FACETED CARNELIAN

These are similar to 242 in that they are irregular shaped drops, but in this case the stone has been cut more or less randomly wherever the facets fit best on the original piece. Space these to hang down neatly because they are a little bulky to push together, and allow them to twist whichever way happens to come about.

Actual size

Hole: *Large*
Stringing: *Heavy tiger tail*
Weight: *8.1g*
Other sizes: *Many*
Color range: *Variable*

Length: *18mm*
Width: *22mm*
Depth: *20mm*

Mix and match

414

550

3

14

244 POINTS SMOKY QUARTZ

These long crystal shapes are natural: they have not been cut except to remove them from the rock on which they were growing and to drill a hole. Raw crystal points (also found in clear quartz) are sometimes considered to have healing or divining uses as well as being beautiful objects in their own right.

Hole: *Medium*
Stringing: *Medium tiger tail*
Weight: *5.5g*
Other sizes: *Many*
Color range: *None*

Length: *10mm*
Width: *33mm*
Depth: *10mm*

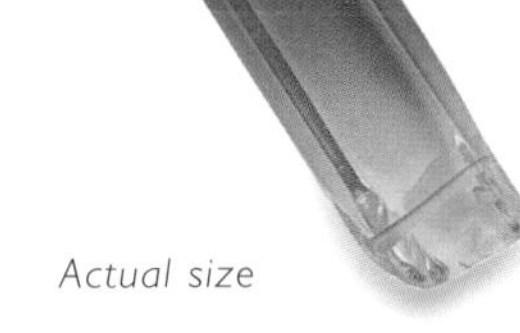

Actual size

Mix and match

300

560

25

3
3
5

245 GRADUATED DROP SET HOWLITE

Graduated sets of flat drops, angled at the base, are available in many semiprecious stones with various numbers in the set, usually an odd number so that there is one longest central drop. They can be used as they are but move better if spaced with small round beads. Howlite is often dyed to simulate turquoise.

Hole: *Small*
Stringing: *Fine tiger tail*
Weight: *9.3g total*
Other sizes: *None*
Color range: *None*

Length: *55mm total*
Width: *30mm longest*
Depth: *3.5mm*

Actual size

Mix and match
2
219

3
3
28

246 STRAND SPACERS MOTHER-OF-PEARL

These pieces are cut from shell, polished and drilled at both ends so they can be used to join two rows of beads. Strung with small beads between them they would make magnificent bracelets, or they could be dangled from a single strand by one hole because they are drilled finely enough for the other not to be noticed in wear.

Actual size

Hole: *Medium*
Stringing: *Medium tiger tail or heavy thread*
Weight: *2.2g*
Other sizes: *None*
Color range: *None*

Length: *9mm*
Width: *35mm*
Depth: *8mm*

Mix and match

2
4
25

247 CORAL BRANCH

These are short pieces of polished but naturally branched, pink coral (red is also available), generally deemed to be semiprecious. Coral is formed very slowly and must be harvested responsibly if at all, so buy from reputable dealers or avoid entirely to ensure that coral reefs are not destroyed by unethical removal of material.

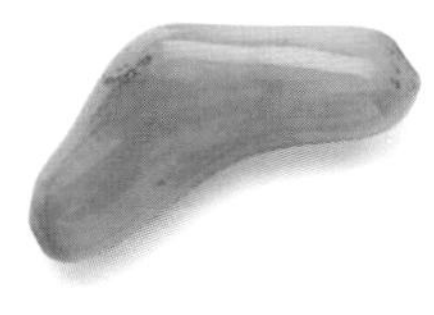

Hole: *Small*
Stringing: *Fine tiger tail*
Weight: *0.2g*
Other sizes: *Many*
Color range: *Small*

Length: *10mm*
Width: *5mm*
Depth: *3mm*

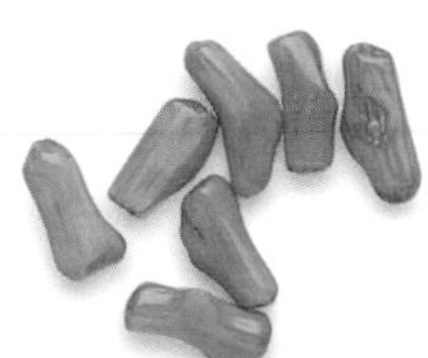

Actual size

Mix and match

248 CHIPS PERIDOT

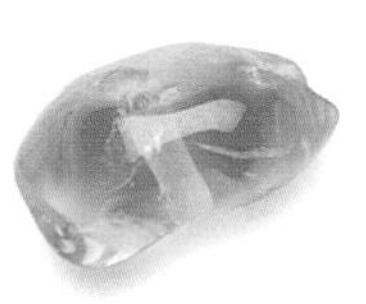

Almost all semiprecious stones are available as tiny tumble-polished and drilled chips because these pieces are leftover from just about any shaping processes. Since they are made mainly from the scraps these are the cheapest way to include such stones in jewelry, on clothing, and so forth. Use on their own, in mixed types, or as spacers.

Hole: *Small*
Stringing: *Fine tiger tail*
Weight: *0.1g*
Other sizes: *Many*
Color range: *None*

Length: *3mm*
Width: *5mm*
Depth: *5mm*

Actual size

Mix and match
397
390

249 ROCOCO FRESHWATER PEARLS

These pearls are flat on one end, so they must have grown near the shell of the oyster, as 211, but are far less regular than those buttons; this is possibly due to the shape of the irritant that started the process. The random shapes are rather striking and would look splendid with tumbled semiprecious stones of a similar size.

Hole: *Small*
Stringing: *Silk*
Weight: *0.2g*
Other sizes: *Many*
Color range: *Small*

Length: *6mm*
Width: *9mm*
Depth: *6mm*

Actual size

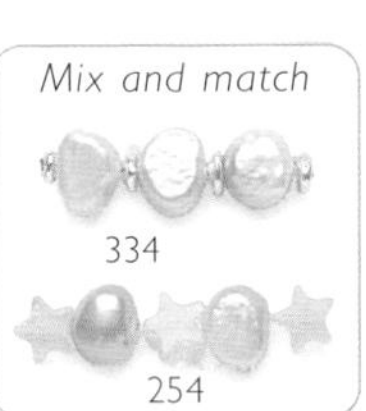
Mix and match
334
254

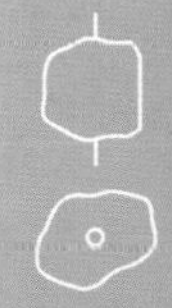

250 UNPOLISHED FLUORITE

Actual size

Roughly cut chunks of some semiprecious stones can look wonderful drilled and strung, as these large fluorite beads show. A whole strand would be both heavy and somewhat jagged, which could be uncomfortable to wear, so a necklace might be best with these spaced out at the front only, with something more comfortable against the back of the neck.

Hole: *Large*
Stringing: *Heavy tiger tail*
Weight: *16.8g*
Other sizes: *Many*
Color range: *Variable*

Length: *22mm*
Width: *19mm*
Depth: *17mm*

Mix and match
269
316

251 FACETED BLUE LACE AGATE

These somewhat random shapes are faceted rather like 243, but their bases are flatter, they are roughly the same depth, and the drill is through the center so the beads lie evenly along a strand. Flat shapes like this are good for jewelry where a substantial look is required but too much height would be inconvenient.

Hole: *Medium*
Stringing: *Medium tiger tail*
Weight: *3.3g*
Other sizes: *None*
Color range: *None*

Length: *17mm*
Width: *14mm*
Depth: *8mm*

Actual size

Mix and match

252 RANDOM MOTHER-OF-PEARL

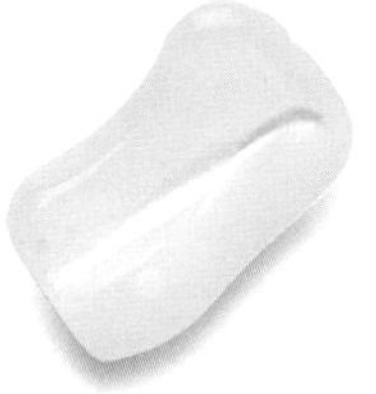

Random pieces of mother-of-pearl, possibly off-cuts from shaping other beads, have been smoothed on the edges and drilled on the longest axis to make these attractive bumpy but fairly flat beads. They would make a comfortable bracelet or choker and would lie neatly if stitched on to embroidery or to decorate clothing.

Hole: *Medium*
Stringing: *Medium tiger tail or heavy thread*
Weight: *1.3g*
Other sizes: *Many*
Color range: *None*

Length: *16mm*
Width: *12mm*
Depth: *4mm*

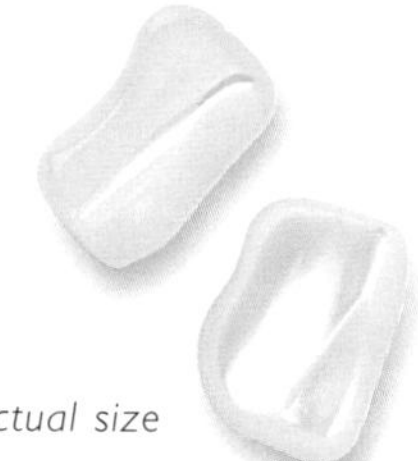
Actual size

Mix and match

253 TUMBLE-POLISHED JADE

Small pebbles of stone are rotated in the barrel of a tumbling machine with various grades of grit until they are smooth and shiny, then drilled to make these random-shaped pieces. They are often graded so that they can be sold in strands of roughly the same size beads.

Hole: *Medium*
Stringing: *Medium tiger tail*
Weight: *2.0g*
Other sizes: *Many*
Color range: *Small*

Length: *13mm*
Width: *11mm*
Depth: *10mm*

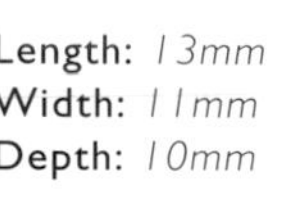

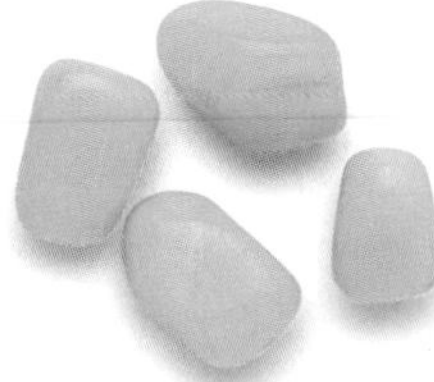
Actual size

Mix and match

254 STAR ROSE QUARTZ

Small fancy shapes such as stars are often cut from more common stones and can be attractive strung on their own and as fillers or spacers. These would be cute at the end of a fringe on clothing for a little girl, or on a tiara for a fairy costume, but because they are flat they could be stitched anywhere.

Hole: *Small*
Stringing: *Fine tiger tail*
Weight: *0.1g*
Other sizes: *None*
Color range: *None*

Length: *6mm*
Width: *7mm*
Depth: *3mm*

Actual size

Mix and match

234

150

255 TOPPER MOSS AGATE

This shape is usually found only in power bracelets at the top hole of beads such as 186, with both ends of the elastic cord passed through one of these in the same direction (from base to tip) before knotting. They also look interesting along a strand with the base either side of a larger round bead.

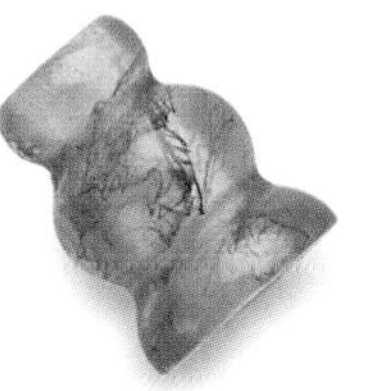

Hole: *Large*
Stringing: *Heavy tiger tail*
Weight: *0.3g*
Other sizes: *None*
Color range: *None*

Length: *8mm*
Width: *6mm*
Depth: *6mm*

Actual size

Mix and match

265

186 2

3

32

256 BEAR FLUORITE

This bear shape is seen in Zuni jewelry and other decorative work. Other animals made of semiprecious stones are also used in fetish pieces. Some fluorite is fluorescent (hence the name), and the color shown under various wavelengths of ultraviolet light may not be the same as that shown in white light.

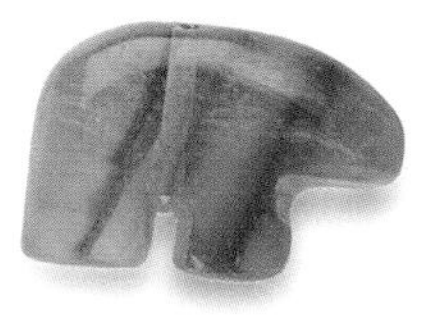

Hole: *Medium*
Stringing: *Medium tiger tail*
Weight: *1.3g*
Other sizes: *None*
Color range: *Variable*

Length: *9mm*
Width: *13mm*
Depth: *5.5mm*

Actual size

3

28

CHAPTER 

Precious metals

The precious metals chapter covers gold, silver, and combinations of those metals with other materials, including types of plating. Platinum is also a precious metal, but beads in this material are not easily available and so have not been included.

Each shape of bead has been shown in one type of precious metal. Many of the shapes shown have no color range within the metal shown, but are also available in other grades of that material (for example, nine-karat gold beads may also be available in eighteen-karat gold) and in other precious metals (some vermeil shapes in sterling silver, for example). Most of the handmade silver beads, however, are not available in other grades or metals.

Precious metal beads tend to be hollow. This can make them difficult to thread, because the end of the stringing material can catch inside the bead, rather than going through the hole on the other side. If possible, use a stiff needle rather than the usual flexible beading needle. Sometimes, when the holes are small, it is necessary to bring a thin thread through the beads with the stiff needle, and then tie or glue this thread to the main stringing material and pull it through.

The glow of precious metals can be emphasized by using matte beads as a contrast. Note that the catch and gold beads are exactly the same color, a result of careful matching.

257 ROUND STERLING SILVER

Most silver on sale today is sterling silver, which means it is at least 925 parts per 1000 silver or 92.5 percent pure. Silver with a higher purity can be too soft for beads, unless the bead is a solid, simple shape. Check before buying because beads are in general too small to require a silver mark.

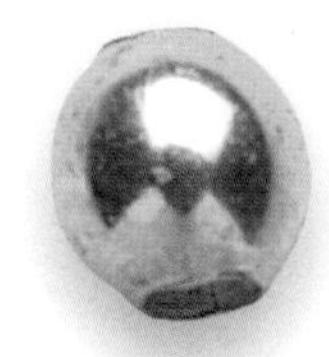

Hole: *Medium*
Stringing: *Fine tiger tail or medium thread*
Weight: *0.05g*
Other sizes: *Many*
Color range: *None*

Length: *2mm*
Width: *2mm*
Depth: *2mm*

2 3 125

Actual size

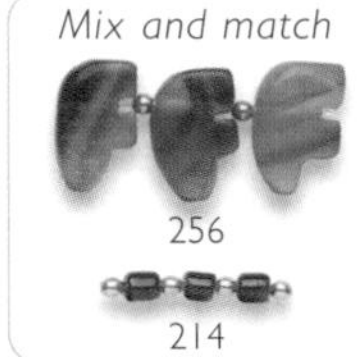
Mix and match
256
214

258 ROUND GOLD-FILLED

"Gold-filled" means that a base metal, usually brass or copper, has had a sheet of gold bonded to its surface. "14K 1/20 gold-filled" would mean that the gold was fourteen-karat (see 259), and the total weight of gold was one twentieth of the total weight of the piece.

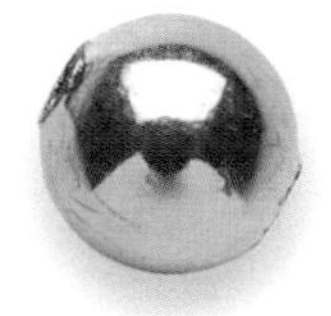

Hole: *Medium*
Stringing: *Fine tiger tail or medium thread*
Weight: *0.05g*
Other sizes: *Many*
Color range: *None*

Length: *3mm*
Width: *3mm*
Depth: *3mm*

2 3 84

Actual size

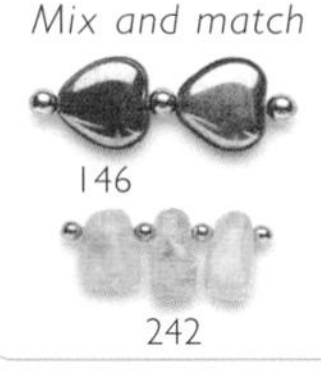
Mix and match
146
242

259 ROUND NINE-KARAT GOLD

Pure gold is twenty-four-karat (carat, in the United Kingdom) and is very soft. Nine-karat gold is nine parts gold and the other fifteen parts other metals, making it too low a grade to count as gold in the United States (ten-karat is the minimum) but commonly used in Britain and elsewhere.

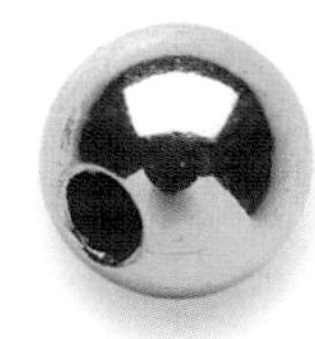

Hole: *Large*
Stringing: *Fine tiger tail or medium thread*
Weight: *0.05g*
Other sizes: *Many*
Color range: *None*

Length: *4mm*
Width: *4mm*
Depth: *4mm*

2 4 63

Actual size

Mix and match
136

218

260 SPARKLE ROUND STERLING SILVER

The sparkle of these beads is caused by the surface texture, hundreds of dents that look as though they have been made by rolling the bead under some pressure between surfaces with tiny, sharp spikes. Some designers will find that these look too glittery and not enough like real silver, even though they are.

Hole: *Large*
Stringing: *Medium tiger tail or medium thread*
Weight: *0.4g*
Other sizes: *3mm, 4mm, 5mm, 8mm*
Color range: *None*
Length: *5mm*
Width: *6mm*
Depth: *6mm*

Actual size

Mix and match

506

122

50

261 WITH CRYSTALS STERLING SILVER

The matte surface of these beads is in deliberate contrast to the bright crystals embedded into the metal. The crystals are fairly evenly spaced and seem quite firm, unlike those in some similar glass beads, so no special care needs to be taken. A whole strand of these with different colored crystals could be very striking.

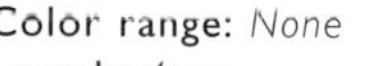

Hole: *Medium*
Stringing: *Medium tiger tail or medium thread*
Weight: *0.1g*
Other sizes: *6mm, 8mm*
Color range: *None*
Length: *4mm*
Width: *4.5mm*
Depth: *4.5mm*

Actual size

Mix and match

217

257

63

262 RIDGED GOLD-FILLED

These ridges, which are quite large for such a small bead, are pressed into the surface of the sheet of metal the beads are made from (the join is just visible) rather than made by folding a flat sheet and shaping the results as in 336. This bead is excellent where a plain bead would be too dull.

Hole: *Medium*
Stringing: *Medium tiger tail or medium thread*
Weight: *0.05g*
Other sizes: *Many*
Color range: *None*
Length: *3mm*
Width: *3mm*
Depth: *3mm*

Actual size

Mix and match

342

152

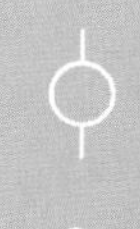

84

72

263 RIDGED STERLING SILVER

A larger bead with finer ridges than 262, created in the same way, these look much more delicate in use than their size would suggest. The wall of the bead is very thin, so they are light, and the hole is larger than usual for this kind of bead making them useful on thin cord.

Hole: *Large*
Stringing: *Medium tiger tail or medium thread*
Weight: *0.1g*
Other sizes: *Many*
Color range: *None*

Length: *3.5mm*
Width: *4mm*
Depth: *4mm*

Actual size

Mix and match

406

122

42

264 FILIGREE GOLD-PLATED

Gold-plated beads are a very thin layer of gold bonded on to a base metal such as copper. The gold can wear away much more easily than with a gold-filled piece (see 258). The openwork pattern was made before the bead was formed, and the join is not quite accurate, but this is not visible in wear.

Hole: *Large*
Stringing: *Medium tiger tail or medium thread*
Weight: *0.3g*
Other sizes: *8mm*
Color range: *None*

Length: *6mm*
Width: *6mm*
Depth: *6mm*

Actual size

Mix and match

19

91

32

265 FILIGREE LAYERS GOLD-PLATED

This is very similar to 264, although larger. The same open mesh has been used on the outside of a plain, round hollow bead, so that the light catches and reflects from all the edges rather than passing through as in a more usual filigree bead. This bead is also heavier than might be expected because there are two thicknesses of metal.

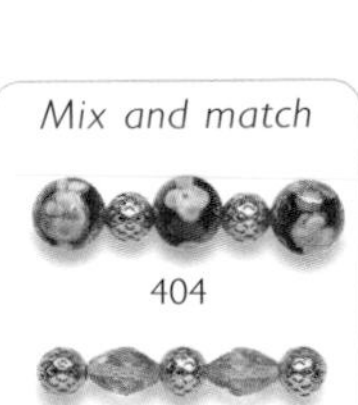

Hole: *Large*
Stringing: *Medium tiger tail or medium thread*
Weight: *1.0g*
Other sizes: *10mm*
Color range: *None*

Length: *8mm*
Width: *8mm*
Depth: *8mm*

Actual size

Mix and match

404

175

266 FACETED STERLING SILVER

This faceted shape made by machine is reminiscent of a 1970s mirror ball and reflects light from different angles as the beads move. These might look best in a style from that period or later rather than in a classical design, unless the other beads were also faceted.

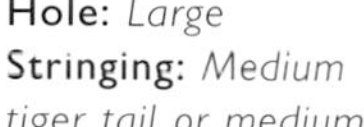

Hole: *Large*
Stringing: *Medium tiger tail or medium thread*
Weight: *0.7g*
Other sizes: *2mm, 3mm, 4mm, 5mm, 7mm, 8mm*
Color range: *None*
Length: *5mm*
Width: *6mm*
Depth: *6mm*

Actual size

Mix and match

216

472

2

3

50

267 SATURN VERMEIL

Vermeil is usually a sterling silver base with a fourteen-karat gold coating, but check when buying because other grades of both silver and gold may be used. There are two strands of twisted wire around the midline of these otherwise plain round beads, giving a more interesting shape and extra texture.

Hole: *Medium*
Stringing: *Medium tiger tail or medium thread*
Weight: *0.9g*
Other sizes: *None*
Color range: *None*
Length: *7mm*
Width: *9mm*
Depth: *9mm*

Actual size

Mix and match

49

158

2

4

36

268 FANCY BALI SILVER

Actual size

One of the most popular contemporary producers of beautiful silver beads is Bali, with a variety of their wares shown in this chapter. This large round bead has been lavishly decorated around the center with twists and loops of wire as well as dots. Just a few of these spaced with simpler pieces would make an impressive necklace.

Hole: *Large*
Stringing: *Medium tiger tail or medium thread*
Weight: *3.6g*
Other sizes: *None*
Color range: *None*
Length: *15mm*
Width: *14mm*
Depth: *14mm*

Mix and match

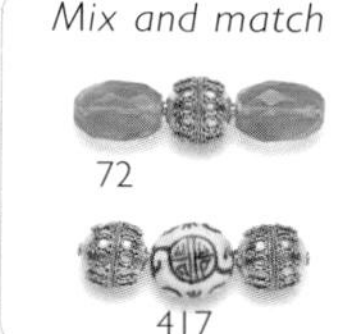

72

417

3

4

17

16

269 FILIGREE VERMEIL

The only really solid parts of these beads are around the holes, the remainder being assembled from two twisted wires around the middle and loops of thicker plain wire attaching those to the hole ends. Because all the parts are quite thick the bead is sturdy but light and very handsome.

Actual size

Hole: *Large*
Stringing: *Medium tiger tail or medium thread*
Weight: *4.8g*
Other sizes: *None*
Color range: *None*

Length: *16mm*
Width: *17mm*
Depth: *17mm*

Mix and match

116

11

18

270 ELECTROPLATED STERLING SILVER

Some of the other plated items mentioned in this chapter may also be electroplated, meaning that the layer of precious metal was laid down on to the base metal out of a chemical solution by means of electricity. This bead is sold as such, perhaps because the bead wall is so thin that it could not be done by any other method.

Actual size

Hole: *Large*
Stringing: *Medium tiger tail or medium thread*
Weight: *1.3g*
Other sizes: *None*
Color range: *None*

Length: *14mm*
Width: *15mm*
Depth: *15mm*

Mix and match

519

34

18

271 GRANULATED VERMEIL

These beads have been decorated with the technique known as granulation where tiny spheres of the same metal are made separately and then fused on to the surface rather than individually soldered. Triangular patterns of dots like this are found on some ancient decorative metalwork including beads and brooches.

Actual size

Hole: *Large*
Stringing: *Medium tiger tail or medium thread*
Weight: *3.3g*
Other sizes: *None*
Color range: *None*

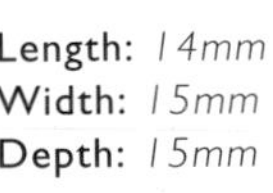

Length: *14mm*
Width: *15mm*
Depth: *15mm*

Mix and match

223

85

272 ANTIQUED BALI SILVER

The dots and arcs of wire on these beads are flattened rather than rounded as on many of the other similarly made beads in this chapter. This is probably because the whole bead was darkened chemically and then the surface polished to bring back the bright silver. This has given an aged look to the finished item.

Hole: *Large*
Stringing: *Medium tiger tail or medium thread*
Weight: *2.5g*
Other sizes: *None*
Color range: *None*

Length: *11mm*
Width: *12.5mm*
Depth: *12.5mm*

Actual size

273 BALI SILVER WITH WIRE COILS

Each piece of the embellishment of these beads is very simple, just a wire coiled at one end, but the arrangement on the plain, flattened round bead gives the impression of hearts. Decorative without being too ornate, these could be used either as the main feature of a piece with simpler items or to balance larger, fussier beads.

Hole: *Large*
Stringing: *Medium tiger tail or medium thread*
Weight: *3.3g*
Other sizes: *None*
Color range: *None*

Length: *12mm*
Width: *13mm*
Depth: *13mm*

Actual size

274 FILIGREE BALI SILVER

The two flower shapes, made of loops of wire soldered to a central ring, that make up these openwork beads, could have been formed into a round bead but have deliberately been pushed further together when attached at the midpoint, so that this bead is somewhat flattened in that direction.

Hole: *Large*
Stringing: *Medium tiger tail or medium thread*
Weight: *0.5g*
Other sizes: *None*
Color range: *None*

Length: *9mm*
Width: *8mm*
Depth: *8mm*

Actual size

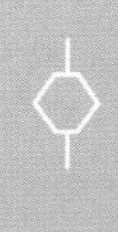

275 COIL FILIGREE BALI SILVER

These are similar in principle to 273 but made as filigree with the coils attached only to rings of wire at the center and ends of the rondelle-shaped bead. This of course makes them much lighter but also far less reflective, so the pattern could go unnoticed unless the beads were seen against a strong color.

2

3

25

Hole: *Large*
Stringing: *Medium tiger tail or medium thread*
Weight: *1.5g*
Other sizes: *None*
Color range: *None*

Length: *10mm*
Width: *12mm*
Depth: *12mm*

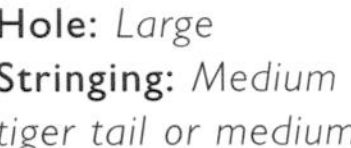

Actual size

Mix and match

111

27

276 END CAPPED BALI SILVER

A decoration of tiny dots arranged around the holes in layers has been added to what would otherwise be a very simple and possibly quite uninteresting flattened round bead. A similar impression would be given by using a plain bead with small bead caps (620). Use small beads next to these in order not to hide the fancy ends.

3

4

25

Hole: *Large*
Stringing: *Medium tiger tail or medium thread*
Weight: *1.8g*
Other sizes: *None*
Color range: *None*

Length: *10mm*
Width: *11mm*
Depth: *11mm*

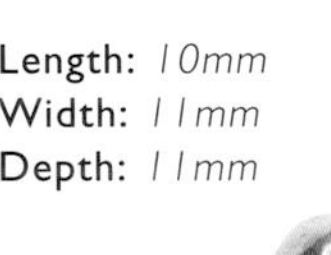

Actual size

Mix and match

45

197

277 SHELL STERLING SILVER

The curves of these beads seem organic, similar to those of a seashell, and would work well with pieces made of real shells or with an ocean theme. They have been shaped in two halves, then soldered at the center line and deliberately darkened in the creases to emphasize the shape.

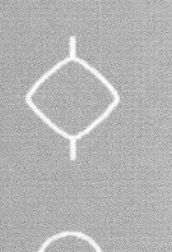

2

3

28

Hole: *Large*
Stringing: *Medium tiger tail or medium thread*
Weight: *0.9g*
Other sizes: *None*
Color range: *None*

Length: *9mm*
Width: *9mm*
Depth: *9mm*

Actual size

Mix and match

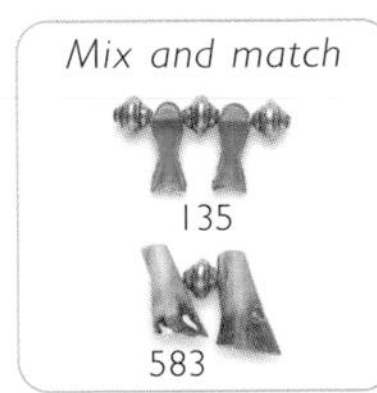

135

583

278 FOLDED THAI SILVER

Thin strips of silver have been woven together to make the middle of these beads, then folded down to overlap each other at the ends. These would be wonderful to wear with a complex textile because they would echo folded fabric or patchwork without distracting colors.

Hole: *Large*
Stringing: *Medium tiger tail or medium thread*
Weight: *2.1g*
Other sizes: *None*
Color range: *None*

Length: *8mm*
Width: *12mm*
Depth: *12mm*

Actual size

32

279 LENTIL GOLD-FILLED

Possibly the most useful spacer beads available. Small lentil shapes allow the beads around them to move well, so that a strand can drape softly but not take up much space, and they are plain and narrow enough not to distract the eye from the main beads. Use to add a touch of gold to almost any piece.

Hole: *Small*
Stringing: *Medium tiger tail or medium thread*
Weight: *0.05g*
Other sizes: *6mm*
Color range: *None*

Length: *2mm*
Width: *4mm*
Depth: *4mm*

Actual size

125

280 RIDGED WHEEL GOLD-FILLED

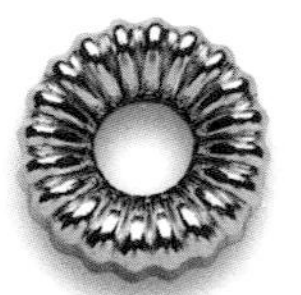

These could be used as spacers or to add a decorative patch of gold. The ends are dented inward to fit against a rounded bead. A little of the length of the bead will be taken up in this overlap, so allow for that when calculating the number of beads you need.

Hole: *Large*
Stringing: *Medium tiger tail or medium thread*
Weight: *0.1g*
Other sizes: *6mm, 8mm*
Color range: *None*

Length: *2mm*
Width: *4mm*
Depth: *4mm*

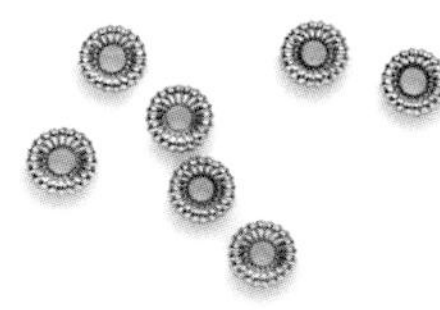

Actual size

Mix and match

151

41

125

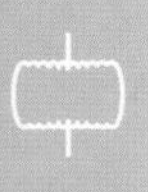

84

281 RIDGED WHEEL STERLING SILVER

The dent in the ends of these beads is larger than that in 280, so the overlap with a rounded bead will be even greater. Note that rounded beads are necessary between these for a strand to move: otherwise it will be completely rigid. A narrow lentil (see 279) just smaller than the wheel will be enough to allow some drape.

Hole: *Large*
Stringing: *Medium tiger tail or medium thread*
Weight: *0.2g*
Other sizes: *4mm, 6mm, 8mm*

Color range: *None*
Length: *3mm*
Width: *5mm*
Depth: *5mm*

Actual size

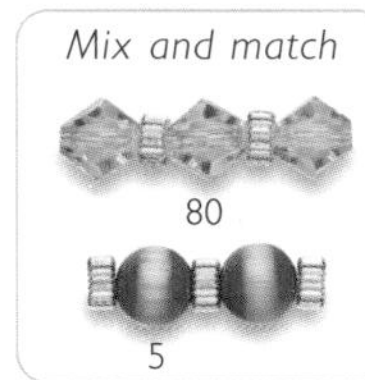

100

282 RONDELLE NINE-KARAT GOLD

Another bead with ridges, but this time shaped into a rondelle that makes it suitable for use not only between pieces such as 281 where it will allow movement but also between any flat-ended beads to improve drape. It can also be used to add a little metal and light-reflection to any piece.

Hole: *Medium*
Stringing: *Medium tiger tail or medium thread*
Weight: *0.05g*
Other sizes: *3mm, 4mm*

Color range: *None*
Length: *2.5mm*
Width: *5mm*
Depth: *5mm*

Actual size

100

283 TWISTED RONDELLE STERLING SILVER

Useful in all the same ways as 282, the twist in these rondelles somehow makes them look wider even though the measurement is the same, and the edges catch and reflect the light more. Both of these factors make the bead more dominant, so these may be better used between plainer beads than with those with a lot of detail.

Hole: *Medium*
Stringing: *Medium tiger tail or medium thread*
Weight: *0.1g*
Other sizes: *None*
Color range: *None*

Length: *2.5mm*
Width: *4.5mm*
Depth: *4.5mm*

Actual size

284 FIVE-BALL SPACER RAJASTHANI SILVER

When strung together, each of these beads locks into the space in the next one to make a very solid looking but quite flexible strand. Used as spacers, they sit neatly just over the ends of any rounded bead and add dots of reflected light. A similar four-ball version is also available.

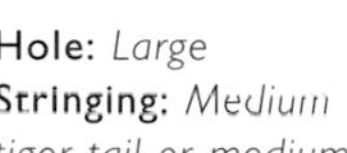

Hole: *Large*
Stringing: *Medium tiger tail or medium thread*
Weight: *0.4g*
Other sizes: *None*
Color range: *None*

Length: *2.5mm*
Width: *6mm*
Depth: *6mm*

Actual size

Mix and match
187
153

285 DISK SILVER-PLATED

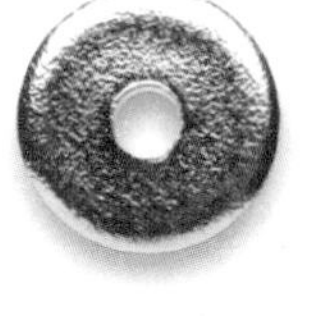

Flat disk beads are just about the only beads with wide flat ends that can be used on their own in strings without making a strand very stiff. This is because they are so thin. Very different looks can be achieved by using disks smaller, the same width, or larger than the main rounded beads of a jewelry piece.

Hole: *Medium*
Stringing: *Medium tiger tail or medium thread*
Weight: *0.2g*
Other sizes: *None*
Color range: *None*

Length: *1.5mm*
Width: *6mm*
Depth: *6mm*

Actual size

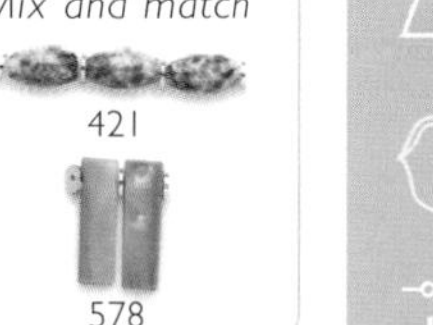

Mix and match
421
578

2
3

286 ROPE RING STERLING SILVER

Although many people think of these as spacers, they cannot really be used in this way because they take up almost no length on a strand: most rounded beads used either side of this shape will meet each other through the hole. Instead, use them to add a little metallic gleam, a touch of light with dark beads, or a change of texture.

Hole: *Large*
Stringing: *Medium tiger tail or medium thread*
Weight: *0.1g*
Other sizes: *None*
Color range: *None*

Length: *1.5mm*
Width: *4.5mm*
Depth: *4.5mm*

Actual size

Mix and match
193
207

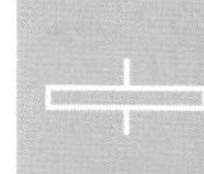

3

4

28

287 CRIMPED HEXAGON TUBE THAI SILVER

Made from a sheet of silver, these have been stamped with little flowers, folded into a hexagonal tube, and then crimped to narrow the ends. Round beads would fit neatly into the crimps, help the movement of a piece, and lessen the slightly sharp feel and the possibility of catching clothing on these ends.

Hole: *Large*
Stringing: *Medium tiger tail or medium thread*
Weight: *0.4g*
Other sizes: *None*
Color range: *None*

Length: *9mm*
Width: *6.5mm*
Depth: *6.5mm*

Actual size

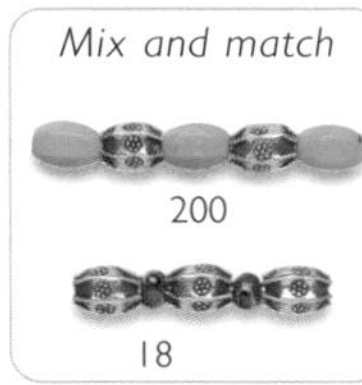

2

4

14

288 ROLLED TUBE THAI SILVER

The makers of these have taken an isosceles triangle of thin silver, hammered a texture on to it, and then rolled it up from the long end around a mandrel and lightly soldered the tip. The result has a good shape and feel. Traditional paper beads (599) are also made this way.

Hole: *Large*
Stringing: *Medium tiger tail or medium thread*
Weight: *1.5g*
Other sizes: *None*
Color range: *None*

Length: *19mm*
Width: *5mm*
Depth: *5mm*

Actual size

2

4

45

289 RIDGED BICONE NINE-KARAT GOLD

This bead is made of crimped metal, shaped so that the folds are tightly together at the ends and more stretched out in the middle. Bicone shapes make good spacers, but those with similar length and width like this can also be used successfully in right-angle weave and in other stitches where they can fit against each other.

Hole: *Medium*
Stringing: *Medium tiger tail or medium thread*
Weight: *0.1g*
Other sizes: *None*
Color range: *None*

Length: *5.5mm*
Width: *4mm*
Depth: *4mm*

Actual size

290 EXTENDED DIAMOND STERLING SILVER

The raised diamond patterns on the surface of these beads emphasize the main shape, making the tube ends look almost like separate parts from a distance. Use small round beads between these on a strand to allow easy movement. Because the shaping is on both sides these will not lie quite flat.

Hole: *Large*
Stringing: *Medium tiger tail or medium thread*
Weight: *0.7g*
Other sizes: *None*
Color range: *None*

Length: *13.5mm*
Width: *7mm*
Depth: *7mm*

Actual size

Mix and match

291 FOLDED BICONE THAI SILVER

This bicone shape is formed by knotting a thin strip of silver and tucking the ends into other parts of the knot. It is sturdy, and the edges of the strip reflect light well, but there are some slightly rough points where the metal is folded, and these might catch on clothing or even skin.

Hole: *Large*
Stringing: *Medium tiger tail or medium thread*
Weight: *0.3g*
Other sizes: *None*
Color range: *None*

Length: *9mm*
Width: *5.5mm*
Depth: *5mm*

Actual size

Mix and match

292 SPINDLE VERMEIL

These look as though a graduated set of rondelle beads have been pushed together, but the shape is of course one hollow piece made in two halves with rather obvious seams. The shape and color would look wonderful against dark fabrics so a bold piece for winter wear, perhaps with festive-colored crystal beads, would be ideal.

Hole: *Large*
Stringing: *Medium tiger tail or medium thread*
Weight: *1.3g*
Other sizes: *None*
Color range: *None*

Length: *16mm*
Width: *9.5mm*
Depth: *9mm*

Actual size

Mix and match

293 ROUND WITH COLLAR BALI SILVER

3
4
20

Starting with a plain round bead, the makers have added rings of twisted wire at the ends and a wide collar consisting of flat wire rings and coils around the middle. The result has then been darkened (antiqued) inside the collar area only with the top surfaces polished to enhance the design.

Hole: *Large*
Stringing: *Medium tiger tail or medium thread*
Weight: *3.0g*
Other sizes: *None*
Color range: *None*

Length: *13mm*
Width: *11mm*
Depth: *11mm*

Actual size

Mix and match

406

75

294 WINGED TUBE THAI SILVER

3
4
11

Actual size

An unusual but wonderful shape, like an African shield or stylized wings, these are made by shaping two sheets of silver together over a narrow mandrel and soldering the edges. The sheets have stamped decoration. Because these are light and lie flat they could be used in almost any jewelry.

Hole: *Large*
Stringing: *Medium tiger tail or medium thread*
Weight: *1.4g*
Other sizes: *None*
Color range: *None*

Length: *23mm*
Width: *13mm*
Depth: *2.5mm*

Mix and match

580

100

295 FLATTENED OVAL THAI SILVER

3
4
12

Actual size

This bead has stamped decoration done with a metal stamp and a hammer as for 294 but a much more rounded overall shape. It was probably formed over a similar sized mandrel, but the sheets, instead of being flattened against it, have been gently curved to meet on each side and soldered at the edges.

Hole: *Large*
Stringing: *Medium tiger tail or medium thread*
Weight: *1.8g*
Other sizes: *None*
Color range: *None*

Length: *22mm*
Width: *9mm*
Depth: *6mm*

Mix and match

110

459

296 FLATTENED OVAL BALI SILVER

This is a plain, flattened oval decorated with the usual wire rings and coils, but it also has flat circles of silver; these give it a somewhat different look, which could be considered more modern. Short flattened beads like these are particularly suitable for bracelets or the backs of necklaces where too much depth would be a disadvantage.

Hole: *Large*
Stringing: *Medium tiger tail or medium thread*
Weight: *1.4g*
Other sizes: *None*
Color range: *None*

Length: *12mm*
Width: *9mm*
Depth: *5.5mm*

Actual size

Mix and match

203

59

297 ROUND-ENDED TUBE BALI SILVER

The wide collar decoration on these beads makes the tubular part draw the eye, but the rounded ends allow easy movement, unlike a flat-ended tube bead. These would be useful in a design that had to drape well while showing mainly straight lines and square edges.

16

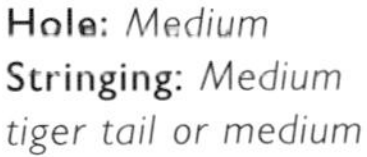

Hole: *Medium*
Stringing: *Medium tiger tail or medium thread*
Weight: *2.5g*
Other sizes: *None*
Color range: *None*

Length: *16mm*
Width: *9mm*
Depth: *9mm*

Actual size

Mix and match

117

555

298 BEADED RONDELLE RAJASTHANI SILVER

Two tiny twisted wire rings with a circle of raised dots in the middle, these are good spacers for any project where the texture would not detract from the main beads. They would also be lovely as the main feature of a slim design, perhaps with tiny brightly colored beads between them.

84

Hole: *Medium*
Stringing: *Medium tiger tail or medium thread*
Weight: *0.2g*
Other sizes: *None*
Color range: *None*

Length: *3mm*
Width: *4mm*
Depth: *4mm*

Actual size

Mix and match

12

239

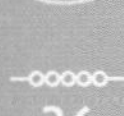

299 RIDGED OVAL STERLING SILVER

These fine ridges are engraved into the surface of the metal, not made by corrugating the sheet as for 289, so they are shallower in texture and less eye-catching. Ovals are always useful to extend the length of pieces using primarily rounded beads where a tube would look out of place.

Hole: *Large*
Stringing: *Medium tiger tail or medium thread*
Weight: *0.2g*
Other sizes: *8mm, 10mm*
Color range: *None*
Length: *7mm*
Width: *4mm*
Depth: *4mm*

Actual size

300 PLAIN OVAL STERLING SILVER

Plain silver beads can add a touch of light and elegance to jewelry made of anything from glass to semiprecious stones and can work well with complex handmade beads. These have a large hole that would allow them to slide along a narrow silk cord, so they could be used sparingly to enhance a focal bead.

Hole: *Large*
Stringing: *Medium tiger tail, heavy thread, or fine cord*
Weight: *0.3g*
Other sizes: *10mm*
Color range: *None*
Length: *8mm*
Width: *5mm*
Depth: *5mm*

Actual size

301 TEXTURED OVAL STERLING SILVER

Lightly texturing the surface of these beads, as if with a stiff wire brush, has given them a satin look, not polished but not completely matte. Compare them with 260, which have been textured with a sharp point to create a sparkle. Use where silver is required but a shine would not fit the design.

Hole: *Large*
Stringing: *Medium tiger tail, heavy thread, or fine cord*
Weight: *0.2g*
Other sizes: *10mm*
Color range: *None*
Length: *7mm*
Width: *4mm*
Depth: *4mm*

Actual size

302 CURVED RIDGE OVAL GOLD-FILLED

These curved ridges are pressed on to the surface of a sheet that is then cut and formed into the beads. They do not catch the light quite as well as a bead made from a corrugated sheet and twisted but are nevertheless very attractive and move well as a spacer.

Hole: *Medium*
Stringing: *Medium tiger tail or medium thread*
Weight: *0.1g*
Other sizes: *None*
Color range: *None*

Length: *5mm*
Width: *3mm*
Depth: *3mm*

Actual size

303 CIRCLED BARREL STERLING SILVER

Pressed silver sheet is wrapped into a tube with a clearly visible seam and rounded at the ends to allow easy movement against other beads, creating a simple and effective spacer. These beads could also make a smoothly draping thin strand on their own, which could be very useful in a multistrand piece.

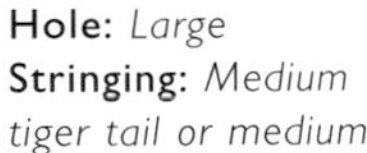

Hole: *Large*
Stringing: *Medium tiger tail or medium thread*
Weight: *0.1g*
Other sizes: *None*
Color range: *None*

Length: *4.5mm*
Width: *3mm*
Depth: *3mm*

Actual size

304 BARREL STERLING SILVER

This barrel shape has spread rings at the ends, so it will not move well against other beads with flat ends. A strand of these with small round beads between them would, however, look very pleasing and drape in an interesting way as the large hole covers part of the spacers.

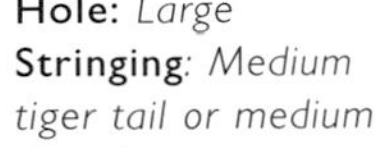

Hole: *Large*
Stringing: *Medium tiger tail or medium thread*
Weight: *0.2g*
Other sizes: *None*
Color range: *None*

Length: *5mm*
Width: *3.5mm*
Depth: *3.5mm*

Actual size

2
3
84

305 TUBE STERLING SILVER

At first glance, these seem to closely resemble 303, but they are shorter and have flat ends with a slightly larger hole, so they would not make good spacers for flat-ended beads but would work on thicker cord. Look carefully at beads that seem similar to see the advantages of each type.

Hole: *Large*
Stringing: *Medium tiger tail or medium thread*
Weight: *0.1g*
Other sizes: *None*
Color range: *None*

Length: *3mm*
Width: *3mm*
Depth: *3mm*

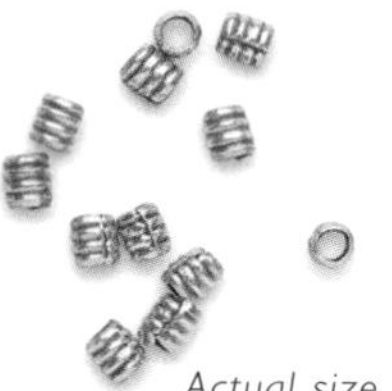

Actual size

Mix and match

212

423

3

4
25

306 STAMPED TUBE THAI SILVER

Because the flowers are sometimes partly obscured by the seam of these beads, the sheet must have been stamped before the tubes were rolled up, which would have been easier in any case. Tubes this size or wider are best used as spacers with larger rounded beads or in strands with small round beads between them to allow movement.

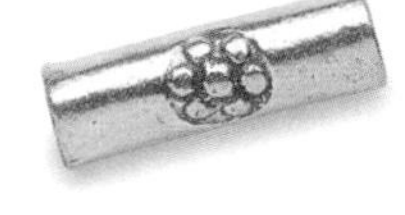

Hole: *Large*
Stringing: *Medium tiger tail or medium thread*
Weight: *0.5g*
Other sizes: *None*
Color range: *None*

Length: *10mm*
Width: *3mm*
Depth: *3mm*

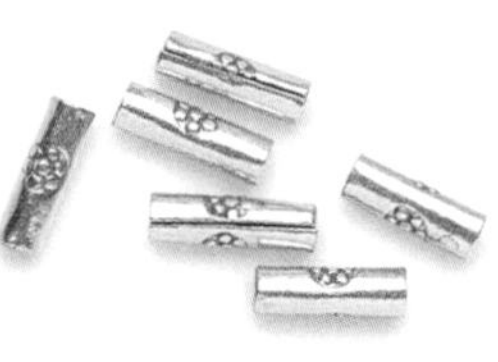

Actual size

Mix and match

192

139

1
3
63

307 LIQUID TUBE GOLD-FILLED

These tiny, fine tubes, whether plain or twisted, are usually used all together in many long strands: the ends are so tiny that they seem to flow rather than bend in movement, so the effect is of a waterfall of beads. They are thus known as liquid gold; liquid silver is also available.

Hole: *Small*
Stringing: *Fine thread*
Weight: *0.01g*
Other sizes: *None*
Color range: *None*

Length: *4mm*
Width: *1.5mm*
Depth: *1.5mm*

Actual size

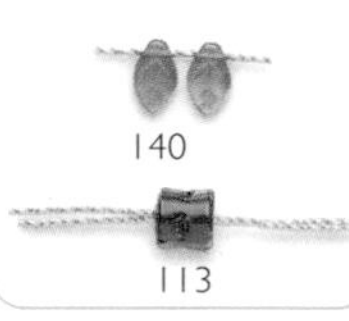

Mix and match

140

113

308 TWISTED TUBE STERLING SILVER

Close up these may seem rather like 307, but because they are so much larger they would not move well at all if it were not for the slight rounding of the ends of the tubes. The twist allows the flat planes to reflect light at various angles making these attractive but not too eye-catching.

Hole: *Large*
Stringing: *Medium tiger tail or medium thread*
Weight: *0.4g*
Other sizes: *None*
Color range: *None*
Length: *12mm*
Width: *3mm*
Depth: *3mm*

Actual size

309 DECORATED TUBE BALI SILVER

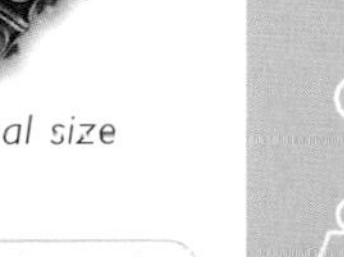

Actual size

The pattern on these tubes, made of loops of wire and dots, is emphasized by the antique effect but somehow looks very up-to-date, although it is also reminiscent of some patterns from the 1970s. Except for a small ring around each hole the ends are flat, so use rounded spacers to allow a piece to drape softly.

Hole: *Large*
Stringing: *Medium tiger tail or medium thread*
Weight: *2.3g*
Other sizes: *None*
Color range: *None*
Length: *17mm*
Width: *8mm*
Depth: *8mm*

310 SPINDLE SILVER-PLATED

More engraved lines than actual ridges, the texture on these beads does not really catch the light much, but it does add interest to what is already an unusual shape. These would probably look out of place in a very classical design but otherwise would be good almost anywhere that curves are required.

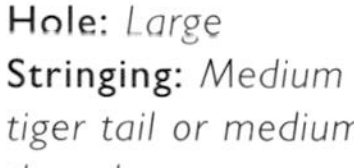

Hole: *Large*
Stringing: *Medium tiger tail or medium thread*
Weight: *0.7g*
Other sizes: *None*
Color range: *None*
Length: *15mm*
Width: *5mm*
Depth: *5mm*

Actual size

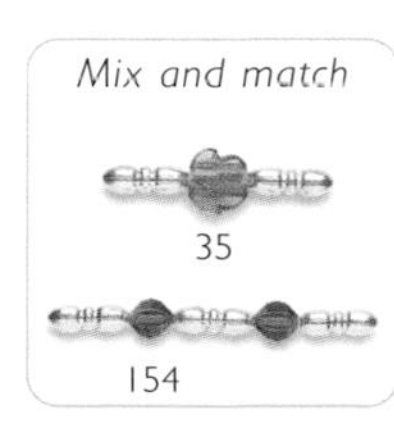

3
4
23

311 FOUR-SECTION TUBE VERMEIL

If four rondelle beads were fixed together and slightly flattened, the result would look like one of these beads. They are probably too plain to be the main beads of a piece but look lovely as spacers with larger or more complex beads and are suitable for classical designs. They could look wrong with round beads because of the flattening.

Hole: *Large*
Stringing: *Medium tiger tail or medium thread*
Weight: *0.6g*
Other sizes: *None*
Color range: *None*

Length: *11mm*
Width: *5mm*
Depth: *5mm*

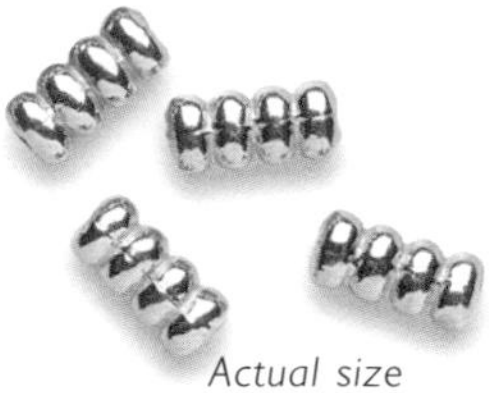

Actual size

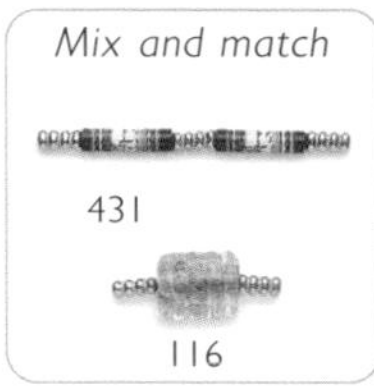

3
4
17

312 FACETED TUBE THAI SILVER

This seems to have been made as a solid piece, then supported inside the hole so that the flower pattern could be stamped on to each face. It is a lovely, sharply defined shape, with slightly matte, angled sections, which manages to look both contemporary and traditional, and so could be used in many styles of jewelry.

Hole: *Large*
Stringing: *Medium tiger tail or medium thread*
Weight: *0.9g*
Other sizes: *None*
Color range: *None*

Length: *15mm*
Width: *3mm*
Depth: *3mm*

Actual size

2
3
63

313 FACED ROUND GOLD-FILLED

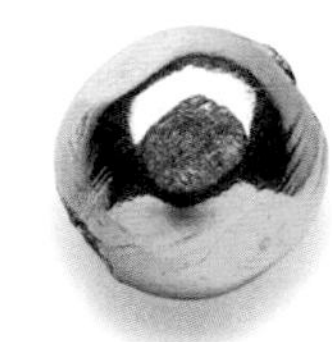

This bead is as generally useful as a small round bead but with the added interest of six little flattened faces that reflect the light in a different way, add a touch of the unusual to any strand. Excellent spacers for just about any style of project, these help with movement without drawing the eye.

Hole: *Medium*
Stringing: *Fine tiger tail or medium thread*
Weight: *0.1g*
Other sizes: *None*
Color range: *None*

Length: *4mm*
Width: *4mm*
Depth: *4mm*

Actual size

314 CUBE THAI SILVER

These have been made by cutting a section of square, stamped tube, then flattening or filing the corners, and folding and soldering the ends to make a slanting section with a generous square hole. The angle of the ends makes these much more mobile on a strand than would a flat end.

50

Hole: *Large*
Stringing: *Medium tiger tail or medium thread*
Weight: *0.6g*
Other sizes: *None*
Color range: *None*

Length: *5mm*
Width: *4.5mm*
Depth: *4.5mm*

Actual size

Mix and match

315 FOLDED CUBE THAI SILVER

The most impressive of the beads made from narrow ribbons of silver, these have been made by weaving the strips along the middle section, then folding them over and tucking them into each other at the ends. These are fairly sturdy but store them carefully as they could be bent or crushed.

4

21

Hole: *Large*
Stringing: *Medium tiger tail or medium thread*
Weight: *1.9g*
Other sizes: *None*
Color range: *None*

Length: *12mm*
Width: *11mm*
Depth: *11mm*

Actual size

Mix and match

316 POLYGON BALI SILVER

The shape of these beads will allow for easy movement of any strand. The middle section is decorated with a collar of wire edges and raised rings made by stacking thin disks of different sizes on top of each other, then antiquing that section and polishing the surface. These could be used in both classic and contemporary designs.

21

Hole: *Medium*
Stringing: *Medium tiger tail or medium thread*
Weight: *2.8g*
Other sizes: *None*
Color range: *None*

Length: *12mm*
Width: *11mm*
Depth: *11mm*

Actual size

Mix and match

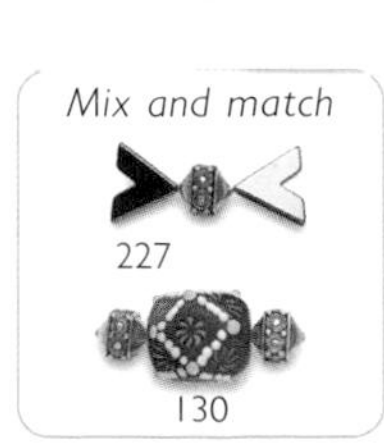

22

317 POLYGON STERLING SILVER AND BRASS

With their brass bumps and fancy ends, like dotted ring beads added at each hole, the interesting geometric shape of these beads may have been a bit over decorated. These are more comfortable to wear than they look because they tend to lie with two of the bumps supporting the bead against the skin, so they do not press in.

Hole: *Large*
Stringing: *Medium tiger tail or medium thread*
Weight: *1.6g*
Other sizes: *None*
Color range: *None*

Length: *11.5mm*
Width: *12mm*
Depth: *12mm*

Actual size

18

318 DIAGONAL SQUARE BALI SILVER

Flat squares can be awkward to use where a good drape is required, but these are pierced diagonally so they will move well and add shape to any piece. They would also be good in embroidery, and a section stitched together using right-angle weave would make a very solid but flexible piece.

Hole: *Large*
Stringing: *Medium tiger tail or medium thread*
Weight: *2.5g*
Other sizes: *None*
Color range: *None*

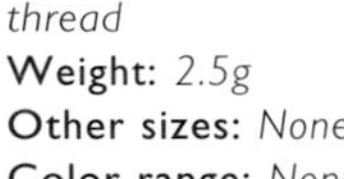

Length: *14mm*
Width: *14mm*
Depth: *5mm*

Actual size

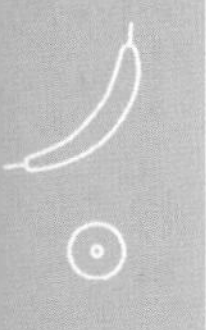

8

319 CURVED WRAPPED TUBE THAI SILVER

Made in the same way as 288 but using a curved mandrel or worked into shape after soldering. Long curved beads are best used at or near the bottom curve of a necklace, depending on the amount of curve, because elsewhere they may pull the strand into an odd shape.

Actual size

Hole: *Large*
Stringing: *Medium tiger tail or medium thread*
Weight: *2.4g*
Other sizes: *None*
Color range: *None*

Length: *35mm*
Width: *5mm*
Depth: *5mm*

320 SHELL CONE RAJASTHANI SILVER

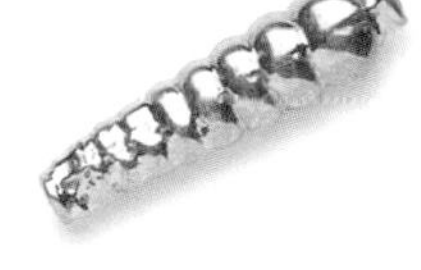

The shape of these beads is reminiscent of a long seashell, making these fun to use in light summer jewelry, perhaps with real shells and pastel colors. A different look would be achieved by using them all threaded in the same direction or using pairs tip to tip or end to end.

Hole: *Medium*
Stringing: *Medium tiger tail or medium thread*
Weight: *0.5g*
Other sizes: *None*
Color range: *None*

Length: *16.5mm*
Width: *4mm*
Depth: *4mm*

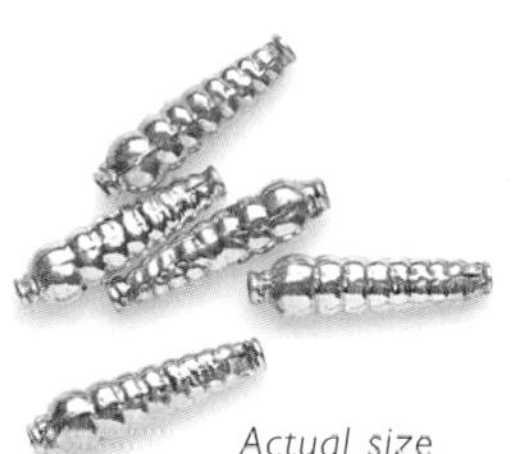

Actual size

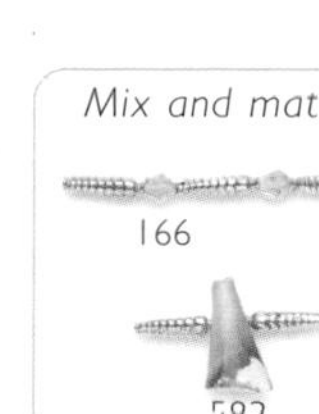

321 DROP GOLD-FILLED

Plain drop shapes are useful at the ends of earrings or as dangles from a strand, but these have such large holes that an extra small bead would be required to hang them on most head pins (629). They could also be used along a strand, arranged in various directions, as for 320.

Hole: *Large*
Stringing: *Medium tiger tail or medium thread*
Weight: *0.05g*
Other sizes: *None*
Color range: *None*

Length: *8mm*
Width: *4mm*
Depth: *4mm*

Actual size

322 TRUMPET NINE-KARAT GOLD

This shape was formed using corrugated gold sheet, so they are sturdy and reflect light from all the folds. The flared shape fits well on either side of a round-ended bead, and a strand made in that way has an interesting texture and moves well. It could also be used with a flat flower bead to give a daffodil look.

Hole: *Medium*
Stringing: *Medium tiger tail or medium thread*
Weight: *0.05g*
Other sizes: *None*
Color range: *None*

Length: *7mm*
Width: *5mm*
Depth: *5mm*

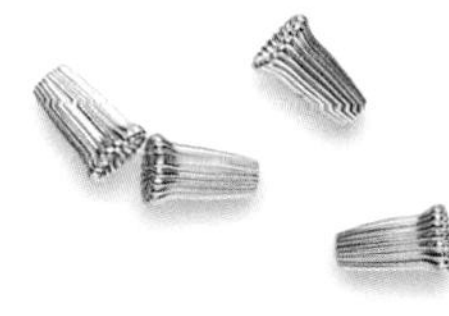

Actual size

323 THREE-TO-ONE SPACER VERMEIL

The holes, one at the tip of the triangle and three at the base, mean that this could be used to bring a three-strand necklace neatly into one, whether for design purposes or to make the fastening simple. With a small strand of beads descending from each hole like a fringe, they would also make good ends for earrings or lariats.

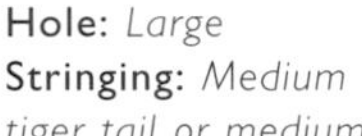

Hole: *Large*
Stringing: *Medium tiger tail or medium thread*
Weight: *2.3g*
Other sizes: *None*
Color range: *None*

Length: *16mm*
Width: *11mm*
Depth: *5mm*

Actual size

Mix and match

324 TRIANGULAR TUBE BALI SILVER

This is unusually chunky for a silver bead. The triangular tube shape will usually sit with one side against the skin so that one edge is always pointing outward, displaying two of the sides. Even so, it is not a good bead for the back of a heavy necklace or a tight bracelet, as the decoration is rather rough and could be uncomfortable to wear.

Hole: *Large*
Stringing: *Medium tiger tail or medium thread*
Weight: *4.3g*
Other sizes: *None*
Color range: *None*

Length: *14mm*
Width: *13mm*
Depth: *13mm*

Actual size

Mix and match

325 LEAF RAJASTHANI SILVER

A lovely, well-made, delicate shape, these beads would work well on earrings, at the ends of a lariat, or anywhere along a strand. They are shaped all the way around, and the side seams are practically invisible, so they are just as pretty from all directions. They would go well with any flower bead.

Hole: *Medium*
Stringing: *Medium tiger tail or medium thread*
Weight: *0.7g*
Other sizes: *None*
Color range: *None*

Length: *14mm*
Width: *6mm*
Depth: *4.5mm*

Actual size

Mix and match

326 SEMICIRCLE THAI SILVER

This is simply a circle of silver wrapped over a mandrel, stamped with a pattern, and then soldered. Because they will hang downward if possible, these beads are probably best used near the bottom curve of a necklace or on a choker, unless it does not matter to the design which way the semicircle is pointing when worn.

Hole: *Large*
Stringing: *Medium tiger tail or medium thread*
Weight: *0.9g*
Other sizes: *None*
Color range: *None*

Length: *16mm*
Width: *8mm*
Depth: *3mm*

Actual size

Mix and match
395
180

16

327 CIRCLE THAI SILVER

This is made in a similar way to 326, but with two circles shaped over the mandrel and soldered together. Because they will lie flat in most circumstances, these are more adaptable in use and would work in almost any piece. They are perhaps especially good for bracelets where thick beads would be awkward.

Hole: *Large*
Stringing: *Medium tiger tail or medium thread*
Weight: *1.2g*
Other sizes: *None*
Color range: *None*

Length: *12mm*
Width: *11mm*
Depth: *3.5mm*

Actual size

Mix and match
205
570

4
21

328 CROSS-HOLE THAI SILVER

Very like 327, this has two holes across the circle at right angles to each other. These could be used at the cross points of a network of beads, to add side or dangling decoration to a piece, or to construct a complex section at the bottom of a necklace.

Hole: *Large*
Stringing: *Medium tiger tail or medium thread*
Weight: *1.2g*
Other sizes: *None*
Color range: *None*

Length: *13mm*
Width: *13mm*
Depth: *3mm*

Actual size

Mix and match
84
44

20

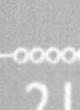

329 FLOWER STERLING SILVER

This thick, rounded flower shape is made even deeper by the dots that form the center and are almost a small flower in themselves. These raise the back of the main flower above the skin or clothing. Rather a cute bead, it is probably most suitable for spring or summer jewelry or fun pieces for children, teens, or young adults.

3 4 21

Hole: *Large*
Stringing: *Medium tiger tail or medium thread*
Weight: *1.5g*
Other sizes: *None*
Color range: *None*

Length: *12mm*
Width: *10mm*
Depth: *10mm*

Actual size

Mix and match

251

506

330 LETTER HEART STERLING SILVER

Letter beads are available in most materials, and precious metals are no exception. The large hole through these hearts allows them to be used on thick cord to make simple bracelets or chokers, but, if small beads were used on either side to allow them to hang neatly, they could be used on more standard stringing materials.

3 4 32

Hole: *Very large*
Stringing: *Cord*
Weight: *1.2g*
Other sizes: *None*
Color range: *None*

Length: *8mm*
Width: *7mm*
Depth: *5.5mm*

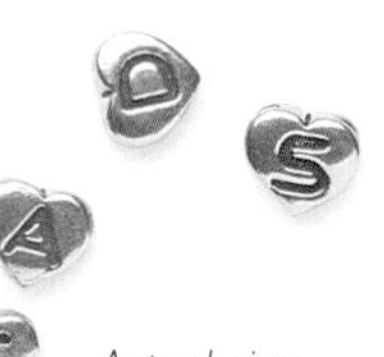

Actual size

Mix and match

468

453

331 PUFFED HEART STERLING SILVER

This heart shape has been puffed (rounded up) and decorated to such an extent that it is almost disguised, which seems a shame. Look closely to see the smaller heart: it is supposed to look tied on to the main shape with raised lines. It is probably best used dangling as the dots are very raised and could catch on the skin.

2 4 20

Hole: *Large*
Stringing: *Medium tiger tail or medium thread*
Weight: *1.5g*
Other sizes: *None*
Color range: *None*

Length: *13mm*
Width: *12mm*
Depth: *10mm*

Actual size

Mix and match

234

143

332 FISH STERLING SILVER

Many creatures are available in silver beads, and these are a good example. The pattern is hammered into the metal with shaped tools to make the details and features of a fish: this is called repoussé work. The fish would work well along a strand or dangled at the end of clear monofilament—as if on a fishing line.

Hole: *Large*
Stringing: *Medium tiger tail or medium thread*
Weight: *1.7g*
Other sizes: *None*
Color range: *None*

Length: *18mm*
Width: *11mm*
Depth: *6mm*

Actual size

Mix and match

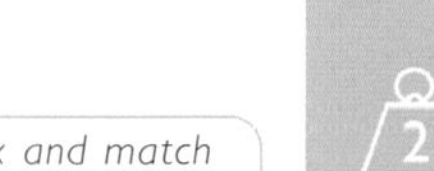

575

82

333 SEAHORSE STERLING SILVER

An example of a creature made in a completely different way to the fish 332, these have been molded in two parts, giving raised rather than impressed details and a more rounded look. As the hole goes across the shoulders these would work best along a strand, and the longer body will prevent too much turning when worn.

Hole: *Medium*
Stringing: *Medium tiger tail or medium thread*
Weight: *1.2g*
Other sizes: *None*
Color range: *None*

Length: *13mm*
Width: *2.3mm*
Depth: *5.5mm*

Actual size

Mix and match

320

247

334 BLOB STERLING SILVER

Random blobs of silver are usually made by dripping molten silver into deep cold water, so that the drop has set before it touches the bottom, then drilling through them for stringing. Dropping silver on to a surface would give a flat side to every piece. Blobs look good with chips of tumbled gemstones.

Hole: *Medium*
Stringing: *Medium tiger tail or medium thread*
Weight: *2.4g*
Other sizes: *None*
Color range: *None*

Length: *2mm*
Width: *5.5mm*
Depth: *5mm*

Actual size

Mix and match

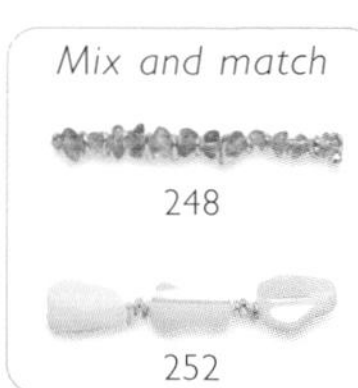

248

252

CHAPTER 5

Base metals

Some base metal beads are mainly one single metal, for example, brass, copper, or aluminum; others are standard alloys (a mixture of metals) such as pewter (some of which is made with lead—check when purchasing and do not allow small children access to such beads). Some alloys are sold simply as "metal."

Gold-colored beads are often called "gilt," to distinguish them from real gold, but silver-colored beads do not have a special name. The majority of base metal alloy beads come in both gold and silver colors, and some in copper, too. Beads may also be available in "bright" or "antiqued," where the metal has been dulled and darkened, using either a coating or a chemical process, to make it look old.

Most metal beads are much lighter than their size and material might imply, because they are hollow. They are, however, heavier than similar "metalized plastic" (plastic beads with a metallic coating). Metal beads, even hollow ones, "clink," whereas plastic beads have a dull sound—this is another way to tell the difference between them. Hollow beads make stringing more difficult—see the introduction to the chapter on precious metals (page 106) for ways around this problem.

The huge range of shapes in metal beads allows for very traditional designs or for more contemporary ones such as this necklace and earring set.

335 HOLLOW ROUND BASE METAL

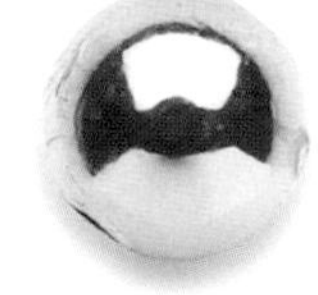

Plain round beads are available in many different metals and in a huge range of sizes. Hollow beads are slightly more difficult to string than solid ones because there is no channel from the hole on one side to that on the other.

Hole: *Large*
Stringing: *Medium tiger tail or heavy thread*
Weight: *0.5g*
Other sizes: *Many*
Color range: *Small*

Length: *6mm*
Width: *6mm*
Depth: *6mm*

Actual size

Mix and match
404
433

42

336 RIDGED ROUND BASE METAL

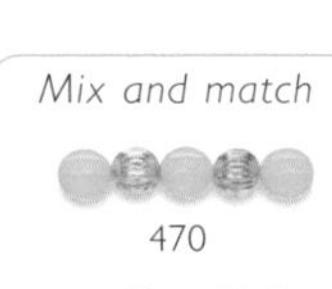

Although they look solid, these beads are made of quite thin metal, made much stronger by the ridged shape. Because the ridges are pushed together at the ends and no seam is visible, these were probably formed from textured tubes of metal cut to size and then worked into shape.

Hole: *Large*
Stringing: *Medium tiger tail or heavy thread*
Weight: *1.0g*
Other sizes: *Many*
Color range: *Small*

Length: *13mm*
Width: *13mm*
Depth: *13mm*

Actual size

Mix and match
470
506

20

337 FINE FILIGREE BASE METAL

Exceptionally light for their size, these beads have been formed from a four-lobed shape, molded or pressed and cut from very thin metal. One end was the middle of the original shape, the other a small round to which the tips of the lobes are fixed after shaping. The four sections are also fixed to each other.

Hole: *Large*
Stringing: *Medium tiger tail or heavy thread*
Weight: *0.5g*
Other sizes: *8mm*
Color range: *Small*

Length: *14mm*
Width: *14mm*
Depth: *14mm*

Actual size

Mix and match
468
153

18

338 WIRE FILIGREE BASE METAL

Rather thicker filigree than 337, two pressed flower shapes surround the holes of these beads, but the flowers on the main section are formed from loops of square wire. Five loops were assembled into one flower, then ten flowers plus the end pieces were shaped and soldered together to form the bead.

Actual size

Hole: *Large*
Stringing: *Medium tiger tail or heavy thread*
Weight: *2.1g*
Other sizes: *None*
Color range: *None*

Length: *15mm*
Width: *15mm*
Depth: *15mm*

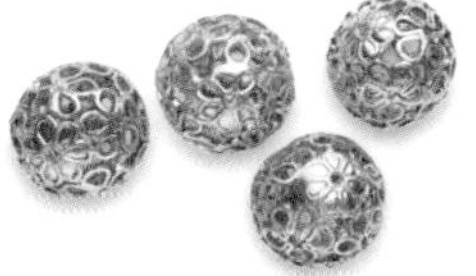

Mix and match

115

126

2

3

17

339 STAMPED BASE METAL

Stamped plates, one at each end and a longer one wrapped around to form the main bead, have been shaped to make these beads. They have oriental designs, so they could be used with traditional Chinese beads such as blue and white ceramics, jade, or red carved cinnabar, and would be suitable for pieces involving fine Chinese knotting.

Actual size

Hole: *Large*
Stringing: *Medium tiger tail or heavy thread*
Weight: *1.9g*
Other sizes: *None*
Color range: *None*

Length: *15mm*
Width: *15mm*
Depth: *15mm*

Mix and match

26

519

1

3

17

340 KNOTTED PEWTER

Molded into the shape of a Chinese button knot, these pewter beads have been antiqued so that there is darker color in the dips of the molding. The seam can be seen but is not obvious. Because they are solid these beads are heavier than any of the larger metal beads we have seen so far.

Hole: *Large*
Stringing: *Medium tiger tail or heavy thread*
Weight: *2.0g*
Other sizes: *None*
Color range: *None*

Length: *8mm*
Width: *9mm*
Depth: *9mm*

Actual size

Mix and match

406

216

3

3

32

341 CURL DECORATED PEWTER

Another solid cast bead, this pewter has been colored gold, and the short spirals and dots of metal on the molded shapes must have been added afterward because the seam lines can just be seen going under some of the raised pattern pieces. Antiquing has been used to emphasize the decoration.

Hole: *Large*
Stringing: *Medium tiger tail or heavy thread*
Weight: *1.8g*
Other sizes: *None*
Color range: *Small*

Length: *7.5mm*
Width: *9mm*
Depth: *9mm*

Actual size

Mix and match

342 CLOISONNÉ COPPER

Cloisonné decoration is used on jewelry and other metal decorative items such as bowls and vases. The base metal for beads is usually copper. Thin, flat wire is assembled into outlines and soldered to the base shape, then filled in with enamel and fired to create the designs. The remaining copper showing is then gilded, if required.

Hole: *Large*
Stringing: *Medium tiger tail or heavy thread*
Weight: *1.3g*
Other sizes: *6mm, 8mm, 12mm*
Color range: *Medium*

Length: *10mm*
Width: *10mm*
Depth: *10mm*

Actual size

Mix and match

343 OPEN CLOISONNÉ COPPER

The work on these beads is a little finer than that on 342, and only the shapes have been filled with enamel, not the background area. This allows a lot more of the metal of the beads to show, and leaves the filled areas raised up against the background for a delicate look.

Hole: *Large*
Stringing: *Medium tiger tail or heavy thread*
Weight: *1.2g*
Other sizes: *6mm, 8mm, 12mm*
Color range: *Medium*

Length: *10mm*
Width: *10mm*
Depth: *10mm*

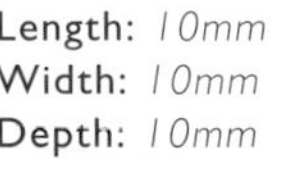

Actual size

Mix and match

344 COIL SPIKES BASE METAL

Almost the opposite of cloisonné, these have an enamel background with raised spikes made with a dot of metal surrounded by a coil of fine wire. These are a little uncomfortable to have pressed into the skin, so avoid use at the back of a necklace if the components at the front are heavy.

Hole: *Large*
Stringing: *Medium tiger tail or heavy thread*
Weight: *2.1g*
Other sizes: *None*
Color range: *Medium*

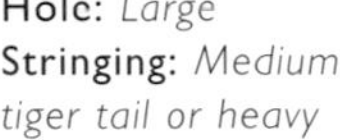

Length: *12mm*
Width: *13mm*
Depth: *13mm*

Actual size

Mix and match

17

338

345 RHINESTONE SET BASE METAL

Made up of two pieces of metal, each with three arms set with two rhinestones, folded together and fixed into each other with tabs, probably after the stones have been set. This forms a hollow shape that is almost round and holds twelve cut stones, so this is a very sparkly bead.

Hole: *Medium*
Stringing: *Medium tiger tail or heavy thread*
Weight: *0.6g*
Other sizes: *4.5mm, 5.5mm, 10mm*

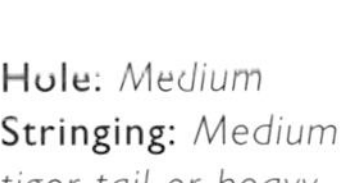

Color range: *Medium*
Length: *7.5mm*
Width: *7.5mm*
Depth: *7.5mm*

Actual size

Mix and match

343

11

346 DOTTED LINES BASE METAL

The ridges on these beads are formed from lines of dots. Because these lines do not go up to the holes the ends are somewhat concave, so that the ends of round beads can fit into the space. This is interesting and allows for a more solid-looking strand, which still moves well.

Hole: *Large*
Stringing: *Medium tiger tail or heavy thread*
Weight: *1.0g*
Other sizes: *None*
Color range: *Small*

Length: *5.5mm*
Width: *7mm*
Depth: *7mm*

Actual size

Mix and match

540

499

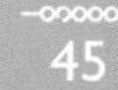

2

4

20

347 NET FILIGREE BASE METAL

Two domes of netting meet at a solid ring collar on the central line, and flat wire decorations have been added on top. These are very dull and were probably made with inexpensive metal allowed to oxidize naturally, rather than antiqued or coated. Avoid using with shiny beads unless a contrast is required.

Hole: *Large*
Stringing: *Medium tiger tail or heavy thread*
Weight: *1.5g*
Other sizes: *None*
Color range: *None*

Length: *12.5mm*
Width: *15mm*
Depth: *15mm*

Actual size

2

3

25

348 WAVE EDGE BASE METAL

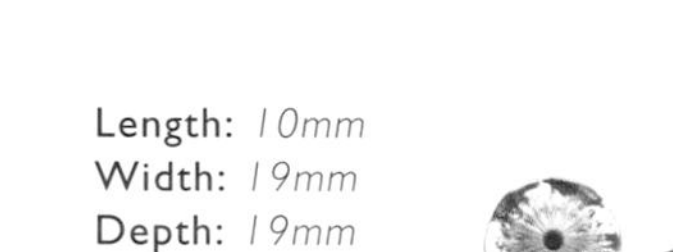

These beads are basically much like 336 but with a smooth wavy collar around the center line. These will stand well away from the skin, so be sure to balance them with other beads as large as the collar or use them regularly along a piece to avoid an uneven hang.

Actual size

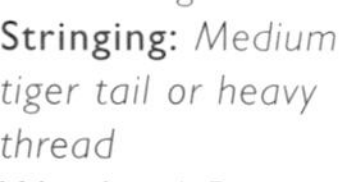

Hole: *Large*
Stringing: *Medium tiger tail or heavy thread*
Weight: *1.5g*
Other sizes: *None*
Color range: *Small*

Length: *10mm*
Width: *19mm*
Depth: *19mm*

3

3

32

349 ANTIQUE RIDGES COPPER

Cast from copper, the ridges on this bead are not folds in the metal as for 336 and 348. This classic shape, in the dulled, antiqued colors available, is particularly suitable for more traditional jewelry and ancient styles, as well as being useful as a spacer for subtle semiprecious stones.

Hole: *Large*
Stringing: *Medium tiger tail or heavy thread*
Weight: *1.9g*
Other sizes: *None*
Color range: *Small*

Length: *8mm*
Width: *8mm*
Depth: *8mm*

Actual size

350 FACETED BASE METAL

Probably molded into its basic shape (a bicone with a central ring) in fairly thin metal, these beads have then been cut so that there are many crisp facets to catch the light. The techniques are ancient, but the result does not look old-fashioned, so these would work equally well in a classic piece or a modern one.

Hole: *Large*
Stringing: *Medium tiger tail or heavy thread*
Weight: *1.1g*
Other sizes: *None*
Color range: *Small*

Length: *7mm*
Width: *7mm*
Depth: *7mm*

Actual size

Mix and match

175

463

351 OVAL WITH LEAVES BASE METAL

The ring of leaves on this bead appears to have been molded separately and then applied to the basic oval shape, as do the two rings of dots at the holes. With the antique finish, this all adds up to very classical looking beads, which would make a lovely strand on their own or could be mixed in with larger pieces.

Hole: *Large*
Stringing: *Medium tiger tail or heavy thread*
Weight: *1.3g*
Other sizes: *None*
Color range: *Small*

Length: *9mm*
Width: *8mm*
Depth: *8mm*

Actual size

Mix and match

139

140

4

3

28

352 WIRE OVAL BASE METAL

Fine colored wire has been wrapped around and around in a spiral to make this bead, which is basically a tight, thin-walled coil. This construction makes an interesting textured shape, but the beads are very easily crushed or bent out of shape, so store both the individual items and the finished jewelry carefully.

Hole: *Large*
Stringing: *Medium tiger tail or heavy thread*
Weight: *0.2g*
Other sizes: *None*
Color range: *Mixed*

Length: *6mm*
Width: *6mm*
Depth: *6mm*

Actual size

Mix and match

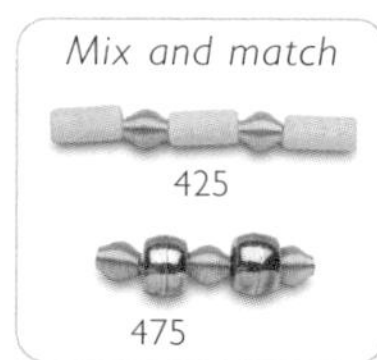

425

475

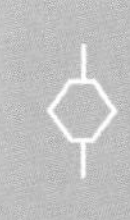

2

2

3
25

353 DRUM SHAPE ALUMINUM

Solid metal but lighter for its size and construction than similar metal beads because of the material. These are roughly shaped, apparently cut from a thick cylinder, drilled, and then rounded toward the ends, although still flat at the holes. Good for chunky jewelry, perhaps on fine cord with knots to hold a few separated along the length.

Hole: *Large*
Stringing: *Medium tiger tail or heavy thread*
Weight: *1.8g*
Other sizes: *None*
Color range: *None*

Length: *10mm*
Width: *11mm*
Depth: *11mm*

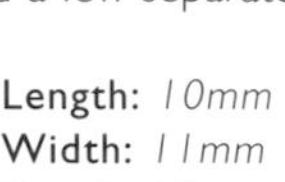

Actual size

Mix and match
407
517

2

2
50

354 RICE SHAPE BASE METAL

Probably the most common shape of metal bead after the plain round, this thin oval is often called the rice shape. It is very useful to extend the length of a piece, as a main bead in multiple thin strands, and as a spacer. It is frequently used with semiprecious stones where silver or gold would be too expensive.

Hole: *Medium*
Stringing: *Medium tiger tail or heavy thread*
Weight: *0.1g*
Other sizes: *Many*
Color range: *Small*

Length: *5mm*
Width: *3.5mm*
Depth: *3.5mm*

Actual size

Mix and match
97
560

1

2
32

355 ROUNDED TUBE BASE METAL

Hollow and with very thin walls, these beads have almost the largest holes in the book, suitable for very thick cord. They could be used to slide over and disguise a knot or even a narrow catch, so that a necklace or bracelet looks continuous, or to join several strands of small beads.

Hole: *Extra large*
Stringing: *Cord*
Weight: *0.6g*
Other sizes: *None*
Color range: *None*

Length: *8mm*
Width: *7mm*
Depth: *7mm*

Actual size

Mix and match
20
498

356 DOUBLE COIL BASE METAL AND COPPER

First, a long coil of the colored wire was wound and threaded on to the copper wire. The copper was wound on the same size mandrel for a short length, then the green coil was pushed up so that it turned along with the copper. When the colored wire was finished, another short length of copper was coiled alone to complete the bead.

Actual size

Hole: *Large*
Stringing: *Medium tiger tail or heavy thread*
Weight: *2.2g*
Other sizes: *None*
Color range: *Medium*

Length: *36mm*
Width: *8mm*
Depth: *8mm*

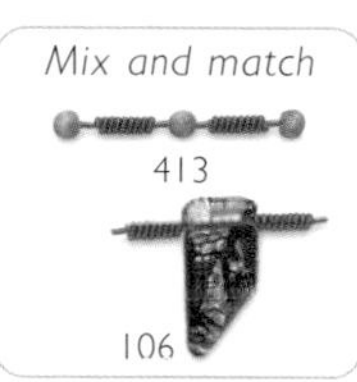

357 HOLLOW DROP BASE METAL

Showing a slight seam, these are made of a sheet of metal shaped into the drop. Because they are hollow they are light and suitable for earrings (use a head pin, 629, to hang them downward); or try them along a strand, either all in the same direction or tip to tip in pairs.

Hole: *Medium*
Stringing: *Medium tiger tail or heavy thread*
Weight: *0.8g*
Other sizes: *None*
Color range: *Small*

Length: *10mm*
Width: *7mm*
Depth: *7mm*

Actual size

358 CAST DROP BASE METAL

These drops are slightly flattened and deeply antiqued. In this case, the seam appears in the decoration as well as in the base bead, so the apparent wire spirals added on top are actually created as part of the casting process. Use in the same was as 357, although sparingly in earrings due to the extra weight.

Hole: *Medium*
Stringing: *Medium tiger tail or heavy thread*
Weight: *1.9g*
Other sizes: *None*
Color range: *Small*

Length: *15mm*
Width: *7mm*
Depth: *7mm*

Actual size

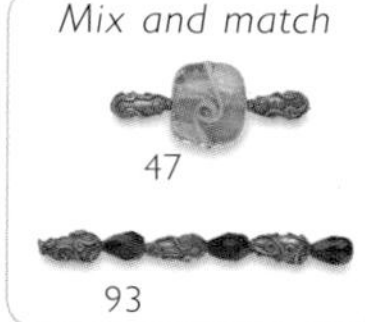

2 2 63

359 FLAT OVAL WITH SIDE HOLE BASE METAL

A flat oval is a fairly standard bead shape, but these are unusual because the hole is through the width of the oval rather than along its length. This gives them a very modern, almost futuristic look, and they would make a striking strand on their own or could be used as spacers in any bright pieces.

Hole: *Medium*
Stringing: *Medium tiger tail or heavy thread*
Weight: *0.4g*
Other sizes: *None*
Color range: *Small*

Length: *4mm*
Width: *6mm*
Depth: *3mm*

Actual size

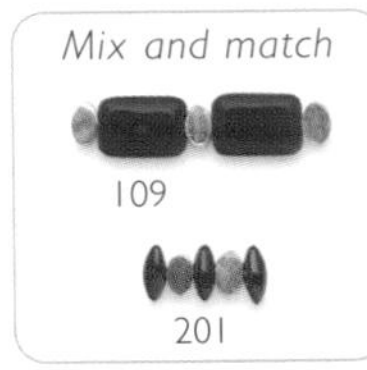

3 3 17

360 FLAT OVAL ROSES BASE METAL

The flat oval shape and the impressed and antiqued rose pattern are classic. The shape is very comfortable to wear so is good at the back of necklaces, and the slim profile is convenient in bracelets that may have to tuck under cuffs.

Hole: *Large*
Stringing: *Medium tiger tail or heavy thread*
Weight: *3.4g*
Other sizes: *None*
Color range: *Small*

Length: *15mm*
Width: *12mm*
Depth: *4.5mm*

Actual size

3 3 36

361 YING YANG DRUM BASE METAL

With dipped sides these do not work well alone in a strand because they tend to overlap unevenly, with one edge slipping into the valley in the next bead. However, when alternated with beads with rounded ends that fit neatly into the dip they unify a piece and make it appear more solid while still moving well.

Hole: *Large*
Stringing: *Medium tiger tail or heavy thread*
Weight: *0.9g*
Other sizes: *None*
Color range: *Small*

Length: *7mm*
Width: *7mm*
Depth: *5mm*

Actual size

362 CORD DRUM BASE METAL

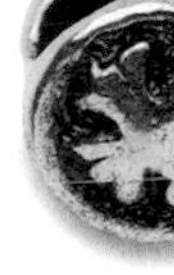

Such a large hole indicates that these were made for use with heavy cord and could hang oddly on slimmer products. Small beads would slip inside them, but beads with a rounded end that just fit into the hole, without going too far in, would work very well with these on thinner stringing materials.

Hole: *Very large*
Stringing: *Cord*
Weight: *1.1g*
Other sizes: *None*
Color range: *Small*

Length: *6mm*
Width: *7mm*
Depth: *7mm*

Actual size

Mix and match
70
127

3
3
42

363 FLOWER SPACER BASE METAL

A little flat disk, cast with a central round texture surrounded with dots to look rather like a simple flower, this is not all that interesting on its own but makes a splendid spacer where a plain bead would be too distracting or too boring, and the slim profile makes it useful if height is not required.

Hole: *Medium*
Stringing: *Medium tiger tail or heavy thread*
Weight: *0.6g*
Other sizes: *None*
Color range: *Small*

Length: *6mm*
Width: *6mm*
Depth: *3mm*

Actual size

Mix and match
205
441

2
2
42

364 FLAT FLOWER BASE METAL

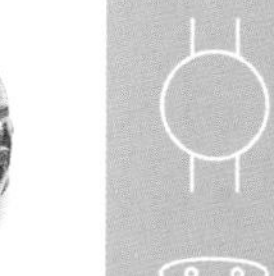

Another flat flower, these beads have two holes. Strung through one hole only, they hang down from the thread and will overlap unless spacers are used. They could also be used with other two-hole items or to connect two rows of smaller beads.

Hole: *Large*
Stringing: *Medium tiger tail or heavy thread*
Weight: *1.8g*
Other sizes: *None*
Color range: *Small*

Length: *12mm*
Width: *12mm*
Depth: *3.5mm*

Actual size

Mix and match
57
488

3
3
21

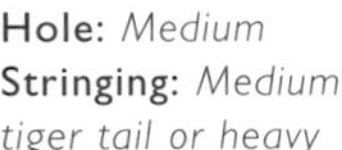

365 ROUND CUSHION COPPER

The copper of these cast beads is very heavily antiqued so that the metal's color only shows on the highest points and even those are dulled. They have a slightly Celtic look. Flattened round beads are useful where the design requires a wide strand without much height, such as for a simple bracelet.

Hole: *Medium*
Stringing: *Medium tiger tail or heavy thread*
Weight: *3.4g*
Other sizes: *None*
Color range: *Small*

Length: *11mm*
Width: *11mm*
Depth: *6.5mm*

Actual size

Mix and match

73

484

366 BRIGHT SPIRAL BASE METAL

Similar in many ways to 365 but even flatter and with the parts of the metal that show above the antiquing very bright; a coating has been used to retain that brightness. The design of a spiral surrounded with dots is an ancient sun symbol, so these beads bring summer days to mind.

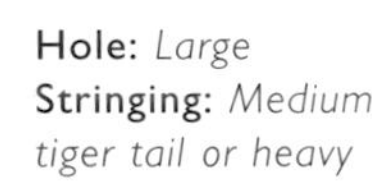

Hole: *Large*
Stringing: *Medium tiger tail or heavy thread*
Weight: *1.9g*
Other sizes: *None*
Color range: *Small*

Length: *13mm*
Width: *13mm*
Depth: *4.5mm*

Actual size

Mix and match

568

48

367 CLOISONNÉ DONUT BASE METAL

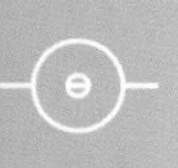

Twisted wire has been used for the outlines of this cloisonné, and the sections are filled with less enamel than in 342 so that the edges stand proud. Unlike many donut shapes, these are pierced on both sides, across the diameter, so they can be used along a strand, perhaps with a small bead in the middle so the thread is covered.

Hole: *Large*
Stringing: *Medium tiger tail or heavy thread*
Weight: *5.5g*
Other sizes: *None*
Color range: *Medium*

Length: *30mm*
Width: *30mm*
Depth: *8mm*

Mix and match

259

265

Actual size

368 **DISK** BASE METAL

Almost flat disks are used most often as spacers between larger beads, but they do make quite interesting strands, rather like textured tubes, on their own. However, these strands tend to be stiff, so try using just a few together to get the look while still allowing your piece to move well.

Hole: *Medium*
Stringing: *Medium tiger tail or heavy thread*
Weight: *0.1g*
Other sizes: *10mm*
Color range: *Small*

Length: *3mm*
Width: *8mm*
Depth: *8mm*

Actual size

Mix and match

573

49

369 **RING** BASE METAL

Because they have such a large hole these rings are rather like tires. Although probably intended as spacers, some round or oval beads can be threaded on either side of one of these and just touch in the middle, so that the ring is held in place but no extra space is taken on the strand.

Hole: *Very large*
Stringing: *Cord*
Weight: *0.4g*
Other sizes: *None*
Color range: *Small*

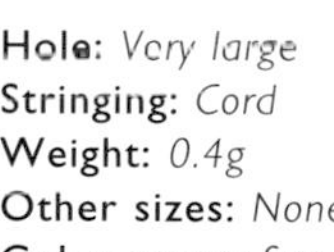

Length: *3mm*
Width: *7mm*
Depth: *7mm*

Actual size

Mix and match

68

187

370 **LENTIL** BASE METAL

Used in much the same way as 368, these are rather longer and allow more movement because they slope in toward their large holes. They are suitable for use on thin cord or leather; if a thinner stringing material is used, small beads may be required on either side to keep these from falling over.

Hole: *Large*
Stringing: *Medium tiger tail or heavy thread*
Weight: *0.6g*
Other sizes: *None*
Color range: *Small*

Length: *4mm*
Width: *7mm*
Depth: *7mm*

Actual size

Mix and match

225

572

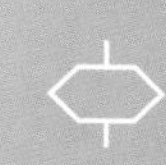

371 DISK SPACER COPPER

These disks, with their rope-twist edging, are probably the most common metal spacer beads and are available in many base and precious metals and finishes, these being antique copper. In use, only the twisted edging shows between the other beads. They are also useful to cover the ends of beaded beads made on tubes.

Hole: *Large*
Stringing: *Medium tiger tail or heavy thread*
Weight: *0.2g*
Other sizes: *4mm, 8mm*
Color range: *Small*
Length: *2mm*
Width: *6mm*
Depth: *6mm*

Actual size

372 COIL SPACER BASE METAL

A coil of fine wire has been shaped into a ring and joined to make these bright little spacers, which allow the light through them. They could be useful where a more common spacer would make the design too solid, where more brightness is required, or where the spacer must be as insubstantial as possible.

Hole: *Large*
Stringing: *Medium tiger tail or heavy thread*
Weight: *0.05g*
Other sizes: *None*
Color range: *None*
Length: *2mm*
Width: *4mm*
Depth: *4mm*

Actual size

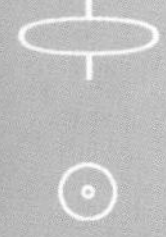

373 SOLID SPACER BRASS

These are heavy disks for their size because they are made of solid brass. They have a rounded edge and are best used as spacers with bigger rounded beads, or where extra weight is required to help a necklace or similar piece to hang correctly without distracting the eye from the main design elements.

Hole: *Medium*
Stringing: *Medium tiger tail or heavy thread*
Weight: *0.5g*
Other sizes: *8mm*
Color range: *None*
Length: *2.5mm*
Width: *6mm*
Depth: *6mm*

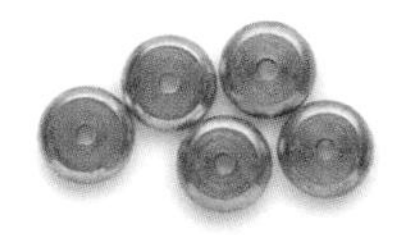

Actual size

374 COMPOUND WHEEL BASE METAL

This shape looks as though it is made of a larger pointed wheel with two smaller coiled rings on either side and another two plain rings at the ends. Distinctly decorative, these beads are a little uncomfortable if pressed into the skin, so avoid using them at the back of a necklace or in a tight-fitting bracelet.

Hole: *Large*
Stringing: *Medium tiger tail or heavy thread*
Weight: *0.9g*
Other sizes: *None*
Color range: *Small*

Length: *6mm*
Width: *8mm*
Depth: *8mm*

Actual size

375 CUT SPACER COPPER

Yet another type of spacer, these are cut into facets along the edge of the wheel to catch the light and are plated with bright copper. There is probably a coating on this metal to keep it bright, because copper dulls easily and forms green verdigris if untreated (which can actually be very attractive).

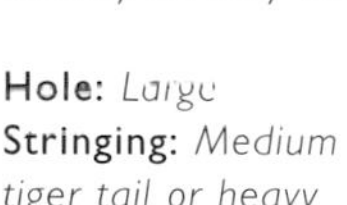

Hole: *Large*
Stringing: *Medium tiger tail or heavy thread*
Weight: *0.2g*
Other sizes: *None*
Color range: *Small*

Length: *3.5mm*
Width: *4mm*
Depth: *4mm*

Actual size

2

72

376 CRYSTAL WHEEL BASE METAL

The edges of the crystals around this wheel shape are held in the channels in the metal. The wheels have concave ends into which round beads can be tucked, making a decorative, solid-looking section that is actually flexible. This adds very little to the length of the piece.

Hole: *Large*
Stringing: *Medium tiger tail or heavy thread*
Weight: *0.2g*
Other sizes: *8mm*
Color range: *Medium*

Length: *3mm*
Width: *6mm*
Depth: *6mm*

Actual size

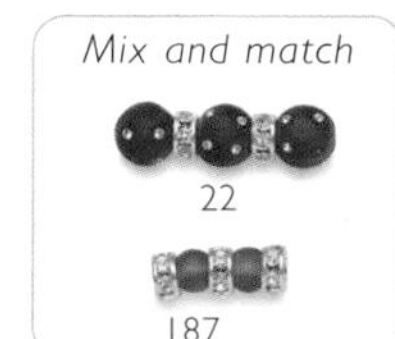

2

84

377 FLORAL TUBE BASE METAL

Slightly flattened so that it lies with one of the larger flowers upward, this heavily decorated shape is cast with lovely floral details; these will probably be lost visually when the beads are used in a strand, unless this bead is used as a focal piece between very plain beads.

Hole: *Large*
Stringing: *Medium tiger tail or heavy thread*
Weight: *1.6g*
Other sizes: *None*
Color range: *Small*

Length: *14mm*
Width: *8mm*
Depth: *6.5mm*

Actual size

42

378 BOW BASE METAL

From the end these show a five-pointed star but looked at from the side they are shaped rather like a bow, narrow in the middle with spreading ends. They would be excellent spacers for beads whose ends are only slightly larger than theirs or as the main beads in a fine strand with very small round beads between them.

Hole: *Large*
Stringing: *Medium tiger tail or heavy thread*
Weight: *0.3g*
Other sizes: *None*
Color range: *Small*

Length: *6mm*
Width: *3mm*
Depth: *3mm*

Actual size

50

379 DOTTY TUBE BASE METAL

The first row of raised dots is just higher than the ring at the end of these tubes and the middle row is a little higher still, so the overall shape of this bead is an oval. These could look interesting spaced with tiny round beads but are more often used as spacers themselves, adding texture without being eye-catching.

Hole: *Medium*
Stringing: *Medium tiger tail or heavy thread*
Weight: *0.4g*
Other sizes: *None*
Color range: *Small*

Length: *6mm*
Width: *5mm*
Depth: *5mm*

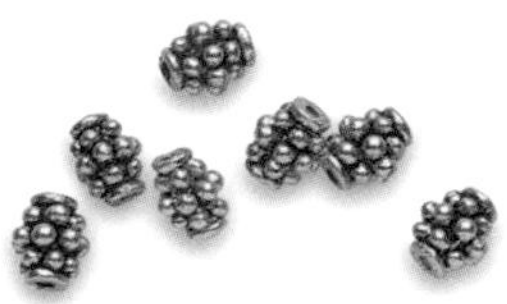

Actual size

380 COLORED PEWTER

Unless they are enameled, few metal beads are colored; if they are, the base is usually pewter as it is here. Although they do still look metallic, colored beads in other materials are easier to find and use, so the main reason to choose these may be that a design needs weight.

Hole: *Large*
Stringing: *Medium tiger tail or heavy thread*
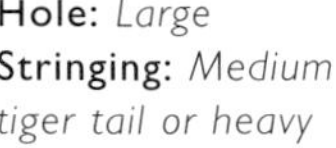
Weight: *1.4g*
Other sizes: *None*
Color range: *Medium*

Length: *8mm*
Width: *6mm*
Depth: *6mm*

Actual size

Mix and match

381 CURVE TUBE BASE METAL

Curved tubes are most commonly used near the lowest point of the hang of a necklace, and this tube also has a loop. This allows the designer to suspend a pendant, possibly on a head pin (629), and provides a good way to show a focal bead that is designed to hang rather than to be threaded along a strand.

Actual size

Hole: *Large*
Stringing: *Medium tiger tail or heavy thread*
Weight: *3.6g*
Other sizes: *None*
Color range: *Small*

Length: *30mm*
Width: *6mm*
Depth: *6mm*

Mix and match

382 CLOISONNÉ TUBE BASE METAL

Instead of making the outlines of the cloisonné sections with wire, as for 342, 343, and 367, the maker of this bead has stamped a pattern on a flat piece of metal and then wrapped the embossed sheet around into a tube. The enamel has then been filled in and fired in the usual way, but the result is not as crisp.

Hole: *Medium*
Stringing: *Medium tiger tail or heavy thread*
Weight: *0.8g*
Other sizes: *None*
Color range: *Small*

Length: *20mm*
Width: *6mm*
Depth: *6mm*

Actual size

Mix and match

50

383 LIQUID METAL BASE METAL

When these tiny fine tubes are strung together on fine thread, the resulting strands move rather like a liquid, so these are sometimes called liquid metal or, in this case, faux (meaning false) liquid silver. A large number of strands used together look great and move wonderfully. Check the holes of other beads used to ensure their holes are not large enough to allow these to slip inside them.

Hole: *Small*
Stringing: *Fine thread*
Weight: *0.01g*
Other sizes: *None*
Color range: *Small*

Length: *5mm*
Width: *1.5mm*
Depth: *1.5mm*

Actual size

50

384 CUT LIQUID METAL BASE METAL

These tubes are very similar to 383 (and are also available in precious metal, see 307) but have flat edges and have been twisted so that the angles catch the light. They can be used exactly as 383, providing even more reflectivity. Try using either kind to dangle beads further from a main strand without showing thread or detracting from the bigger beads.

Hole: *Small*
Stringing: *Fine thread*
Weight: *0.01g*
Other sizes: *None*
Color range: *Small*

Length: *5mm*
Width: *1.5mm*
Depth: *1.5mm*

Actual size

385 CUT HEXAGON BASE METAL

This cutting pattern is often called "sunray" because the facets spread out from the middle. These hexagons do look good in a strand next to each other, but because the flat ends prevent movement a rounded spacer is required if you need a soft drape or any movement without showing thread.

Hole: *Large*
Stringing: *Medium tiger tail or heavy thread*
Weight: *1.0g*
Other sizes: *None*
Color range: *Small*

Length: *6.5mm*
Width: *9mm*
Depth: *3mm*

Actual size

38

386 FLAT DIAMOND PEWTER

A Celtic knotwork pattern has been created on the surfaces of this diamond-shaped bead, with a very black coating added in the depths; this coating technique is rather like antiquing but has a crisper effect that does not dull the Britannia metal, a high-tin-content pewter. This shape would work well in right-angle weave, as well as on a strand.

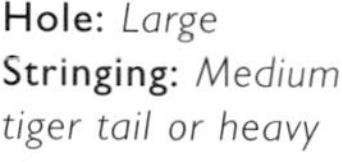

Hole: *Large*
Stringing: *Medium tiger tail or heavy thread*
Weight: *0.8g*
Other sizes: *None*
Color range: *Small*

Length: *11mm*
Width: *12mm*
Depth: *4mm*

Actual size

Mix and match

97

433

387 TWO-STRAND SPACER BASE METAL

As well as having a place in the center to stick a pointed-back stone or crystal, these have two holes so they can be used to connect two narrow strands of beads. They would also make great bracelets with single beads between them top and bottom. Although hollow on the back, they are unlikely to turn over when worn.

Hole: *Large*
Stringing: *Medium tiger tail or heavy thread*
Weight: *1.1g*
Other sizes: *None*
Color range: *Small*

Length: *8mm*
Width: *9mm*
Depth: *4mm*

Actual size

Mix and match

2

199

388 CLOISONNÉ SQUARE CUSHION BASE METAL

These padded-looking squares are pierced diagonally so they move better and look more interesting than would a similar shape with the hole across the flat sides. These seem to have been made as two squares, then domed slightly, and joined at the sides with plain wire before enameling, even though the outlines are twisted wire.

Hole: *Large*
Stringing: *Medium tiger tail or heavy thread*
Weight: *1.3g*
Other sizes: *None*
Color range: *Small*

Length: *11.5mm*
Width: *9mm*
Depth: *6mm*

Actual size

Mix and match

367

345

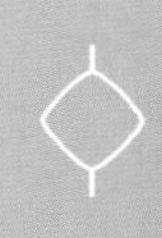

389 FLAT SQUARE BASE METAL

3
4
19

Similar to 386 but slimmer despite being larger overall. This shape would make a very solid-looking panel if used in right-angle weave, but it would actually move well because, although the beads would fit into each other when lying flat, they would be able to turn on their threads without restriction.

Hole: *Large*
Stringing: *Medium tiger tail or heavy thread*
Weight: *2.0g*
Other sizes: *7mm*
Color range: *Small*

Length: *13.5mm*
Width: *14mm*
Depth: *3.5mm*

Actual size

Mix and match
44
577

390 HANGING SQUARE BASE METAL

4
3
17

With the hole across one corner, these squares hang down from the string and will overlap on themselves unless spacers are used. They are rather too thick to overlap successfully. Make sure they are all facing the same way because the spiral is only on one side. They are not suitable for bracelets because they could turn over when worn.

Actual size

Hole: *Large*
Stringing: *Medium tiger tail or heavy thread*

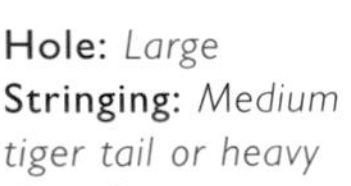

Weight: *3.6g*
Other sizes: *None*
Color range: *None*

Length: *15mm*
Width: *15mm*
Depth: *5mm*

Mix and match
199
395

391 STONE-SET SQUARE BASE METAL

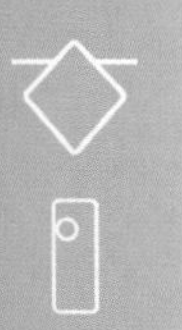

3
4
28

Although similar in shape to 390, these are much less likely to turn over or to overlap because the hole here is made more toward the back of the thick square. However, spacers will still be required if the thread between them is not to be seen. Unlike 387, these come with stones already set in place.

Hole: *Large*
Stringing: *Medium tiger tail or heavy thread*

Weight: *1.1g*
Other sizes: *None*
Color range: *Medium*

Length: *9mm*
Width: *9mm*
Depth: *5mm*

Actual size

Mix and match
164
3

392 INLAID ENAMEL CUBES BASE METAL

The shapes of moons and stars are either molded into these cubes or engraved, then filled with enamel and fired. The technique is similar to cloisonné, but the result looks more like pieces of semiprecious stone inlaid into the metal. Probably intended to slide tightly along a cord, these can also be used on thinner materials if spaced with small rounded beads.

Hole: *Very large*
Stringing: *Cord*
Weight: *2.0g*
Other sizes: *None*
Color range: *None*

Length: *6.5mm*
Width: *7.5mm*
Depth: *7.5mm*

Actual size

393 SPLIT SQUARE BASE METAL

Each of these beads is effectively a short tube with squares added on to the ends and rounded off. They would be useful in a design requiring a number of dangles on head pins (629) or similar because the main strand could be made, and then the loops of the hanging pieces fitted into the space between the ends of these beads.

Hole: *Large*
Stringing: *Medium tiger tail or heavy thread*
Weight: *0.2g*
Other sizes: *None*
Color range: *None*

Length: *3mm*
Width: *4mm*
Depth: *4mm*

Actual size

394 ROUNDED CUBE BASE METAL

Either a rounded cube drilled diagonally or a round bead flattened a little on six sides, these are actually molded because the seam line can clearly be seen. When strung together these look very much like random chunks of metal, which is attractive, but a whole strand would be very heavy.

Hole: *Medium*
Stringing: *Medium tiger tail or heavy thread*
Weight: *2.1g*
Other sizes: *None*
Color range: *None*

Length: *7.5mm*
Width: *7.5mm*
Depth: *7.5mm*

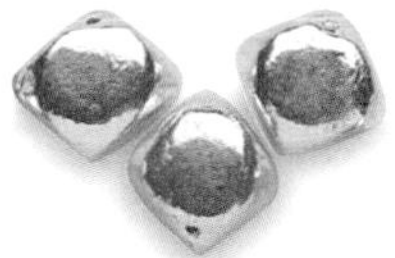

Actual size

28

395 NUGGET PEWTER

Another colored pewter bead cast as a flat, slightly irregular diamond shape with the seam along the edge. In use these look more random than this description suggests. They are good to add to a very casual piece, especially if more weight is required to help with the drape of a necklace or lariat.

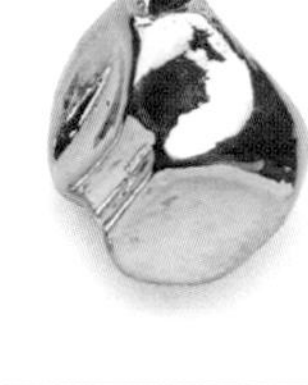

Hole: *Medium*
Stringing: *Medium tiger tail or heavy thread*
Weight: *1.7g*
Other sizes: *None*
Color range: *Medium*

Length: *9mm*
Width: *8mm*
Depth: *5.5mm*

Actual size

25

396 TUBE WITH WING BASE METAL

This tube shape has a triangular section, somewhat like a wing, extending out from the side. The design makes the whole piece look woven. The shaping is on both sides, so this could be used anywhere. Although the bead may turn over in use it will not matter, unless the direction it is pointing is critical to the piece.

Hole: *Large*
Stringing: *Medium tiger tail or heavy thread*
Weight: *0.9g*
Other sizes: *None*
Color range: *Small*

Length: *10mm*
Width: *8mm*
Depth: *4mm*

Actual size

84

397 TRIANGLE TUBE BASE METAL

Three tiny triangles are fixed together to make each of these tubes. When they are worn, they sit on one flat side so the opposite point always faces outward. They are probably most useful as a spacer in a very geometric design, or six would fit together into a ring that could be used to bring six strands together at the end of a necklace.

Hole: *Large*
Stringing: *Medium tiger tail or heavy thread*
Weight: *0.1g*
Other sizes: *None*
Color range: *None*

Length: *3mm*
Width: *3.5mm*
Depth: *3.5mm*

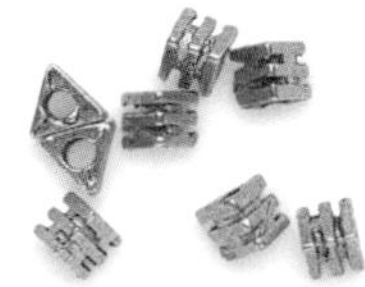
Actual size

398 TWO-STONE DANGLE BASE METAL

This is simply a geometric shape drilled across the top, narrow but with the lower part hanging below the line of the strand. It may turn over when worn and the back is plain so is not suitable for use in bracelets, and the sides are flat so avoid using them next to each other if the piece needs to be able to bend.

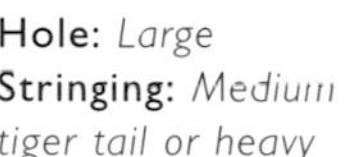

Hole: *Large*
Stringing: *Medium tiger tail or heavy thread*
Weight: *0.8g*
Other sizes: *None*
Color range: *Medium*

Length: *4.5mm*
Width: *10mm*
Depth: *4.5mm*

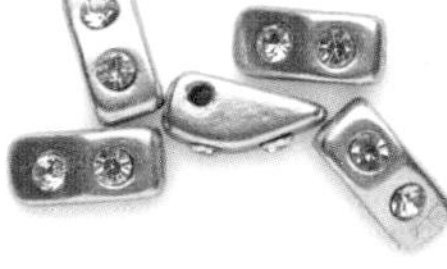

Actual size

Mix and match

219

359

399 FACE BASE METAL

Cast with the same face on both sides, these could possibly be used as the head of a beaded doll but are probably too serious looking. They could be used instead at the sides of a necklace or along a bracelet, or hung from a strand using a head pin (629); if the pin head is smaller than the hole, a small bead can be used to secure it.

Hole: *Large*
Stringing: *Medium tiger tail or heavy thread*
Weight: *4.4g*
Other sizes: *None*
Color range: *Small*

Length: *12mm*
Width: *10mm*
Depth: *8mm*

Actual size

Mix and match

112

374

400 CLOISONNÉ BUTTERFLY BASE METAL

One last cloisonné type, this is really just a pressed pattern on a cut-out metal shape, domed and soldered at the sides to make the puffy hollow butterfly, then painted with enamel to roughly follow, or in some cases overlap, the raised lines. This example is much lower in quality than 342, 343, or 367.

Actual size

Hole: *Large*
Stringing: *Medium tiger tail or heavy thread*
Weight: *1.4g*
Other sizes: *None*
Color range: *Small*

Length: *18mm*
Width: *19mm*
Depth: *4mm*

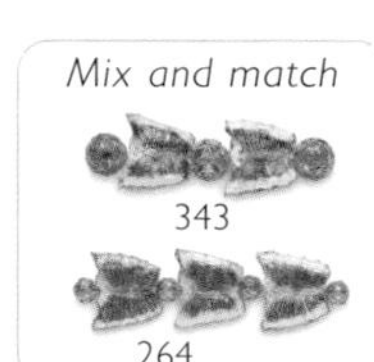

Mix and match

343

264

CHAPTER 6

Clay

Ceramic beads are made of standard ceramic clay, usually fired in a kiln, and often decorated with a fancy glaze. Alternatively, a pattern may be added underneath a clear glaze. Ceramic glaze is basically glass once it has been fired. Ceramic beads are sometimes hollow—see the introduction to the chapter on precious metals (page 106) for ideas on stringing such beads. Clay beads are heavier than plastic and "clink," though not with as sharp a sound as glass. If the material is not obvious, look into the hole to see the unglazed ceramic.

Polymer clay is an oven-bake clay, which comes in many colors, and can be used in the home to make your own beads without the need for a kiln. Technically a plastic, it is used as a clay, and results look more like unglazed ceramic (or even glazed, when varnished or polished), so these beads fit more sensibly here than in the chapter on plastic beads. The polymer clay beads shown here are professionally made, some in large quantities and others individually, by designers. These beads are usually solid (not hollow) and are lighter than might be expected for their size. They make a dull sound, not a "clink," when tapped together.

Simple ceramic beads combined with dull metal give this necklace an almost ancient feel, and yet it is still wearable with today's fashions.

401 UNGLAZED ROUND PORCELAIN

Unglazed porcelain has a matte surface and is absorbent, so these beads could be stained easily; they would not wipe clean like most glazed ceramic. This can be a positive thing because they would take dye well if you needed a special color and can also absorb scents if kept boxed with perfumed items.

2

3

23

Hole: *Large*
Stringing: *Medium tiger tail or heavy thread*
Weight: *2.0g*
Other sizes: *None*
Color range: *Mixed*

Length: *11mm*
Width: *11mm*
Depth: *11mm*

Actual size

Mix and match

478

187

402 TRANSFER DECORATION CERAMIC

These beads have been glazed and fired, then an on-glaze transfer with gilt edges has been applied to each, and finally the beads have been fired again. This is a less time-consuming method than hand painting every bead, so more delicate decorations can be applied without adding too much to the cost.

2

3

23

Hole: *Large*
Stringing: *Medium tiger tail or heavy thread*
Weight: *2.0g*
Other sizes: *None*
Color range: *Mixed*

Length: *11mm*
Width: *12mm*
Depth: *12mm*

Actual size

Mix and match

237

8

403 LUCK SYMBOL CERAMIC

The oriental gold pattern on the thin, slightly mottled glaze of these beads could be a transfer, but because each one is very slightly different they are probably hand painted. Because there are four good luck symbols on each bead they would be very time-consuming to produce by hand.

2

3

25

Hole: *Large*
Stringing: *Medium tiger tail or heavy thread*
Weight: *1.2g*
Other sizes: *None*
Color range: *None*

Length: *10mm*
Width: *10mm*
Depth: *10mm*

Actual size

Mix and match

533

370

404 HAND PAINTED CERAMIC

These beads were hand painted; the floral design first, then the background, both of which have been fired at a high temperature to set the glaze. The gold lines were then applied on top and a lower temperature firing performed because too high a heat would burn off the gilding.

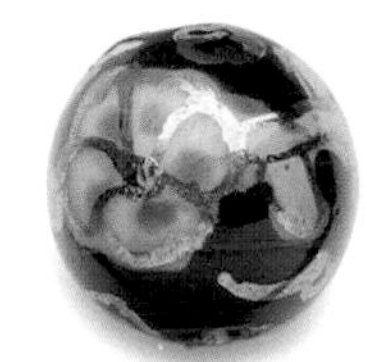

Hole: *Large*
Stringing: *Medium tiger tail or heavy thread*
Weight: *1.7g*
Other sizes: *None*
Color range: *None*

Length: *11mm*
Width: *12mm*
Depth: *12mm*

Actual size

405 FLOWER GARDEN POLYMER CLAY

These polymer clay beads are made by the designer Leigh Ross and are assembled from many handmade canes (see 427) with different flower patterns in each. Tiny slices are applied to a base bead, then shaped, baked in an oven (not a kiln), and polished in many stages to achieve the high gloss.

Hole: *Medium*
Stringing: *Medium tiger tail or heavy thread*
Weight: *1.2g*
Other sizes: *None*
Color range: *None*

Length: *11mm*
Width: *12mm*
Depth: *12mm*

Actual size

406 MOLDED GLAZED CERAMIC

Molded from white clay, these beads have been dipped into colored glaze that has been allowed to settle into the impressed lines, making a thicker coating. Because the glaze is translucent it appears darker there, while the edges of the lines (where there is very little glaze) show as almost white.

Hole: *Large*
Stringing: *Medium tiger tail or heavy thread*
Weight: *2.4g*
Other sizes: *None*
Color range: *Medium*

Length: *11mm*
Width: *13mm*
Depth: *13mm*

Actual size

407 MOLDED PAINTED CERAMIC

Dark blue color has been painted into the impressed lines and spaces in these molded beads to make it look as though they are covered with woven strips. The beads were then finished with a clear glaze. This is a traditional technique and color combination for Chinese beads.

Actual size

Hole: *Large*
Stringing: *Medium tiger tail or heavy thread*
Weight: *3.7g*
Other sizes: *None*
Color range: *None*

Length: *15mm*
Width: *15mm*
Depth: *15mm*

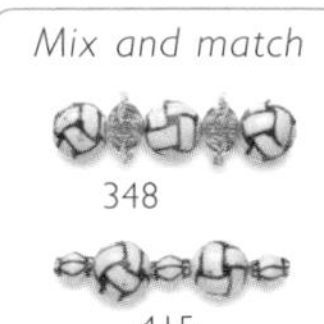

Mix and match

348

415

408 PLANET POLYMER CLAY

Polymer clay can be purchased with fine fibers of prebaked clay of a slightly different shade already mixed in, to give a mottled, stonelike look. Two colors of this clay have been randomly kneaded together, enough to make a solid shape but without blending them, resulting in these beads that look a little like planets seen from space.

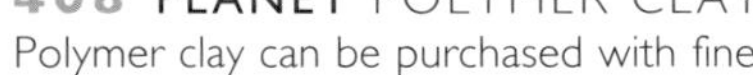

Actual size

Hole: *Medium*
Stringing: *Medium tiger tail or heavy thread*
Weight: *3.2g*
Other sizes: *None*
Color range: *None*

Length: *16mm*
Width: *17mm*
Depth: *17mm*

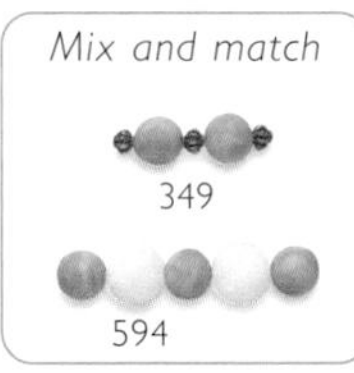

Mix and match

349

594

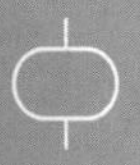

409 PAINTED BEARS CERAMIC

Rounded with flattened ends, these beads are unglazed and have a splendid painted design of black outlined bears decorated with blue and red patterns. These would work well in a piece inspired by Native American traditions and would tone in with natural items such as bone, wood, or horn beads.

Actual size

Hole: *Medium*
Stringing: *Medium tiger tail or heavy thread*
Weight: *4.9g*
Other sizes: *None*
Color range: *None*

Length: *15mm*
Width: *20mm*
Depth: *20mm*

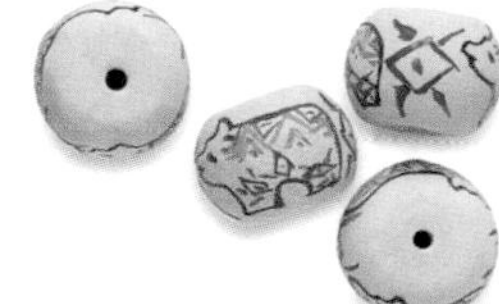

Mix and match

223

541

410 OFF ROUND CERAMIC

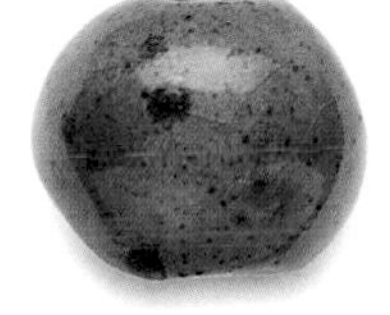

These beads were probably made in the hand rather than molded because they are not perfectly shaped and are flattened in the direction of the hole. The glaze is very uneven and cracked in places. The dots were created as part of the glaze mixture, not separately applied.

Hole: *Large*
Stringing: *Medium tiger tail or heavy thread*
Weight: *1.4g*
Other sizes: *None*
Color range: *Medium*

Length: *10mm*
Width: *13mm*
Depth: *13mm*

Actual size

Mix and match

523

368

411 BASIC TRANSFER CERAMIC

These beads are very irregular, and there are pinprick faults in the glaze. The transfer seems to be a little large for the size of bead, and the bead is of a lower quality than 402, with a wide space on the other side of the bead.

Hole: *Large*
Stringing: *Medium tiger tail or heavy thread*
Weight: *1.5g*
Other sizes: *None*
Color range: *Medium*

Length: *10mm*
Width: *13mm*
Depth: *13mm*

Actual size

412 GEOMETRIC POLYMER CLAY

This bead is slightly roughly shaped. It is made from slices of a cane, with a simple geometric pattern consisting of black lines and colors, rather like a stained-glass window. The beads have not been polished, so they have the matte surface usual on baked polymer clay.

Hole: *Medium*
Stringing: *Medium tiger tail or heavy thread*
Weight: *0.8g*
Other sizes: *None*
Color range: *None*

Length: *10mm*
Width: *11mm*
Depth: *11mm*

Actual size

21

413 BLOBS CRACKED CLAY

Deliberately made with clay too dry to roll into a perfect ball, these irregular shapes have been colored yellow and then dipped into green, taking advantage of the natural cracks in the clay that hold a larger quantity of dye to give the darker pattern. They are unglazed so the rough surface remains.

Hole: *Large*
Stringing: *Medium tiger tail or heavy thread*
Weight: *1.6g*
Other sizes: *None*
Color range: *None*

Length: *12mm*
Width: *12mm*
Depth: *12mm*

Actual size

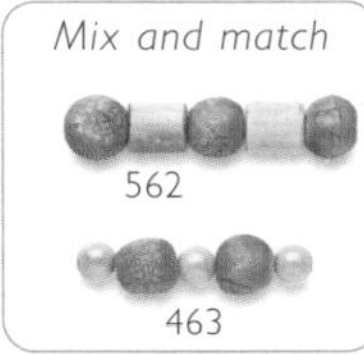

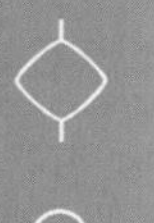

21

414 WIDE BICONE CERAMIC

This shape is a bicone, so called because it is two cone shapes base to base. Bicones are rarely this wide in comparison to their length; if it were a little flatter in that direction, it could be called a lentil. The cream underglaze color has been decorated with precise fine lines and finished with a clear glaze.

Actual size

Hole: *Large*
Stringing: *Medium tiger tail or heavy thread*
Weight: *2.7g*
Other sizes: *None*
Color range: *None*

Length: *12mm*
Width: *16mm*
Depth: *16mm*

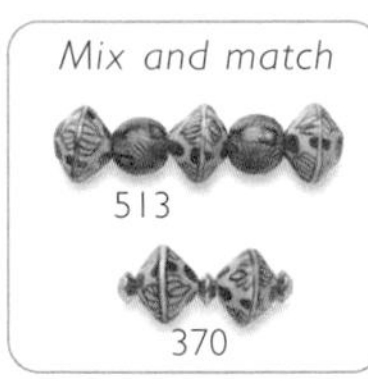

23

415 MOLDED DIAMOND CERAMIC

Traditional blue-and-white Chinese ceramic, this pretty molded shape is useful as a spacer or at the back and sides of a necklace, allowing the eye to be drawn to a few larger or more detailed (and more expensive) beads elsewhere on the piece.

Hole: *Large*
Stringing: *Medium tiger tail or heavy thread*
Weight: *0.6g*
Other sizes: *None*
Color range: *None*

Length: *11mm*
Width: *8mm*
Depth: *8mm*

Actual size

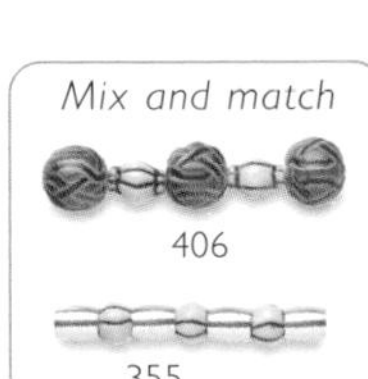

416 FLAT OVAL CERAMIC

A flattened oval shape, domed more on one side than the other, this is decorated with a glaze that includes random spots of a second color. These dots are not added separately. Simple beads like this are suitable for multistrand pieces where a detailed pattern or shape would be too confusing to the eye.

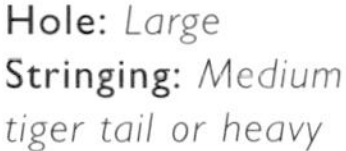

Hole: *Large*
Stringing: *Medium tiger tail or heavy thread*
Weight: *1.9g*
Other sizes: *None*
Color range: *Medium*

Length: *15mm*
Width: *12mm*
Depth: *9mm*

Actual size

Mix and match

550

477

2

3

17

417 GOOD LUCK CERAMIC

The same good luck symbol as on 403 has been molded into the faces of this flat oval bead. Simple rings and stars decorate the sides in a traditional pattern. Flattened ovals can be more comfortable to wear than similar-sized round beads because they do not stand as high, but they have a similar area for the design.

Actual size

Hole: *Large*
Stringing: *Medium tiger tail or heavy thread*
Weight: *3.2g*
Other sizes: *None*
Color range: *None*

Length: *18mm*
Width: *15mm*
Depth: *10mm*

Mix and match

491

460

2

3

14

418 PAINTED OVAL CERAMIC

The shaded blocks of color have been painted directly on to the black background of this oval bead, with the fine rings, outlines, and details added on top. Made in Peru, it is typical of that area's designs and color combination and has not been glazed.

Hole: *Large*
Stringing: *Medium tiger tail or heavy thread*
Weight: *2.9g*
Other sizes: *None*
Color range: *None*

Length: *20mm*
Width: *12mm*
Depth: *12mm*

Actual size

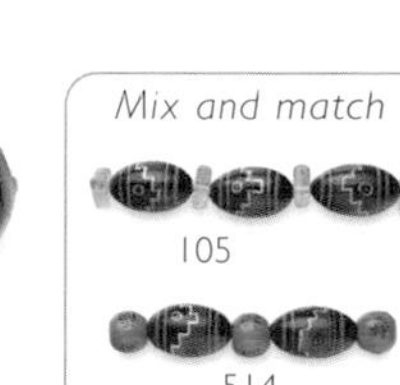

Mix and match

105

514

2

3

13

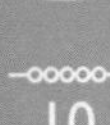

3 3 10

419 GLAZED OVAL CERAMIC

White spaces between the bright shades and a slightly raised feel to the flowers indicate that this decoration was hand painted directly on to the bead in colored glaze. The gold lines have been added, also by hand, after the first glaze firing, and the bead would then have been refired to a lower temperature.

Actual size

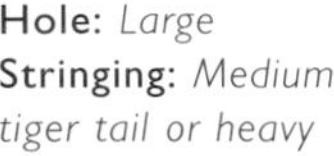

Hole: *Large*
Stringing: *Medium tiger tail or heavy thread*
Weight: *5.9g*
Other sizes: *None*
Color range: *None*

Length: *25mm*
Width: *15mm*
Depth: *15mm*

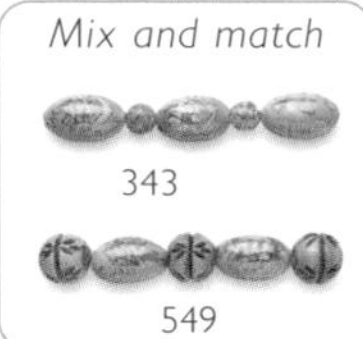

Mix and match

343

549

3 3 14

420 RINGED OVAL CERAMIC

Dipped first into yellow glaze (and possibly fired), these beads have then been overpainted with darker colors, probably by holding a fine brush still and turning the bead against it to get accurate rings. Part of the central decoration has been brushed on, and the finest strokes may be done by pulling the color with a sharp spike.

Actual size

Hole: *Large*
Stringing: *Medium tiger tail or heavy thread*
Weight: *3.7g*
Other sizes: *None*
Color range: *None*

Length: *18mm*
Width: *13mm*
Depth: *13mm*

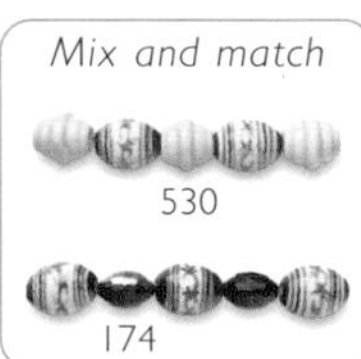

Mix and match

530

174

2 2 17

421 LONG OVAL CERAMIC

This long oval shape, almost a tube, is useful for extending the length of a piece without spending too much on special beads or drawing the eye away from the main features. Because the ends are rounded they move well against each other, as a plain tube does not. The mottled pattern is in the glaze.

Hole: *Large*
Stringing: *Medium tiger tail or heavy thread*
Weight: *1.1g*
Other sizes: *None*
Color range: *Small*

Length: *15.5mm*
Width: *8mm*
Depth: *8mm*

Actual size

Mix and match

346

16

422 TRANSFER BEAN CERAMIC

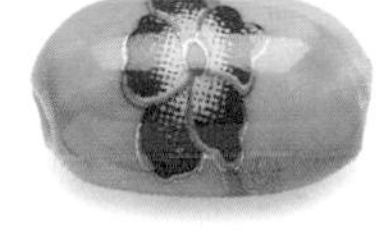

Note that the glaze on this bean-shaped bead is slightly uneven under the transfer. This is probably not intentional, but it does add an interesting textured look to the simple shape. The transfers match those on 402 but are less well applied so are slightly cracked and not as bright.

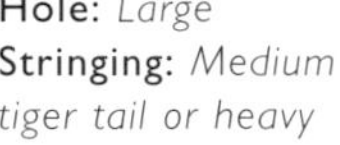

Hole: *Large*
Stringing: *Medium tiger tail or heavy thread*
Weight: *1.2g*
Other sizes: *None*
Color range: *Mixed*

Length: *13.5mm*
Width: *8mm*
Depth: *8mm*

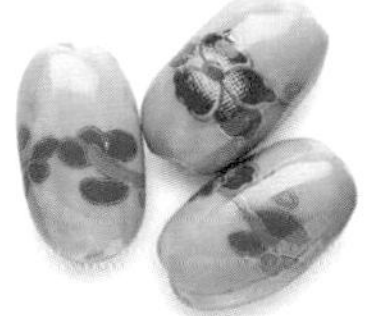

Actual size

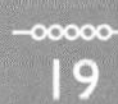

423 FLAT BAND CERAMIC

The middle decorated band on these unglazed beads is flat, but the ends are rounded. The black lines have been painted directly on to the white clay of the bead, with the green applied over the top. They are suitable for pieces in the Native American style and as spacers for anything with a geometric look.

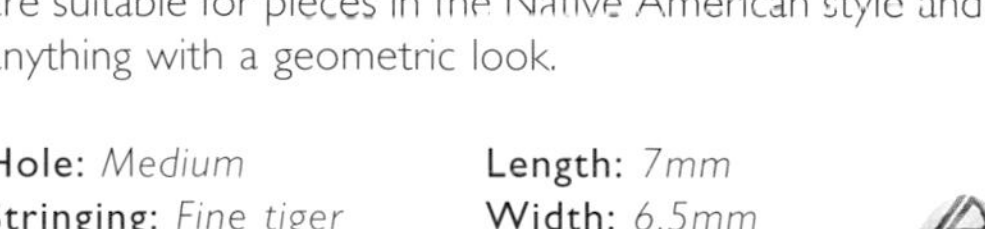

Hole: *Medium*
Stringing: *Fine tiger tail or medium thread*
Weight: *0.4g*
Other sizes: *None*
Color range: *None*

Length: *7mm*
Width: *6.5mm*
Depth: *6.5 mm*

Actual size

424 IMPRESSED CLAY

The rings and dot markings on these little beads have been impressed by hand using very basic tools. The clay has then been fired and finally painted gold. These would be attractive just strung on their own but could also be used as spacers in many kinds of projects.

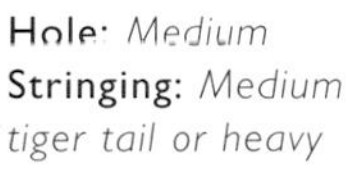

Hole: *Medium*
Stringing: *Medium tiger tail or heavy thread*
Weight: *0.2g*
Other sizes: *None*
Color range: *None*

Length: *5.5mm*
Width: *5.5mm*
Depth: *5.5mm*

Actual size

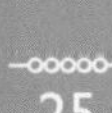

2
2
25

425 BRIGHT TUBES CERAMIC

Accurately shaped round tubes dipped into a very bright, almost fluorescent dye, these are unglazed. Such a strong color could probably only be used in a psychedelic or futuristic design but might be useful to decorate light pulls and similar items in the home to help find them in low light levels.

Hole: *Large*
Stringing: *Medium tiger tail or heavy thread*
Weight: *0.3g*
Other sizes: *None*
Color range: *Medium*

Length: *10mm*
Width: *5mm*
Depth: *5mm*

Actual size

Mix and match

423
463

2
3
20

426 CLASSIC TUBES CERAMIC

These are classically shaped round tubes dipped in one color of glaze and fired. It would be hard to find a simpler bead, and this kind of thing has been made more or less since glazed ceramic was first invented. The ends are flat, so to allow a piece to move well rounded spacers should be used between these beads.

Hole: *Large*
Stringing: *Medium tiger tail or heavy thread*
Weight: *1.3g*
Other sizes: *None*
Color range: *Mixed*

Length: *13mm*
Width: *8mm*
Depth: *8mm*

Actual size

Mix and match

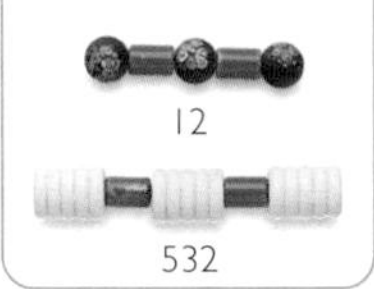
12
532

2
3
25

427 TUBE POLYMER CLAY

Canes are made of polymer clay shapes, stacked and pressed together to make a pattern that goes all the way along the cane. They can be made large to make it simpler to do small details and then stretched and rolled to reduce the diameter. Two slices of such a cane have been used to decorate this tube.

Hole: *Medium*
Stringing: *Medium tiger tail or heavy thread*
Weight: *0.5g*
Other sizes: *None*
Color range: *None*

Length: *17mm*
Width: *10mm*
Depth: *10mm*

Actual size

Mix and match

476
467

428 STAMPED TUBE CERAMIC

The gold symbol has been stamped on top of the black glaze on these tubes. Because only one symbol has been applied the plain black will show a lot of the time in wear, so a few of these scattered throughout a piece could look unimpressive, but a whole strand with small spacers would be striking.

Hole: *Large*
Stringing: *Medium tiger tail or heavy thread*
Weight: *1.0g*
Other sizes: *None*
Color range: *Medium*

Length: *16mm*
Width: *7mm*
Depth: *7mm*

Actual size

Mix and match

515

350

16

429 NETTED TUBE CERAMIC

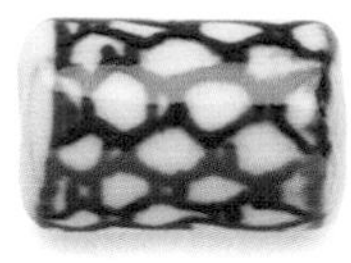
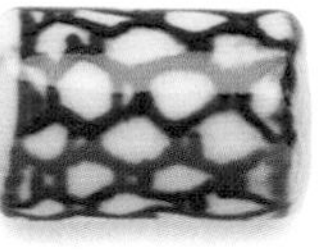

These look similar to the other blue-and-white ceramic beads (407, 417, and 415), but here the netting decoration is painted on to a flat surface, rather than into pressed indentations as on those beads. It is of course difficult to work quite as accurately in this manner, so the pattern seems a little squashed in places.

Hole: *Large*
Stringing: *Medium tiger tail or heavy thread*
Weight: *1.9g*
Other sizes: *None*
Color range: *None*

Length: *14mm*
Width: *10mm*
Depth: *10mm*

Actual size

Mix and match

591

106

18

430 ZEBRA POLYMER CLAY

The stripes on this polymer clay tube have been created as a large black-and-white block, probably pulled and squashed to make them look as random as possible. Fine slices from this block have been applied to a black tube of polymer clay and smeared at the join lines to make the stripes look continuous around the bead.

Hole: *Large*
Stringing: *Medium tiger tail or heavy thread*
Weight: *0.9g*
Other sizes: *6mm*
Color range: *None*

Length: *19mm*
Width: *7mm*
Depth: *7mm*

Actual size

Mix and match

535

545

14

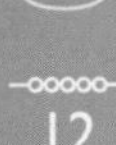

431 PERUVIAN TUBE CERAMIC

A whole scene has been painted on to this tube, showing what appear to be a llama and a cactus against desert colors, hills, and a shaded sky with tiny birds. These must take considerable time to paint, but it must be hand done because there is no indication that they are printed, and they are all very slightly different.

Hole: *Medium*
Stringing: *Medium tiger tail or heavy thread*
Weight: *0.8g*
Other sizes: *None*
Color range: *None*

Length: *22mm*
Width: *5mm*
Depth: *5mm*

12

Actual size

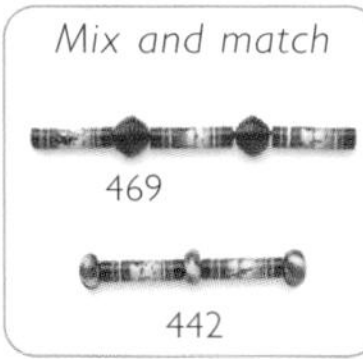
Mix and match
469
442

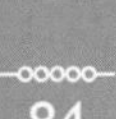

432 RINGS CERAMIC

Little unglazed ceramic rings are useful as spacers but if used on their own in a strand, they will either gap where the piece curves or if strung too tightly, will be stiff and not flex at all. An interesting textured tube that moves well can be made by alternating these with small round beads.

Hole: *Large*
Stringing: *Medium tiger tail or heavy thread*
Weight: *0.1g*
Other sizes: *None*
Color range: *Medium*

Length: *3mm*
Width: *6mm*
Depth: *6mm*

84

Actual size

Mix and match
14
353

433 KNOTWORK TUBES CERAMIC

These tubes have been molded with a texture based on Celtic knotwork and dipped into colored glaze: more liquid stays in the impressions than on the surface, making the tone deeper and emphasizing the pattern without adding a second color. This is aided by the simple shape of the tube.

Hole: *Large*
Stringing: *Medium tiger tail or heavy thread*
Weight: *2.0g*
Other sizes: *None*
Color range: *Medium*

Length: *21mm*
Width: *7mm*
Depth: *7mm*

12

Actual size

Mix and match
187
265

434 ANIMAL-SKIN TUBE CERAMIC

The shape of this bead is roughly a tube, but it is slightly squared off and was made in the hand rather than molded. The background color was painted directly on to the clay, the dark patches added on top of that with a translucent paint, and the raised outlines added last.

3

17

Hole: *Large*
Stringing: *Medium tiger tail or heavy thread*
Weight: *2.6g*
Other sizes: *None*
Color range: *None*

Length: *15mm*
Width: *12.5mm*
Depth: *12mm*

Actual size

435 TUBE TERRA-COTTA CLAY

Actual size

Made to simulate very ancient beads, these are unglazed terra-cotta clay beads with a line and dot pattern created using a simple pointed tool. After firing, they have been covered with a white paint, and the surface wiped completely clean so that the color remains and sets in the impressed areas only.

2

2

10

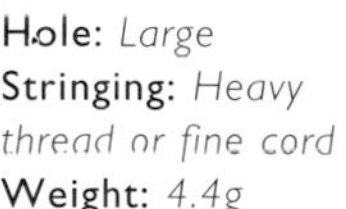

Hole: *Large*
Stringing: *Heavy thread or fine cord*
Weight: *4.4g*
Other sizes: *None*
Color range: *None*

Length: *25.5mm*
Width: *12.5mm*
Depth: *12mm*

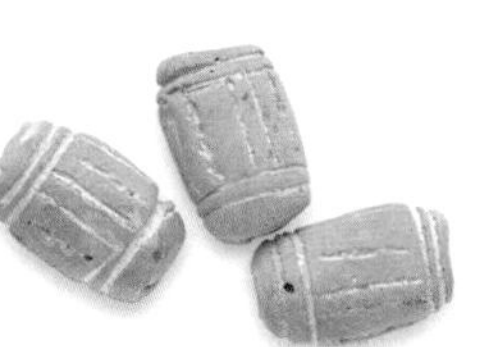

436 CURVED TUBE CERAMIC

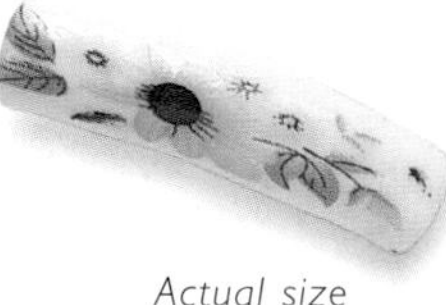

Actual size

Curved tubes are useful only in certain circumstances because they can interfere with the hang of a strand of beads if used in the wrong place. They usually work well in the middle of a necklace, near the lowest point as it is worn. Shallow curves make good bracelet components, although sharper curves will not sit neatly on the wrist.

8

Hole: *Large*
Stringing: *Medium tiger tail or heavy thread*
Weight: *3.8g*
Other sizes: *None*
Color range: *Mixed*

Length: *33mm*
Width: *9mm*
Depth: *9mm*

20

437 TWISTED TUBE CERAMIC

The clay itself has been colored for this unglazed tube, which would be very plain if it were not for the flattened faces. An eight-sided rod of clay has been molded, twisted, and finally cut into sections before drying and firing. These would work well with small, round, natural material spacers.

Hole: *Medium*
Stringing: *Medium tiger tail or heavy thread*
Weight: *1.0g*
Other sizes: *None*
Color range: *None*

Length: *12.5mm*
Width: *7mm*
Depth: *7mm*

Actual size

Mix and match

555

474

20

438 SPINDLE CERAMIC

This shape can be called a spindle, cotton reel, or diablo (after the juggling prop of similar shape). It is also reminiscent of the spinal bones of small animals that were used as early beads because they have a hole along the middle. These could be used to add length to a piece without attracting attention away from a focal bead.

Hole: *Large*
Stringing: *Medium tiger tail or heavy thread*
Weight: *1.0g*
Other sizes: *None*
Color range: *None*

Length: *13mm*
Width: *8mm*
Depth: *8mm*

Actual size

Mix and match

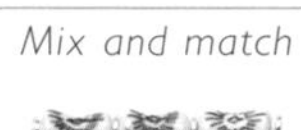

285

5

14

439 MULTIBEAD SHAPE CERAMIC

This bead looks as though it is one large round bead with two smaller ones pressed into the sides. The shape seems most common in beads made in South America (these are from Peru), and the strong, outlined colors and stepped design are also typical of the area, although this is much less fine than 431.

Hole: *Medium*
Stringing: *Medium tiger tail or heavy thread*
Weight: *1.2g*
Other sizes: *None*
Color range: *None*

Length: *18mm*
Width: *9mm*
Depth: *9mm*

Actual size

Mix and match

491

486

440 SCARAB CERAMIC

A simulated ancient scarab beetle bead, this is made to look as though it comes from early Egypt. These are made in the same area today, molded in clay and glazed to look like faience. Faience is a quartzite clay containing copper salts that form a blue surface when fired. It is thought to be the world's first artificial material.

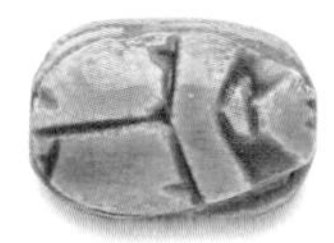

Actual size

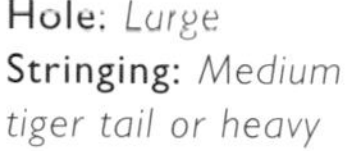

Hole: *Large*
Stringing: *Medium tiger tail or heavy thread*
Weight: *3.5g*
Other sizes: *Variable*
Color range: *None*

Length: *18mm*
Width: *12mm*
Depth: *9mm*

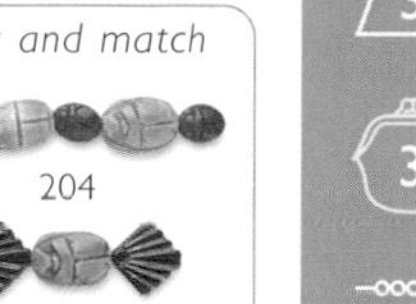

Mix and match

204

85

3

3

14

441 WHALE CANE SLICE POLYMER CLAY

The image of the whale goes all the way through this coin-shaped bead because it is a slice from a polymer clay cane. The detailed design was made much larger than this and carefully rolled and pulled down to the required size without distorting the pattern, then sliced, pierced, and baked.

Hole: *Medium*
Stringing: *Medium tiger tail or heavy thread*
Weight: *0.2g*
Other sizes: *None*
Color range: *None*

Length: *9mm*
Width: *9mm*
Depth: *3mm*

Actual size

Mix and match

385

415

2

3

28

442 BRIGHT RING CERAMIC

These slightly uneven rings have been painted with patches of four bright glazes, fired, overpainted with the gold lines, and finally refired. They are charming as spacers, adding more color to a dull piece or could be used as the main bead, separated with others small enough almost to fit into their holes.

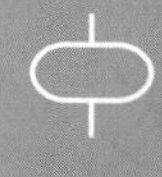

Hole: *Large*
Stringing: *Medium tiger tail or heavy thread*
Weight: *0.6g*
Other sizes: *None*
Color range: *None*

Length: *5mm*
Width: *10mm*
Depth: *9.5mm*

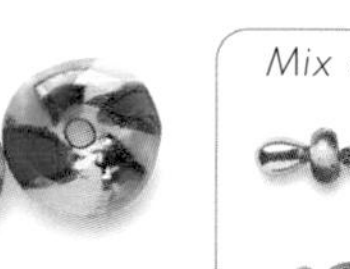

Actual size

Mix and match

357

33

2

2

50

14

443 PIERCED DONUT CERAMIC

Donut shapes are made in almost as many materials as round beads, but many are intended to be strung through the large hole in the middle or are pierced through one side of the ring only. Because this has a double piercing it could be used along a strand, with or without a small bead in the center.

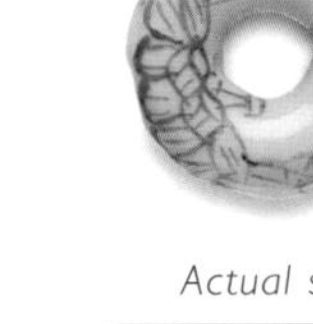

Actual size

Hole: *Medium*
Stringing: *Fine tiger tail or medium thread*
Weight: *1.8g*
Other sizes: *None*
Color range: *None*

Length: *18mm*
Width: *18mm*
Depth: *5mm*

Mix and match

264

570

15

444 PILLOW CERAMIC

A rounded rectangular bead or pillow shape, this is glazed and decorated with a transfer consisting mainly of gold lines, with only a little color. Despite the rounded corners and sides, the ends are still fairly flat, so rounded spacers may be needed if these are strung together and the piece needs a lot of movement.

Actual size

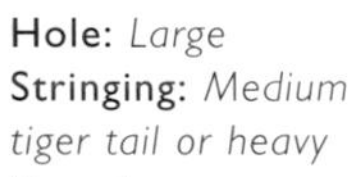

Hole: *Large*
Stringing: *Medium tiger tail or heavy thread*
Weight: *4.0g*
Other sizes: *None*
Color range: *Mixed*

Length: *17mm*
Width: *14mm*
Depth: *9mm*

Mix and match

222

311

25

445 LETTERS POLYMER CLAY

Made by the cane method (see 427), these letters are pierced across the top so that they hang down from the thread. Because the letter will be backward from the wrong side of the bead take care when stringing, and do not use on projects where the beads can flip over, such as bracelets.

Actual size

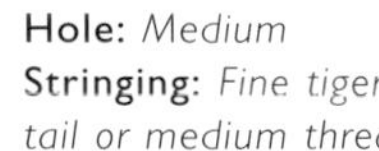

Hole: *Medium*
Stringing: *Fine tiger tail or medium thread*
Weight: *0.5g*
Other sizes: *None*
Color range: *Mixed*

Length: *10mm*
Width: *17mm*
Depth: *5mm*

Mix and match

441

485

446 PAINTED CUBE CERAMIC

This cube has been hand painted over a cream glaze, with Chinese text on one side. Like all cube beads, these will make a stiff strand if strung tightly next to each other and will show thread when worn if used more loosely: to avoid these problems, add rounded spacers.

Hole: *Large*
Stringing: *Medium tiger tail or heavy thread*
Weight: *2.0g*
Other sizes: *None*
Color range: *None*

Length: *11mm*
Width: *10mm*
Depth: *10mm*

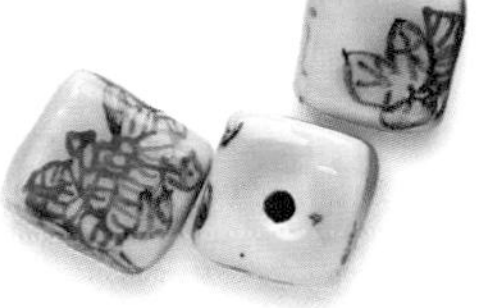

Actual size

23

447 MOTTLED CUBE CERAMIC

Fractionally too long to be a true cube, this has an interesting mottled glaze that has either been wiped off of all the edges or has shrunk in on firing to leave the angles pale. The hole in some of them is slightly off-center, so pointed beads could sit awkwardly next to these.

Hole: *Large*
Stringing: *Medium tiger tail or heavy thread*

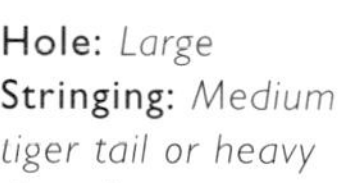

Weight: *1.1g*
Other sizes: *None*
Color range: *Medium*

Length: *10mm*
Width: *9mm*
Depth: *9mm*

Actual size

28

448 FAT DROPS CERAMIC

These lovely fat drops are quite wide for their length. The swirls of color for the snakes and leaves have been painted first, followed by the black "background," and the fine lines added on the top. If hung on a head pin (629), a small bead may have to be added first because the hole is larger than most pin heads.

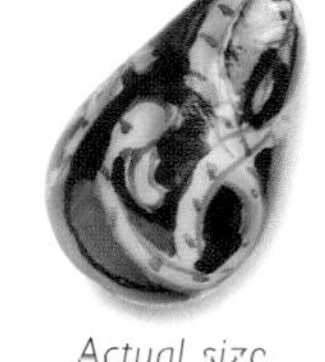

Actual size

Hole: *Large*
Stringing: *Medium tiger tail or heavy thread*
Weight: *4.4g*
Other sizes: *None*
Color range: *None*

Length: *23mm*
Width: *15mm*
Depth: *15mm*

Mix and match

412

478

11

449 SLIM DROP CERAMIC

A much slimmer drop than 448, these have been painted in layers rather than glazed, starting with the background color and the blue lines. The apparent fine black outlines on the white design (a stylized bird) are actually a thicker black background painting with the white on the top.

Actual size

Hole: *Medium*
Stringing: *Medium tiger tail or heavy thread*
Weight: *2.9g*
Other sizes: *None*
Color range: *None*

Length: *31mm*
Width: *10mm*
Depth: *10mm*

Mix and match

460

511

450 GLAZED DROP CERAMIC

The decoration on these slim drops is done in underglaze colors with the black lines painted last, before glazing. The work is much rougher than the other similar designs such as 418 and 439, with smudges, gaps in the color, and ring lines not meeting on some of the beads.

Actual size

Hole: *Large*
Stringing: *Medium tiger tail or heavy thread*
Weight: *2.9g*
Other sizes: *None*
Color range: *None*

Length: *33mm*
Width: *10mm*
Depth: *10mm*

Mix and match

545

490

451 VASE CERAMIC

Shaped like a vase with a long neck, these make splendid ends for tassels, drops, and earrings, as well as eye-catching additions to bead strands. A different look can be achieved by threading a number of them all in the same direction or in pairs with either the neck or base ends together.

Actual size

Hole: *Large*
Stringing: *Medium tiger tail or heavy thread*
Weight: *2.5g*
Other sizes: *None*
Color range: *None*

Length: *29mm*
Width: *11mm*
Depth: *11mm*

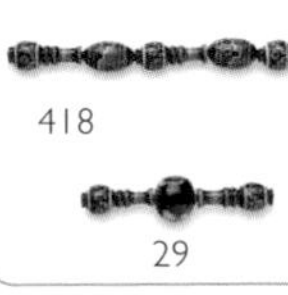

Mix and match

418

29

452 TINY ANGEL CERAMIC

These molded angels are also available pierced across the head so that they will hang down without the need for a head pin (629). The wings are plain ceramic, and the hair and skin are painted; only the robe is actually glazed, so parts of these could be scented (or stained, intentionally or otherwise) as for 401.

Hole: *Medium*
Stringing: *Fine tiger tail or medium thread*
Weight: *0.7g*
Other sizes: *None*
Color range: *Mixed*

Length: *15mm*
Width: *12mm*
Depth: *5mm*

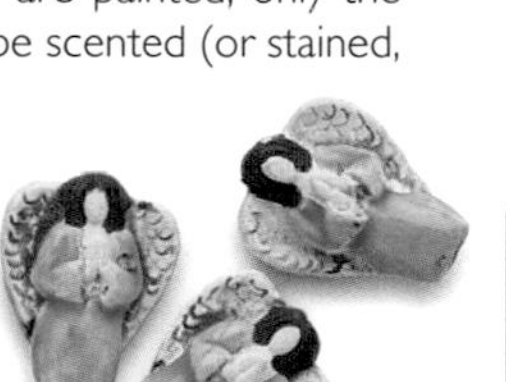

Actual size

Mix and match

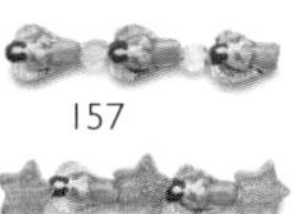

157

505

3

2

17

453 BEAR CERAMIC

Many molded ceramic animal beads are available, some painted more or less realistically, like this bear, and others stylized, for example, 454 and 455. The bears are pierced across their neck and so would be good for fun strands of beads, but they are wider at the bottom than at the hole, so spacers would be needed to allow them to hang neatly.

Actual size

Hole: *Large*
Stringing: *Heavy thread or fine cord*
Weight: *3.7g*
Other sizes: *None*
Color range: *None*

Length: *12mm*
Width: *19mm*
Depth: *13mm*

Mix and match

414

514

3

21

454 DOG CERAMIC

The molded shape of this dog is not at all detailed, but the blue decoration makes up for that. It even includes a cute bow at the dog's neck. Use a head pin (629) to hang this dog downward or use a few in a strand with other classic blue-and-white ceramic beads for an entertaining extra touch.

Hole: *Large*
Stringing: *Medium tiger tail or heavy thread*
Weight: *1.9g*
Other sizes: *None*
Color range: *None*

Length: *14mm*
Width: *13mm*
Depth: *10mm*

Actual size

Mix and match

331

415

18

13

455 RABBIT CERAMIC

Look very carefully at these beads, and you will see that they are rabbits with pink inside the ears and red eyes. The stylization, however, seems to have gone a little too far because they are not immediately recognizable as such, especially in a strand with other beads of similar style.

Actual size

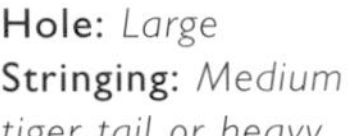

Hole: *Large*
Stringing: *Medium tiger tail or heavy thread*
Weight: *4.8g*
Other sizes: *None*
Color range: *None*

Length: *20mm*
Width: *20mm*
Depth: *13.5mm*

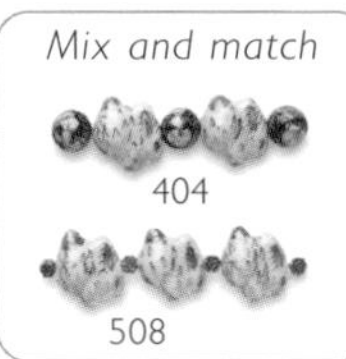

Mix and match

404

508

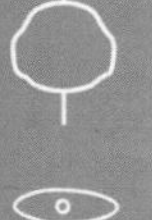

25

456 BUDDHA FACE CERAMIC

Antiqued unglazed ceramic with a brown color left only in the dips, these molded faces are one-sided and may turn over when worn. They could be used to good effect in an embroidery, fixed flat on the top of a background of beadwork, or as the head of a beaded man.

Hole: *Medium*
Stringing: *Medium tiger tail or heavy thread*
Weight: *0.7g*
Other sizes: *None*
Color range: *None*

Length: *10mm*
Width: *10mm*
Depth: *6mm*

Actual size

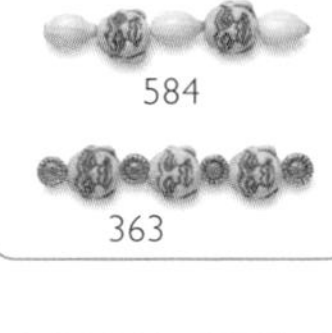

Mix and match

584

363

28

457 PLAIN HEART CERAMIC

Sometimes a plain shape is exactly what is required for a bead design. The simplicity of these hearts, which are neatly molded and drilled to hang down from a strand, could be teamed with much more elaborate beads or used alone to create an understated piece. They are useful on embroideries and cards, too.

Hole: *Large*
Stringing: *Medium tiger tail or heavy thread*
Weight: *0.5g*
Other sizes: *None*
Color range: *None*

Length: *9mm*
Width: *10mm*
Depth: *6mm*

Actual size

Mix and match

520

506

458 FLOWER-GARDEN HEART POLYMER CLAY

Slices of incredibly detailed polymer clay canes (see 427), including blended colors and translucent clay (separate canes for each flower), have been applied to these beads by their designer Leigh Ross, worked into the main shape, and then baked. Repeated sanding and polishing with increasingly fine grit papers have given a beautiful shine.

50% of actual size

Hole: *Medium*
Stringing: *Medium tiger tail or heavy thread*
Weight: *8.3g*
Other sizes: *None*
Color range: *None*

Length: *37mm*
Width: *33mm*
Depth: *8mm*

7

459 IMPRESSED TRIANGLE CERAMIC

An unusual shape to be pierced across the tip, these flat triangles have been molded with a deep pattern and antiqued with the dipping color wiped off of the highlights only (compare with 456). At least 20mm of other beads would be needed between these to allow them to hang neatly.

Hole: *Large*
Stringing: *Medium tiger tail or heavy thread*
Weight: *4.6g*
Other sizes: *None*
Color range: *None*

Length: *7mm*
Width: *28mm*
Depth: *7mm*

Actual size

13

460 FLOWER CERAMIC

These flowers are not a very detailed molding, but they are decorated in the traditional blue on white, front and back. The odd number of petals means that the tip of one will fit into the dip in the next if they are strung together, so allow for this when working out the length or add small beads in between them.

Hole: *Medium*
Stringing: *Medium tiger tail or heavy thread*
Weight: *0.9g*
Other sizes: *None*
Color range: *None*

Length: *12mm*
Width: *6mm*
Depth: *8mm*

Actual size

21

CHAPTER 7

Plastic

When plastic was first commercially available, beads made from this material were particularly interesting and sought after. More recently, many people have looked down on plastic beads as cheap, low-quality substitutes for glass and other materials—this is certainly true of some of them, but by no means all.

The range of plastic beads today includes some very beautiful pieces, shapes that would be very difficult to make in other materials (those used to fit together for craft projects, for example), and colors with special properties such as luminosity (glow-in-the-dark). There are also beads aimed at children, although these often work in "fun" pieces for adults too.

One advantage of plastic beads is that they generally survive a gentle, low-temperature wash—this, combined with their light weight, makes them very suitable for decorating clothing. Garments should be turned inside out for washing, however, to reduce the risk of breaking or scratching the beads.

Plastic beads can be distinguished by their light weight for the size and the fact that there is no "clink" when they are tapped together (instead, they make rather a dull clunk). They are warm (room temperature) to the touch even when not in wear, unlike glass and stone, which feel cool.

Bright interlocking plastic beads make simple but effective bracelets strung onto elastic cord, to be worn singly or in groups.

25

461 PLAIN ROUND

Probably the simplest plastic bead, generally intended to simulate a clear glass bead, although also available in opaque colors that often do not look very glasslike. When buying, look out for air bubbles, visible seam lines, and rough holes, all of which should be avoidable in a good-quality plastic bead.

Hole: *Large*
Stringing: *Medium thread*
Weight: *0.6g*
Other sizes: *Many*
Color range: *Large*

Length: *10mm*
Width: *10mm*
Depth: *10mm*

Actual size

Mix and match
562
368

34

462 CRACKLE ROUND

This bead is also intended to imitate glass but in this case with a special crackle effect (see 15). Just as pretty as the glass but lighter, which may be an advantage or a disadvantage depending on the type and design of the jewelry and on the other beads you are using.

Hole: *Medium*
Stringing: *Medium thread*
Weight: *0.5g*
Other sizes: *None*
Color range: *Small*

Length: *7.5mm*
Width: *8.5mm*
Depth: *8.5mm*

Actual size

Mix and match
457
301

34

463 MIRACLE

Called "miracle beads," these have a special coating that catches and returns the light in a bright patch with lustrous color around it. It looks like something between a colored pearl and an opaque moonstone, seeming almost to glow. Unlike some coatings, these are as interesting in natural light as they are under bright artificial lighting.

Hole: *Medium*
Stringing: *Medium thread*
Weight: *0.3g*
Other sizes: *6mm, 10mm*
Color range: *Medium*

Length: *7.5mm*
Width: *8mm*
Depth: *8mm*

Actual size

Mix and match
537
362

464 DYEABLE ROUND

Especially made for the jewelry artist who needs specific colors, this plastic has been designed to take any acrylic dye and many permanent inks or paints. This is very useful if you want to match a special item of clothing. The results usually look frosted but can be very lovely. There are several other shapes and sizes available in this material.

Hole: *Large*
Stringing: *Heavy thread or fine cord*
Weight: *0.5g*
Other sizes: *14mm*
Color range: *None*

Length: *9mm*
Width: *10mm*
Depth: *10mm*

Actual size

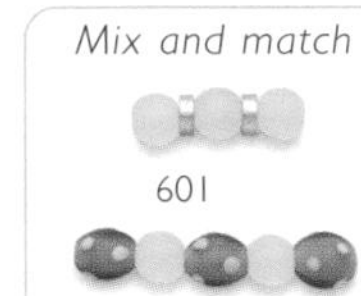

Mix and match

601

65

465 ROSE TRANSFER

A very good simulation of a porcelain bead with a transfer pattern, this bead manages to have a shiny glazed look without seeming plastic at all. Only the weight and lack of a "clink" give away the material, and there is no real reason not to use these as a substitute for the heavier and more expensive ceramic version.

Hole: *Medium*
Stringing: *Medium thread*
Weight: *1.1g*
Other sizes: *None*
Color range: *None*

Length: *12mm*
Width: *12.5mm*
Depth: *12.5mm*

Actual size

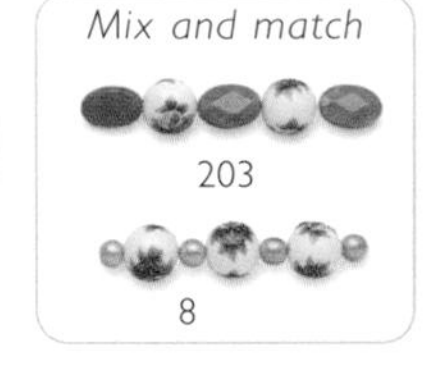

Mix and match

203

8

466 SIMULATED FLAMEWORK

At first glance, this looks like a flameworked glass bead right down to the white showing in the hole. The flowers inside the bead look wonderful, and there is no sign of a seam or any other indication of its material. A strand of these would be very impressive without being heavy to wear.

Actual size

Hole: *Large*
Stringing: *Heavy thread or fine cord*
Weight: *4.9g*
Other sizes: *15mm*
Color range: *Small*

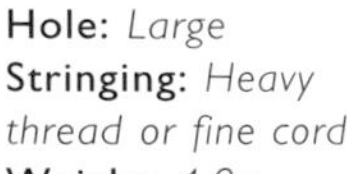

Length: *19mm*
Width: *20mm*
Depth: *20mm*

Mix and match

293

250

14

467 LAMINATED ROUND

This bead is made of laminated layers of plastic, in this case pastel shades of blue and white with thin white layers in between. The lamination is probably done in large sheets and the beads shaped afterward. It is a good example of a lovely bead using the properties of plastic without trying to simulate another material.

Hole: *Large*
Stringing: *Heavy thread*
Weight: *1.0g*
Other sizes: *6mm, 8mm, 20mm*
Color range: *Medium*

Length: *10.5mm*
Width: *12mm*
Depth: *12mm*

Actual size

Mix and match

122

531

24

468 PURPLE PRINT

Another bead that is not trying to look like any other material, this has been cast in white with an impressed pattern filled with color. Seam lines have not been removed but are left as part of the overall design. The middle of the flower is flattened, possibly to help the beads to line up in wear.

Hole: *Large*
Stringing: *Heavy thread*
Weight: *0.5g*
Other sizes: *None*
Color range: *Medium*

Length: *9mm*
Width: *9mm*
Depth: *9mm*

Actual size

Mix and match

363

449

28

469 BLACK LAYERS

Cast to look as though it is carved or assembled in layers, this bead catches the light in a similar way to a faceted bead but with a less classical look and so may be more suitable for some fashion jewelry designs. The overall effect is of a more-or-less round bead, but the shape is actually more like a bicone.

Hole: *Large*
Stringing: *Heavy thread*
Weight: *0.6g*
Other sizes: *8mm*
Color range: *Mixed*

Length: *9.5mm*
Width: *11mm*
Depth: *11mm*

Actual size

Mix and match

483

348

27

470 MELON

The shape of this bead is sometimes called "melon" due to the rounded ridges, rather like some types of the fruit. In glass beads, this is done by making a round bead and then pressing the dent lines in while the glass is molten, but these have been cast. The surface has been frosted, but the lines are shiny.

Hole: *Medium*
Stringing: *Heavy thread*
Weight: *1.4g*
Other sizes: *None*
Color range: *Medium*

Length: *14mm*
Width: *13mm*
Depth: *13mm*

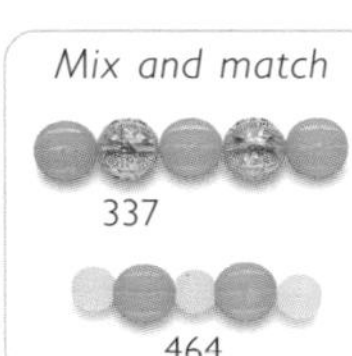

Actual size

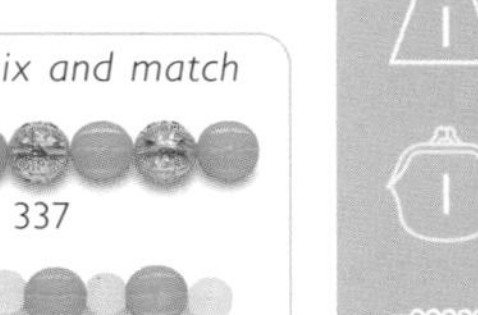

Mix and match

337

464

18

471 FACETED

Imitating a faceted glass bead, this version has been well cast with any seam lines removed, so the plastic is clear and does reflect some light, although nothing like as much as would a similar glass or crystal bead. It is not really a satisfactory substitution for glass but pretty enough for an inexpensive piece of jewelry.

Hole: *Medium*
Stringing: *Heavy thread*
Weight: *0.9g*
Other sizes: *Many*
Color range: *Large*

Length: *12mm*
Width: *12mm*
Depth: *12mm*

Actual size

Mix and match

266

495

21

472 POINTS

Probably impractical to make in any material other than plastic, this faceted shape is hollow and covered with tiny pyramidal points; because of the metallic coating these points reflect the light. Very modern, geometric and bright, these would be good beads to include in pieces to wear at a club or party.

Hole: *Medium*
Stringing: *Heavy thread*
Weight: *0.2g*
Other sizes: *None*
Color range: *Mixed*

Length: *8mm*
Width: *7mm*
Depth: *7mm*

Actual size

Mix and match

15

468

32

21

473 OFF CENTER

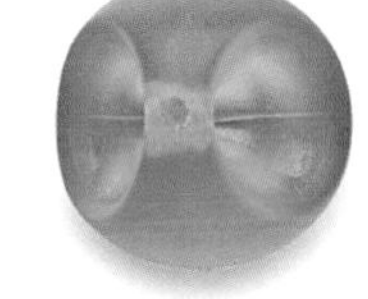

With its off-center hole, this type of bead is useful for the ends of drops of any kind and also as an end-ball in a fastening: make a loop of small beads at the other end of a necklace or bracelet to fit over it. This bead is also often seen on elastics made to hold a ponytail.

Hole: *Large*
Stringing: *Elastic or cord*
Weight: *0.9g*
Other sizes: *None*
Color range: *Mixed*

Length: *12mm*
Width: *12mm*
Depth: *12mm*

Actual size

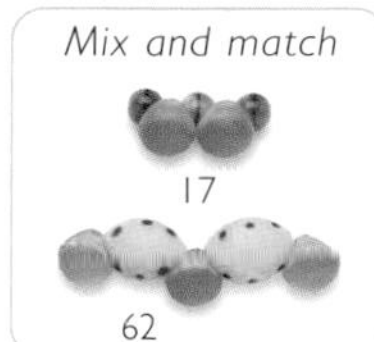

Mix and match

17

62

28

474 SIMULATED CERAMIC

This unglazed bead, with darker slip-coloring in the dips, is plastic simulating ceramic. The seam line has again been included in the design rather than eliminated. This version is probably longer-lasting and less prone to damage than the original it is imitating, which is also less commonly available.

Hole: *Large*
Stringing: *Heavy thread or fine cord*
Weight: *0.4g*
Other sizes: *None*
Color range: *None*

Length: *9mm*
Width: *9.5mm*
Depth: *9.5mm*

Actual size

Mix and match

434

510

475 PONY

The classic pony shape of bead is available in clear, opaque, and other styles, as well as with this colored-metallic coating. It can be used for bead creatures, leatherwork, and macramé, among other things, and is also useful in large-size beadweaving for patterns and pictures due to their almost square shape in cross-section.

Hole: *Very large*
Stringing: *Cord*
Weight: *0.3g*
Other sizes: *None*
Color range: *Large*

Length: *6mm*
Width: *9mm*
Depth: *9mm*

Actual size

Mix and match

440

464

42

476 FLORAL OVAL

Metal-coated plastic beads are sometimes bright and shiny, as this one is, and are often very detailed with good seams and impressed patterns. Being hollow, like most metal beads, they are often difficult to tell from pure metal, but this rarely matters. They are less likely to tarnish than uncoated plain metal beads.

Actual size

Hole: *Medium*
Stringing: *Heavy thread*
Weight: *2.2g*
Other sizes: *None*
Color range: *Small*

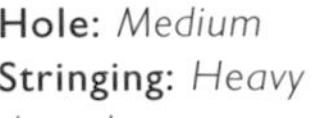

Length: *20mm*
Width: *15mm*
Depth: *15mm*

13

477 GILDED OVAL

The pattern on this slightly frosted clear bead has been filled with metallic color, making it look rather sophisticated and classical. The oval shape is complemented by the diamond in the middle of the patterned stripes. Some of these could be used to bring a little light to a dark composition, without adding too much secondary color.

Hole: *Medium*
Stringing: *Heavy thread*
Weight: *0.6g*
Other sizes: *None*
Color range: *Medium*

Length: *14mm*
Width: *9mm*
Depth: *9mm*

Actual size

18

478 PILLOW RONDELLE

A round, cushion-shaped bead is useful either as a focal bead or as a spacer for larger beads. This one has a rather classical pattern, and the metal coating has been antiqued (dulled a little) and the dips filled with black.

Hole: *Large*
Stringing: *Cord*
Weight: *1.8g*
Other sizes: *None*
Color range: *Small*

Length: *12mm*
Width: *15.5mm*
Depth: *15.5mm*

Actual size

21

479 WHEEL

Thick disk beads or wheels are most useful as separators because a long run of them together can make a rather stiff tube, although of course that may be what the design requires. This one has a faceted edge and is clear, so it could be used to add light to a piece.

Hole: *Medium*
Stringing: *Heavy thread*
Weight: *0.1g*
Other sizes: *None*
Color range: *Mixed*

Length: *3mm*
Width: *7mm*
Depth: *7mm*

Actual size

Mix and match
476
471

84

480 SIMULATED AMBER

Actual size

It can be quite difficult to tell a good-quality plastic simulated amber bead from the real thing. This one has no seam lines or bubbles, there are saw marks on the end, and the hole is drilled just like the real thing. Weight and warmth are similar, too, so only the smell will reveal the difference (see 198).

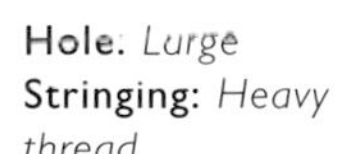

Hole: *Large*
Stringing: *Heavy thread*
Weight: *2.0g*
Other sizes: *None*
Color range: *None*

Length: *19mm*
Width: *10.5mm*
Depth: *10.5mm*

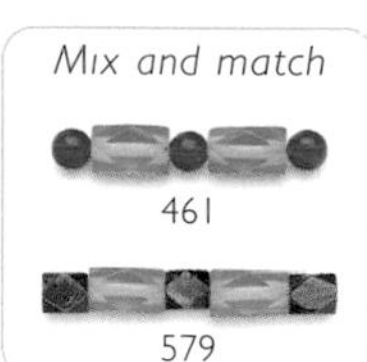
Mix and match
461
579

14

481 GLOW TUBE

These tubular beads glow in the dark. They also come in a large range of clear and opaque colors but are not intended mainly for jewelry making. They are used on spiked, shaped mats to assemble designs and pictures, then ironed to melt them slightly and stick them together. Because they are very regular they are also good for beadweaving.

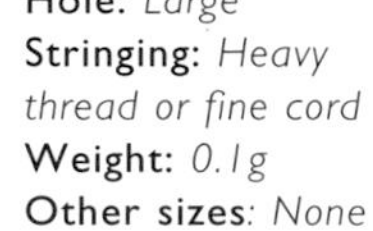

Hole: *Large*
Stringing: *Heavy thread or fine cord*
Weight: *0.1g*
Other sizes: *None*
Color range: *Large*

Length: *5mm*
Width: *4.5mm*
Depth: *4.5mm*

Actual size

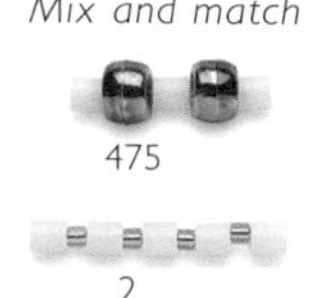
Mix and match
475
2

50

482 TRANSFER CURVED TUBE

With its black, shiny background and printed, gilded pattern, this looks like a high-quality lacquered or even enameled bead. Curved tubes are particularly useful near the middle of loose necklaces because they can influence the shape the strand falls into in wear, but be careful of using them elsewhere, especially on a bracelet where the curve may be too sharp.

Actual size

Hole: *Medium*
Stringing: *Heavy thread*
Weight: *1.1g*
Other sizes: *None*
Color range: *Small*

Length: *30mm*
Width: *6.5mm*
Depth: *6.5mm*

Mix and match
8
404

483 SQUARE CUSHION

This bead could be an imitation of carved, antiqued bone, especially given the classic pattern and shape, which I would call a square puffed cushion. The hole is large enough to use with cord, and a few beads of this type strung onto leather could make a quick, simple piece for summer.

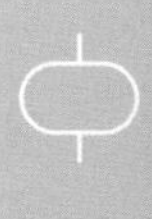

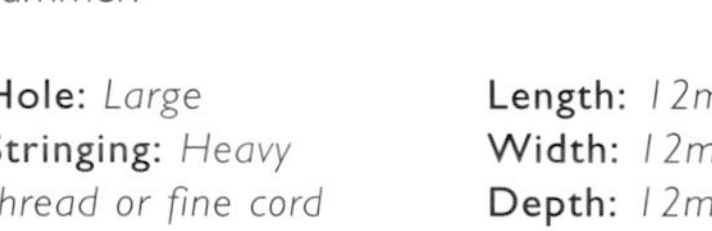

Hole: *Large*
Stringing: *Heavy thread or fine cord*
Weight: *1.1g*
Other sizes: *None*
Color range: *Small*

Length: *12mm*
Width: *12mm*
Depth: *12mm*

Actual size

Mix and match
272
543

21

484 DIAGONAL PUFFED CUBE

Despite being a big bead, these are very light because they are hollow. This makes them easy to wear. The seam line is visible, but the overall pattern disguises it, and the unusual shape (a slightly distorted, rounded cube with pressed-in sides) makes it visually interesting without needing bright colors to draw the eye.

Actual size

Hole: *Large*
Stringing: *Heavy thread or fine cord*
Weight: *4.0g*
Other sizes: *None*
Color range: *None*

Length: *21mm*
Width: *22mm*
Depth: *22mm*

Mix and match
507
459

12

38

485 DIAGONAL DICE

These fun little beads, in a pearly colored plastic, are cast and painted to look like dice. You could not use them as real dice though because the balance is uneven due to the hole. Some dice beads have the hole going through the sides of the cube rather than the points, but this looks more interesting.

Hole: *Small*
Stringing: *Medium thread*
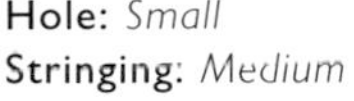
Weight: *0.1g*
Other sizes: *None*
Color range: *Mixed*

Length: *6.5mm*
Width: *5mm*
Depth: *5mm*

Actual size

Mix and match

126

172

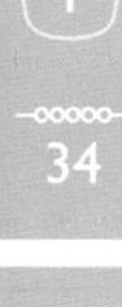

34

486 BRIGHT LAMINATE CUBE

Brightly colored laminated layers of plastic make up this cube bead. If you thread cubes with holes through the sides like this right next to each other, be sure to use a stringing material that can show without spoiling the look of the piece, and leave enough "give" when finishing the ends to allow the piece to move well.

Hole: *Medium*
Stringing: *Heavy thread*
Weight: *0.5g*
Other sizes: *10mm*
Color range: *Medium*

Length: *7.5mm*
Width: *7.5mm*
Depth: *7.5mm*

Actual size

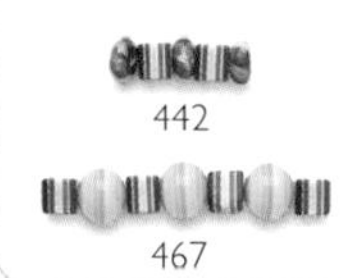

Mix and match

442

467

18

487 RECTANGLE

The flat, rectangular shape of this bead is given extra interest by the pattern and by the disks added around the hole at both ends. This metal-coated, antiqued, hollow shape, is comfortable to wear and so could be useful at the back of a necklace or on a bracelet, as well as to give different heights within a design.

Hole: *Medium*
Stringing: *Heavy thread*
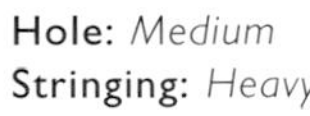
Weight: *0.6g*
Other sizes: *None*
Color range: *Small*

Length: *14mm*
Width: *10.5mm*
Depth: *6.5mm*

Actual size

Mix and match

218

84

488 TWO-HOLE RECTANGLE

These have an opal look without being opaque and reflect light in interesting ways. The two holes allow them to be used as spacers for multirow pieces or alone in a choker or bracelet. When using them as the main bead in a necklace, help them to lie flat by adding small beads between the holes at the bottom.

Hole: *Medium*
Stringing: *Heavy thread*
Weight: *0.5g*
Other sizes: *None*
Color range: *Mixed*

Length: *9.5mm*
Width: *11mm*
Depth: *6mm*

Actual size

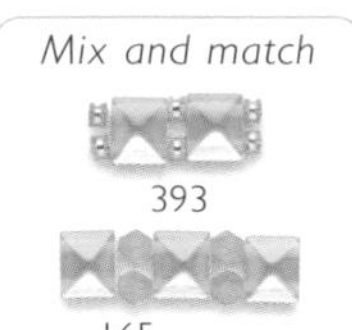

27

489 TWO-HOLE ARCH

Similar to the previous bead in use, these are more domed on the top (although flat at the sides) and made of a clear plastic, so they catch the light in a different way. They are also smaller, so their holes are closer together, and the other beads in multistrand works might have to be narrower as a result.

Hole: *Medium*
Stringing: *Heavy thread*
Weight: *0.3g*
Other sizes: None
Color range: *Mixed*

Length: *8mm*
Width: *10mm*
Depth: *6mm*

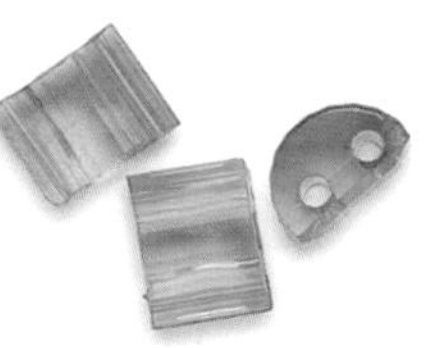

Actual size

32

490 ANCIENT SYMBOLS

Made to look a bit like antiqued bone with rune-like symbols and a slightly uneven shape, these beads might make good counters for board games as well as interesting jewelry. Because a flat bead with a central hole like this will turn over in wear both sides are marked, and the fact that the sides are different adds interest.

Hole: *Large*
Stringing: *Heavy thread*
Weight: *2.4g*
Other sizes: *None*
Color range: *None*

Length: *26mm*
Width: *18.5mm*
Depth: *5.5mm*

Actual size

10

2
13

491 DOMED DISK

The very sharp geometric pattern on these slightly domed disks and their antiqued metallic coating gives them a look that could be used in anything from Aztec to Art Deco themed pieces. Flat round shapes can be useful to make a necklace or bracelet larger and more impressive, without making it inconveniently bulky to wear.

Actual size

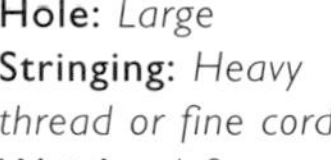

Hole: *Large*
Stringing: *Heavy thread or fine cord*
Weight: *1.8g*
Other sizes: *None*
Color range: *Small*

Length: *20mm*
Width: *20mm*
Depth: *7mm*

Mix and match

17

483

1
20

492 DISK FACE

Happy faces on both sides of yellow, flat, round beads, these are cheerful and bright; good for summer jewelry, these would also surely be popular with children. A few scattered into a mix of strong colored shapes and sizes is probably enough because a whole strand could be rather overwhelming and spoil the effect.

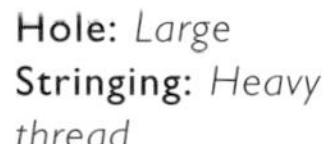

Hole: *Large*
Stringing: *Heavy thread*
Weight: *0.5g*
Other sizes: *None*
Color range: *None*

Length: *13mm*
Width: *13mm*
Depth: *5mm*

Actual size

Mix and match

486

10

1
36

493 DISK LETTERS

Letter beads are available in many materials and often come in this small, round format. Plastic beads probably provide more colors of alphabet than any others, and these pretty pastels are popular with little girls. Make names, phrases such as "I love beads," or slogans; either as jewelry or stitched onto clothing.

Hole: *Medium*
Stringing: *Heavy thread*
Weight: *0.1g*
Other sizes: *None*
Color range: *Mixed*

Length: *7mm*
Width: *7mm*
Depth: *3.5mm*

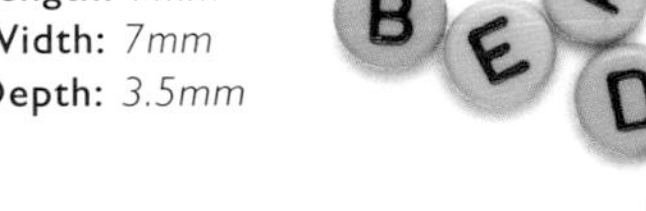

Actual size

Mix and match

457

506

494 SIMULATED PEARL DROP

Simulated pearl drops come in many more colors than do real pearls. Plastic pearls are lighter than glass and less lustrous, but they are useful for inexpensive pretty pieces. This is a through-drilled drop, but drops drilled across the narrow end are also readily available. This is a good shape to put on a head pin (629) for earrings or dangles.

Hole: *Medium*
Stringing: *Heavy thread*
Weight: *0.2g*
Other sizes: *14mm*
Color range: *Medium*

Length: *12mm*
Width: *6mm*
Depth: *6mm*

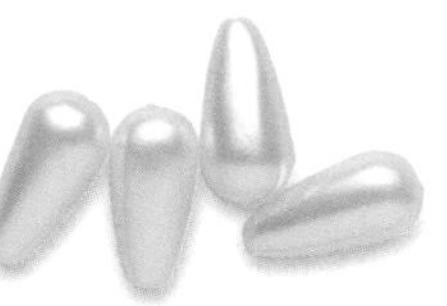

Actual size

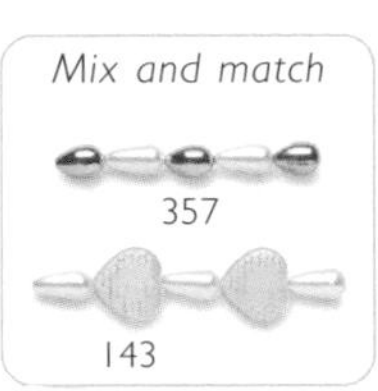

21

495 FACETED DROP

Rather an unusual drop shape, this has a flat, angled base and the hole across the top. The plastic is very clear, and the facets are sharp, so light passes through and is refracted in all directions; this, together with the reflection of light, probably gives this bead the best sparkle available for plastic.

Hole: *Large*
Stringing: *Heavy thread*
Weight: *0.7g*
Other sizes: *None*
Color range: *Mixed*

Length: *11mm*
Width: *19mm*
Depth: *19mm*

Actual size

23

496 SIMULATED TORTOISE SHELL

A substantial drop simulating tortoise shell, which is no longer available. The dark honey color with deeper speckles is realistic, and there are no seams visible, but the hole does not look drilled. However, these look lovely, and there is no reason why they should not be used as a substitute for the real thing.

Actual size

Hole: *Medium*
Stringing: *Heavy thread*
Weight: *1.5g*
Other sizes: *None*
Color range: *None*

Length: *20mm*
Width: *12mm*
Depth: *12mm*

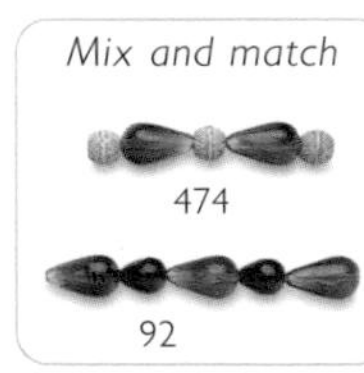

13

32

497 HEART

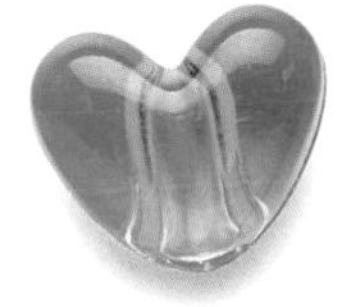

Sometimes known as a pony heart, these are widely available and go well with pony beads of similar size. If used end to end, the tip of each heart will fit in between the bumps on top of the next one, reducing the total length slightly, so allow for this if buying just enough beads for a project.

Hole: *Large*
Stringing: *Cord*
Weight: *0.5g*
Other sizes: *None*
Color range: *Medium*

Length: *8mm*
Width: *12mm*
Depth: *8mm*

Actual size

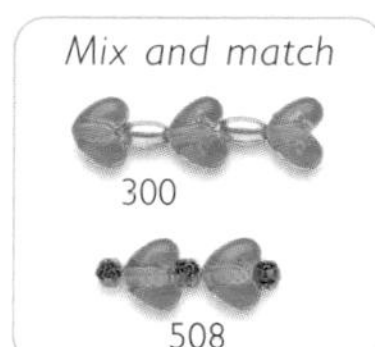

72

498 TRIBEAD

Tribeads look a little strange on their own because they are designed to fit into each other, making flexible, textured tubes of color. Take care not to thread them too tightly, or the tubes will be so stiff that they cannot bend around a wrist or hang well in a necklace.

Hole: *Large*
Stringing: *Heavy thread*
Weight: *0.2g*
Other sizes: *None*
Color range: *Large*

Length: *3.5mm*
Width: *10mm*
Depth: *10mm*

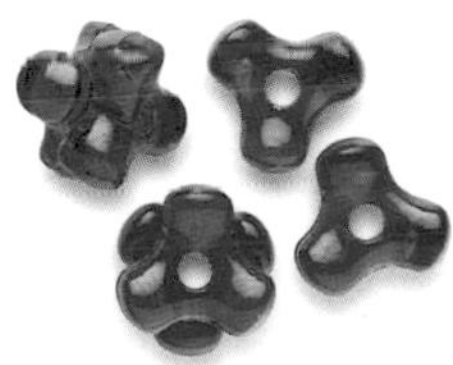

Actual size

22

499 STARFLAKE

Starflakes are pretty as they are stitched onto clothing or used as spacers but really come into their own when fitted together to make tubes and shapes. The different sizes are made to fit neatly into each other so can be stacked to make an icicle or one point of a star.

Hole: *Medium*
Stringing: *Heavy thread*
Weight: *0.5g*
Other sizes: *12mm, 14mm, 18mm, 20mm*
Color range: *Small*

Length: *1.5mm*
Width: *10mm*
Depth: *5.5mm*

Actual size

500 OWLS

These cute little owls are representative of the large range of molded plastic animal-shape beads available; most have good detail, and many are metal-coated. Similar beads may have the hole across the head rather than down the body, which may be more convenient depending on the jewelry design. Use these as a drop by hanging them on a head pin (629).

Hole: *Medium*
Stringing: *Heavy thread*
Weight: *0.5g*
Other sizes: *None*
Color range: *Small*

Length: *11.5mm*
Width: *10mm*
Depth: *5.5mm*

Actual size

Mix and match

151

378

22

501 MICE

This little white mouse is printed onto a more standard shape of bead, rather than molded as for the previous bead. As with the owl, the face appears on both sides of the bead, so that it does not matter which way around they lie in wear.

Hole: *Medium*
Stringing: *Heavy thread*
Weight: *0.4g*
Other sizes: *None*
Color range: *Small*

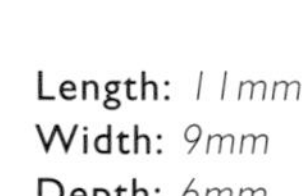
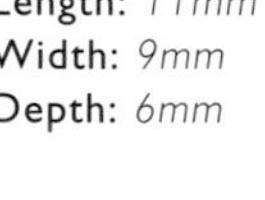

Length: *11mm*
Width: *9mm*
Depth: *6mm*

Actual size

Mix and match

493

500

23

502 BUTTERFLY

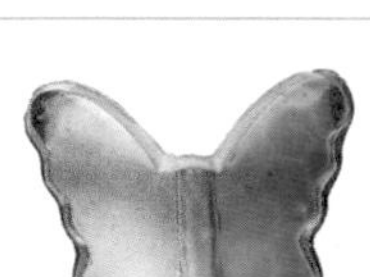

There are no details on this butterfly bead, but the facets and mix of colors make it rather appealing. A strand of these beads will leave a gap between the tip and tail, due to the size of the wings, so add small beads to fill in the space and to prevent the thread showing.

Hole: *Large*
Stringing: *Heavy thread*
Weight: *0.6g*
Other sizes: *None*
Color range: *Mixed*

Length: *13mm*
Width: *16mm*
Depth: *6mm*

Actual size

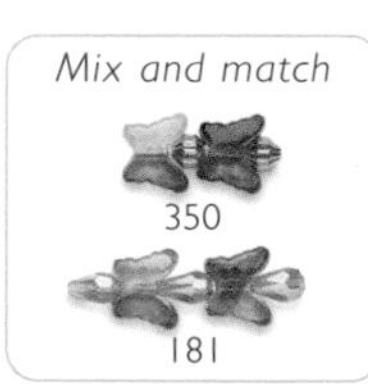

Mix and match

350

181

20

503 STARS

These little flat stars are pretty on their own and also useful as spacers between more impressive beads. They tuck into each other in wear, so more are needed along the length of a piece than might be calculated from their tip-to-tip measurement, but if using them next to larger beads, you may need a tiny bead to fill the gap.

Hole: *Medium*
Stringing: *Medium thread*

Weight: *0.05g*
Other sizes: *None*
Color range: *Mixed*

Length: *6mm*
Width: *6mm*
Depth: *3mm*

42

Actual size

Mix and match

492

308

504 ANGLED STARS

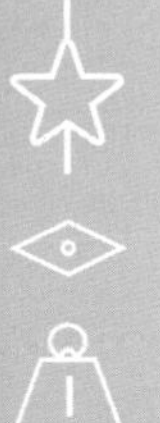

Hollow plastic with a metallic coating, crisply shaped edges, and a raised point in the middle, these stars would be good in decorations or at the tips of spikes on holiday tiaras. Like 503, they would fit into each other if threaded together so allow for this in length or add smaller beads between them.

Hole: *Medium*
Stringing: *Heavy thread*
Weight: *0.4g*
Other sizes: *None*
Color range: *Small*

Length: *14mm*
Width: *14mm*
Depth: *5mm*

18

Actual size

Mix and match

462

503

505 PONY STARS

A more rounded star, with more-or-less flat faces, and with glitter in the translucent plastic, these would make appealing sparkly jewelry for little girls. They can be threaded onto cord so would make good ends for a fringe at the neckline of a party dress, held on with a knot.

Hole: *Large*
Stringing: *Cord*
Weight: *0.5g*
Other sizes: *None*
Color range: *Medium*

Length: *12.5mm*
Width: *12.5mm*
Depth: *7mm*

20

Actual size

Mix and match

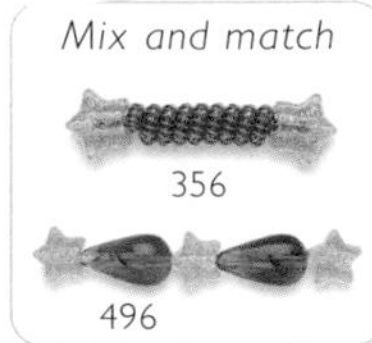

356

496

506 FLOWERS

More sophisticated than many plastic flowers, these are well cast in strong but not bright colors with metallic details, and the dip in the center is faceted to suggest the presence of a cut stone or crystal. A small pointed-back stone could be glued into this space to make the beads even more attractive.

Hole: *Medium*
Stringing: *Heavy thread*
Weight: *0.3g*
Other sizes: *None*
Color range: *Medium*

Length: *11mm*
Width: *11mm*
Depth: *4.5mm*

Actual size

Mix and match

378

169

23

507 PONY FLOWER

The pearly color of this bead adds charm to what is really a very simple molded shape, most suitable for light, inexpensive jewelry. The fun shape and large holes make these suitable for a child's first attempt at beadwork, particularly because they are large enough to hold and will not roll away as easily as round beads could.

Hole: *Large*
Stringing: *Cord*
Weight: *0.4g*
Other sizes: *None*
Color range: *Medium*

Length: *10mm*
Width: *12mm*
Depth: *7mm*

Actual size

Mix and match

152

508

25

508 ANTIQUED ROSE

These little antiqued roses are very popular as spacers in many types of jewelry, and similar beads come in pure metal as well as in metal-coated plastic like these. They are also quite attractive in a strand on their own, perhaps twisted into a group with strands of small toning beads.

Hole: *Medium*
Stringing: *Medium thread*
Weight: *0.05g*
Other sizes: *None*
Color range: *Small*

Length: *5mm*
Width: *5mm*
Depth: *3mm*

Actual size

Mix and match

427

343

50

CHAPTER 8

Wood

Wooden beads are probably most commonly used for children's projects and were the only beads used for them before plastic became widely available. More recently, new methods of printing patterns onto wood have been developed, and lathes, formerly used only by hand, have been automated to create more shapes more quickly. This has led to the availability of delicate, finely decorated wooden beads, in addition to the standard bulky offerings.

A large number of wooden beads are left unfinished, with no color or varnish, for the user to decorate. These are particularly suitable for covering with smaller beads, using techniques such as brick stitch, peyote, netting, and stranding. They are also easy to paint or dye (most fabric dyes work well). To ensure that the beads do not touch a surface or each other while drying, they can be loosely strung and the string suspending at both ends.

It is generally easy to recognize wooden beads by weight and feel (wood usually feels warm), although it is possible to confuse them with some other natural materials. Look into the hole to see the drilled-out wood if necessary, although even that may be painted in some cases.

Simple knots separate these graduated printed wood beads to create an easy but effective necklace.

13

509 NATURAL ROUND

Made of a light-colored wood left in its natural state, these beads could be used as they are or dyed, painted, or varnished as required. Unfinished wood will also take up a scent if stored with aromatic materials such as lavender. The grain is visible, adding to the interest, and may show more clearly if a dye is used.

Actual size

Hole: *Large*
Stringing: *Heavy thread or fine cord*
Weight: *3.6g*
Other sizes: *Many*
Color range: *None*

Length: *20mm*
Width: *20mm*
Depth: *20mm*

Actual size

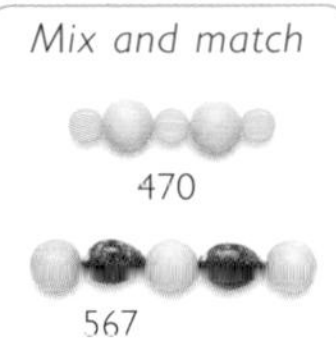
Mix and match
470
567

20

510 SOFT ROUND

As well as having a far larger hole than 509, these beads are made of a far softer and lighter wood. They could be finished in the same ways but are far easier to scratch or dent, and would also pick up unintentional stains easily. This makes such softwood beads more suitable for decorative projects than for jewelry.

Hole: *Large*
Stringing: *Cord*
Weight: *0.7g*
Other sizes: *18mm, 22mm*
Color range: *None*

Length: *12.5mm*
Width: *14mm*
Depth: *14mm*

Actual size

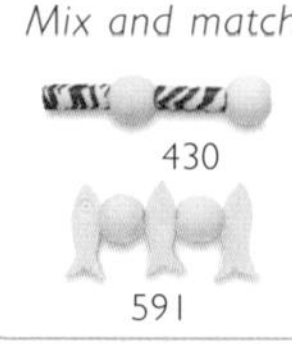
Mix and match
430
591

15

511 DYED ROUNDS

Similar to 509, these have been both dyed and varnished. Bright wood beads are excellent for large, lively jewelry, and are not too heavy to wear. Colored wooden beads are probably the safest to give to small children (although no bead should be given to a child young enough to swallow it).

Actual size

Hole: *Large*
Stringing: *Heavy thread or fine cord*
Weight: *2.5g*
Other sizes: *8mm, 10mm, 12mm*
Color range: *Medium*

Length: *17.5mm*
Width: *18mm*
Depth: *18mm*

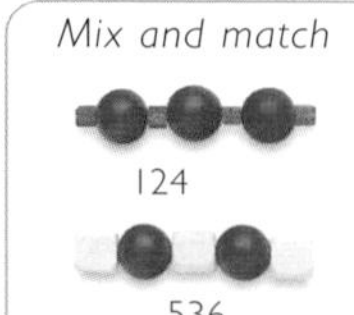
Mix and match
124
536

512 EXOTIC ROUND

The pattern in these beads is natural; the wood has only been shaped and varnished. Exotic woods, with their own intrinsic patterns and strong colors, are very beautiful, and scraps from bowl making or other large projects can be economically used to make beads, but they are not very common.

Actual size

Hole: *Large*
Stringing: *Heavy thread or fine cord*
Weight: *2.0g*
Other sizes: *10mm*
Color range: *None*

Length: *16mm*
Width: *16.5mm*
Depth: *16.5mm*

Mix and match

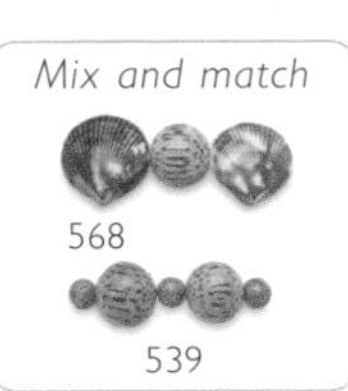

513 PRINTED ROUND

A light wooden bead, with the colored pattern printed or otherwise transferred onto it, then varnished. The basic color of the wood is allowed to show through, and the colors are not too vivid, so some of the natural feel of the beads is retained. These would be useful to add a bright splash without much weight.

Hole: *Large*
Stringing: *Heavy thread or fine cord*
Weight: *0.6g*
Other sizes: *8mm, 10mm*
Color range: *Small*

Length: *11.5mm*
Width: *12.5mm*
Depth: *12.5mm*

Actual size

Mix and match

22

514 PAINTED ROUND

The grain of the wood is almost completely hidden by the paint on these beads. Each has the same four Chinese symbols, all about good luck and fortune; these are printed over the paint but are under the varnish so will not rub off. However, some are poorly printed and unclear.

Hole: *Large*
Stringing: *Heavy thread or fine cord*
Weight: *0.3g*
Other sizes: *None*
Color range: *Small*

Length: *9mm*
Width: *10mm*
Depth: *10mm*

Actual size

Mix and match

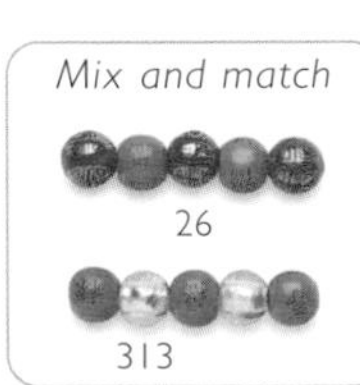

28

16

515 LEAF PATTERN

The subtle leaves on these beads point in opposite directions on either side, so there is no need to worry about the orientation when threading. The crackles in the varnish may not be intentional but add to the beauty of the beads and was perhaps done to make them look vintage.

Actual size

Hole: *Large*
Stringing: *Heavy thread or fine cord*
Weight: *1.3g*
Other sizes: *None*
Color range: *None*

Length: *16mm*
Width: *16mm*
Depth: *16mm*

Mix and match
596
549

13

516 MULTISECTION

A checkerboard cane of wood has been made using square rods of two colors, possibly the same wood but with half the pieces dyed a deeper brown. This has then been shaped into round beads, probably on a lathe, creating this attractive pattern. The construction can be seen more easily from the ends.

Actual size

Hole: *Large*
Stringing: *Heavy thread or fine cord*
Weight: *3.2g*
Other sizes: *None*
Color range: *None*

Length: *20mm*
Width: *20mm*
Depth: *20mm*

Mix and match
522
265

17

517 CARVED DYED

The four segments of this pattern have been simply created by carving lines along the bead from hole to hole. This basic shaping, along with the black dye, gives the beads an ancient look. Be aware that dyed and unvarnished beads can sometimes leak color onto clothing or skin when allowed to get damp.

Actual size

Hole: *Large*
Stringing: *Heavy thread or fine cord*
Weight: *1.3g*
Other sizes: *None*
Color range: *None*

Length: *15mm*
Width: *17mm*
Depth: *17mm*

Mix and match
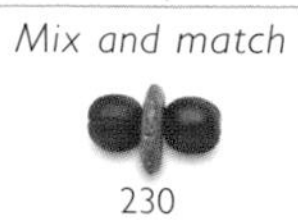
230

542

518 TURNED PATTERN ROUND

The many ridges on these beads are not a spiral but separate rings. This has probably been done on a lathe, using a tool with teeth shaped to produce just this effect because it would be far too time-consuming to do each ring separately. The wood is similar to 510.

Actual size

Hole: *Large*
Stringing: *Cord*
Weight: *1.3g*
Other sizes: *None*
Color range: *None*

Length: *16mm*
Width: *17mm*
Depth: *17mm*

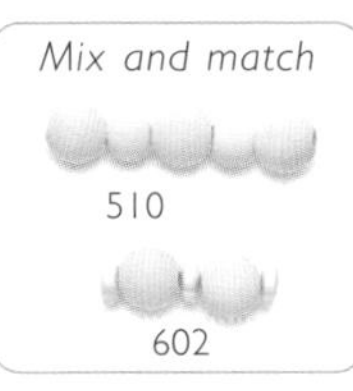

16

519 CARVED

Hand carved in Indonesia, these richly colored hardwood beads have oriental patterns and good luck symbols deeply engraved. Such beads are light for their size and are lovely on their own but would be more eye-catching if used with smooth beads, perhaps in exotic woods, such as 512, or other natural materials.

Actual size

Hole: *Large*
Stringing: *Heavy thread or fine cord*
Weight: *1.8g*
Other sizes: *None*
Color range: *None*

Length: *15mm*
Width: *16mm*
Depth: *16mm*

17

520 RONDELLES

Varnished but not colored, the characteristic shade of these redwood beads would add depth to a piece made primarily of natural woods and other such materials. The rondelle shape is particularly useful as a spacer, allowing larger beads to move more easily on a strand and adding length without drawing the eye too much.

Hole: *Large*
Stringing: *Medium tiger tail or heavy thread*
Weight: *0.2g*
Other sizes: *None*
Color range: *None*

Length: *5.5mm*
Width: *8mm*
Depth: *8mm*

Actual size

Mix and match
349
380

521 PAINTED BARREL

This shape of bead is frequently used in macramé, a form of knotting that creates patterns and is often done with jute, hemp, or other cords for use as jewelry or home decor items. The large hole could accommodate several strands of such materials, a heavy braid, or a thicker leather cord.

Hole: *Very large*
Stringing: *Cord*
Weight: *0.3g*
Other sizes: *None*
Color range: *Medium*

Length: *10mm*
Width: *10mm*
Depth: *10mm*

Actual size

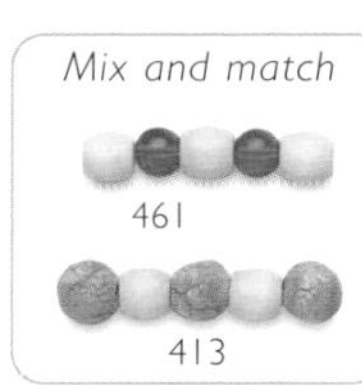

25

522 SHORT BARREL

The flat ends of this short barrel shape make it unsuitable for threading alone in a strand because the beads would not be able to move well against each other, resulting in a very stiff strand that would not drape properly. To avoid this, use rounded spacers in between flat-ended items.

Hole: *Large*
Stringing: *Heavy thread or fine cord*
Weight: *0.4g*
Other sizes: *None*
Color range: *Small*

Length: *8mm*
Width: *10mm*
Depth: *10mm*

Actual size

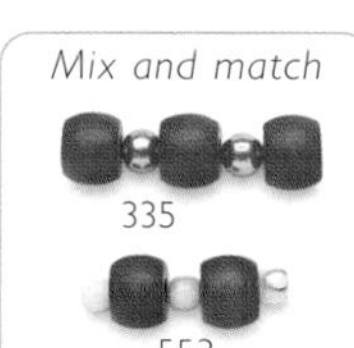

32

523 OPEN BARREL

Actual size

This bead is very light for its size because of the huge hole, which would take not just a cord but a slim rope. If used on a thinner stringing material, rounded beads that just fit snugly into the hole without actually going inside the bead can be used on either side to keep it in place.

Hole: *Extra large*
Stringing: *Cord*
Weight: *1.2g*
Other sizes: *None*
Color range: *Medium*

Length: *16mm*
Width: *16mm*
Depth: *16mm*

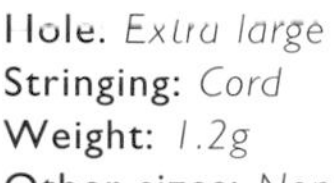

Actual size

16

524 CARVED BARREL

Similar to 523, this dyed bead has simple lines carved into it to add interest. These go around the bead rather than along, though, and are perhaps intended to look like the metal bands on the barrels that this shape is named after. Wood colored in this way may be intended to imitate horn or bone.

Actual size

Hole: *Large*
Stringing: *Heavy thread or fine cord*
Weight: *1.5g*
Other sizes: *None*
Color range: *Small*

Length: *22mm*
Width: *14mm*
Depth: *14mm*

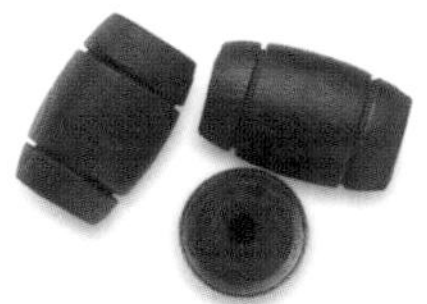

Actual size

12

525 ALMOST OVAL

This shape appears to have started out as a round tube, then had the two ends turned to form conical shapes, making the whole look almost oval even though the ends are flat. The wood is light, similar to 510, but the hole is not as large. This bead is best used as a base for decoration rather than in its own right.

Actual size

Hole: *Large*
Stringing: *Heavy thread or fine cord*
Weight: *7.0g*
Other sizes: *None*
Color range: *None*

Length: *28mm*
Width: *25mm*
Depth: *25mm*

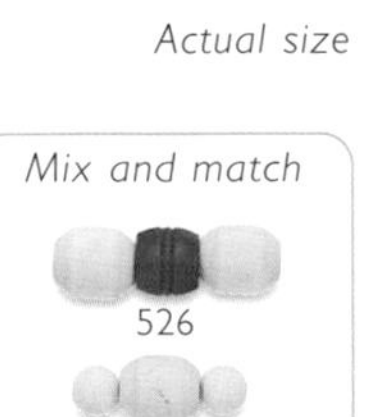

9

526 RINGED BARREL

A ring such as that around the center of these beads is usually created in a single step by turning the piece on a lathe and using a double-pointed tool. Such a substantial bead could be used in macramé for home decor or as part of a light pull but may be too bulky for jewelry.

Actual size

Hole: *Very large*
Stringing: *Cord*
Weight: *5.4g*
Other sizes: *None*
Color range: *Medium*

Length: *21mm*
Width: *25mm*
Depth: *25mm*

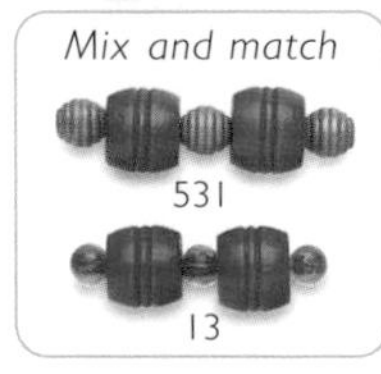

12

17

527 PRINTED OVAL

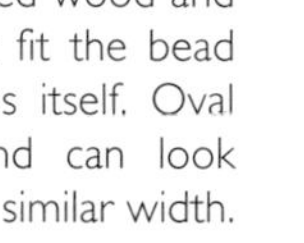

The pattern here has been printed onto the light-colored wood and then varnished over. Note that the pattern does not fit the bead exactly: there is a discontinuity line where it overlaps itself. Oval beads provide length without too much width and can look particularly effective if alternated with round beads of a similar width.

Hole: *Large*
Stringing: *Heavy thread or fine cord*
Weight: *0.2g*
Other sizes: *12mm*
Color range: *Small*

Length: *15mm*
Width: *7mm*
Depth: *7mm*

Actual size

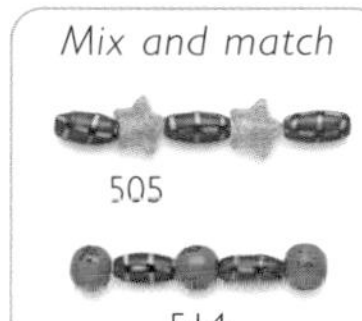

10

528 DROP FROG

A simple drop, this bead has been made into a delightful frog by painting rather than shaping. Because of the direction of the hole it could be used at the sides of a fun necklace, perhaps with fish or water-lily shapes, or hung using head pins (629) and a small bead or beads for back feet.

Actual size

Hole: *Large*
Stringing: *Heavy thread or fine cord*
Weight: *2.3g*
Other sizes: *None*
Color range: *None*

Length: *27mm*
Width: *15mm*
Depth: *15mm*

21

529 CARVED BEAR

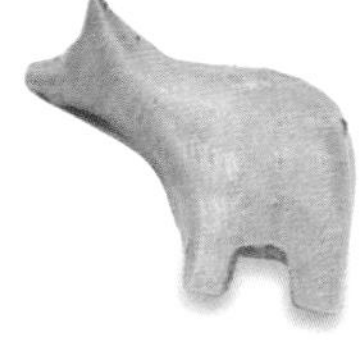

These beads are carved into the shape of bears, as seen in some Native American fetishes, and very little paint is used. They are drilled top to bottom so look best hung the right way up in a vertical strand or on a head pin (629) or to make a bracelet.

Hole: *Medium*
Stringing: *Medium tiger tail or heavy thread*
Weight: *0.5g*
Other sizes: *None*
Color range: *None*

Length: *12mm*
Width: *18mm*
Depth: *8mm*

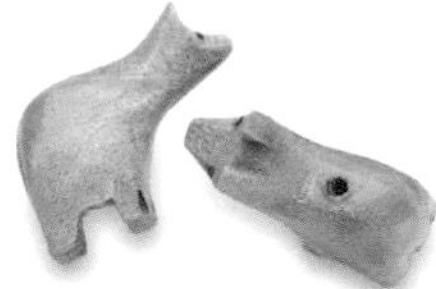

Actual size

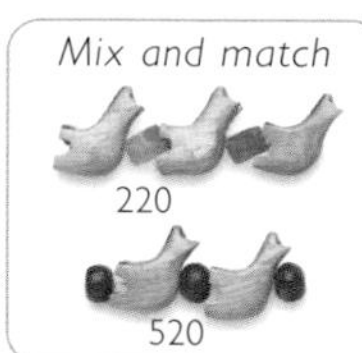

530 RINGED OVAL

This wood is similar to 509, but it has been varnished, which deepens the color somewhat. A single lathe tool has been made to create this attractive shape. These beads would be appealing as ends for pull cords or as toggles on clothing, as well as in simple jewelry.

Actual size

Hole: *Large*
Stringing: *Heavy thread or fine cord*
Weight: *0.9g*
Other sizes: *None*
Color range: *None*

Length: *15mm*
Width: *15mm*
Depth: *15mm*

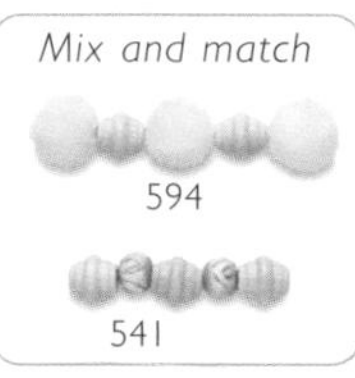

531 RIDGED OVAL

This bead is reminiscent of an old-fashioned beehive. The dye has been allowed to soak more deeply into the dips, emphasizing the shape, and they have been varnished on the outside (but not inside the hole) so the color is less likely to run, although it could rub off onto the stringing material.

Actual size

Hole: *Large*
Stringing: *Heavy thread or fine cord*
Weight: *1.0g*
Other sizes: *None*
Color range: *Medium*

Length: *15mm*
Width: *14.5mm*
Depth: *14.5mm*

532 RIDGED TUBE

A fairly soft, unfinished wood, this is not, however, as soft as 510. These would take the same finishing processes as 509; they could even be made to look like five disk beads used together by carefully painting the bumps in different colors or dividing them with a fine line. They have flat ends so use a rounded spacer to allow movement.

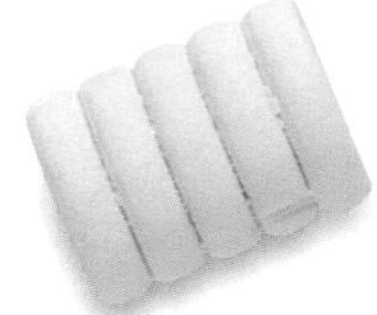

Actual size

Hole: *Very large*
Stringing: *Cord*
Weight: *1.1g*
Other sizes: *None*
Color range: *None*

Length: *19mm*
Width: *13.5mm*
Depth: *13.5mm*

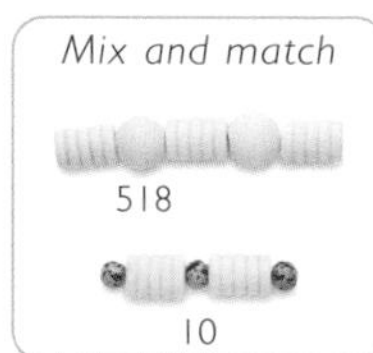

533 PRINTED TUBE

The print, or possibly transfer, on these tubes has not been sized to fit the tube, so there is a line where the pattern fails to meet up, but this is not really noticeable in wear. As with all flat-ended tubes, rounded spacers will be required if these are to be strung together because otherwise the strand will not drape properly.

16

Hole: *Large*
Stringing: *Heavy thread or fine cord*
Weight: *0.2g*
Other sizes: *None*
Color range: *Small*

Length: *16mm*
Width: *6mm*
Depth: *6mm*

Actual size

534 SQUARED TUBE

Cut as a square tube and then rounded on the corners and ends, this wood has been dyed a deeper color than its natural one, then varnished. The shape will move well due to the rounded ends, so this bead would be good on its own, as a subtle spacer, or to add length at the back of a piece.

21

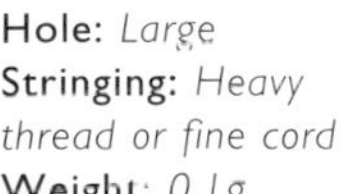

Hole: *Large*
Stringing: *Heavy thread or fine cord*
Weight: *0.1g*
Other sizes: *None*
Color range: *Small*

Length: *12mm*
Width: *15mm*
Depth: *15mm*

Actual size

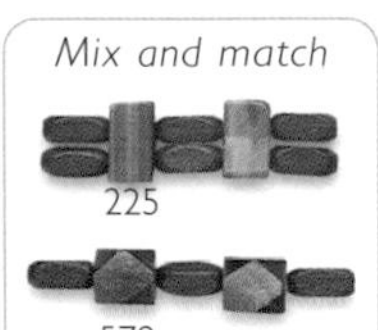

535 OCTAGONAL TUBE

This roughly cut octagon probably started as a square tube, that has had its corners removed. The hole is not drilled centrally so a strand of these would not hang evenly. Dyed black and varnished, these may be intended to look like ebony, which would be heavier and much more expensive.

Actual size

10

Hole: *Large*
Stringing: *Heavy thread or fine cord*
Weight: *3.6g*
Other sizes: *None*
Color range: *Medium*

Length: *25mm*
Width: *15mm*
Depth: *15mm*

536 ROUNDED CUBE

This is similar to 535, but the corners have been rounded off rather than removed to make an octagon shape; the ends are also rounded. The wood is similar to 510 and could be finished as for 509. Flat ends mean that a rounded spacer would be required if these are to be strung together.

Hole: *Large*
Stringing: *Heavy thread or fine cord*
Weight: *1.0g*
Other sizes: *None*
Color range: *None*

Length: *14mm*
Width: *13.5mm*
Depth: *13.5mm*

Actual size

537 DYED CUBES

These regular little cubes would need a spacer if used together in a string but could also be used in large scale beadweaving, peyote, or brick stitch because they would fit into each other neatly and give a very solid-looking flat surface, which could be used for table mats or hangings.

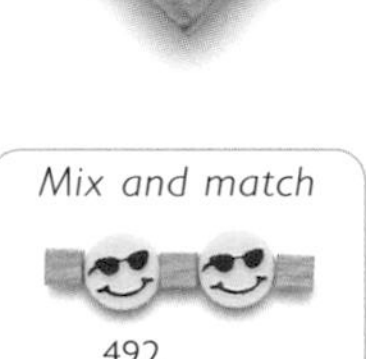

Hole: *Large*
Stringing: *Medium tiger tail or heavy thread*
Weight: *0.2g*
Other sizes: *None*
Color range: *Medium*

Length: *6mm*
Width: *6mm*
Depth: *6mm*

Actual size

Mix and match
492
10

538 DIAMOND CUT

If these beads were made of stone, glass, or crystal, this dyed and varnished shape would be described as faceted, but the term is not usually applied to wood. Despite their size, these could look quite elegant if alternated with a lighter-colored wood in a round bead of similar or slightly smaller width.

Actual size

Hole: *Large*
Stringing: *Heavy thread or fine cord*
Weight: *2.0g*
Other sizes: *None*
Color range: *Small*

Length: *18mm*
Width: *14.5mm*
Depth: *14.5mm*

Mix and match

CHAPTER 9

Other natural materials

As mentioned in the main introduction, shells are the oldest materials used to make beads. However, as will be shown in this chapter, other natural materials such as bones, seeds, and nuts can also be used. Such beads can be extremely simple (just a seed with a hole, for example); others are cut, shaped, drilled, and polished.

Some of these materials look very much like semiprecious stones, but are lighter. Others are almost indistinguishable from wood. Bone and some horn beads are very similar to ivory, and are a much more responsible alternative (ivory is now illegal in most countries). Bone beads would not be acceptable to many vegetarians, but horn beads could be—although some horn is a byproduct of the meat industry, other types are collected after deer have naturally shed their antlers.

Most beads made of these materials retain their natural colors, sometimes varnished to bring out the beauty. Others are dyed—shell beads are often dyed to give a range of shades, usually pastels, while bone and horn are often darkened, to give the impression of age.

Also included here are beads that have natural materials on the outside, although they may have synthetic resin or similar materials as the main base bead.

The sheer ribbon used with these shell beads softens the look of the necklace, which might otherwise appear rough and sharp.

2

2

32

539 ROUND BURI NUT

The nut of the tropical buri tree is used to make several different kinds of beads. The speckles in these are natural, but the color has been darkened for an antique look. Betel nut can look very similar (see 552). The feel is very similar to bone, and small carvings can look like ivory.

Hole: *Medium*
Stringing: *Medium tiger tail or heavy thread*
Weight: *0.3g*
Other sizes: *6mm, 10mm*
Color range: *Small*
Length: *8mm*
Width: *8mm*
Depth: *8mm*

Actual size

Mix and match
202
10

2

2

32

540 ROUND SEA URCHIN

It would be hard to guess exactly what these beads were made out of: they seem like a stone but are too light for that. Actually they are made from sea urchins. The curves and natural colors give these a very interesting look, and they would work well with agates or wood.

Hole: *Medium*
Stringing: *Medium tiger tail or heavy thread*
Weight: *0.4g*
Other sizes: *6mm, 7.5mm*
Color range: *None*
Length: *8mm*
Width: *9mm*
Depth: *9mm*

Actual size

Mix and match
219
8

2

3

23

541 CARVED ROUND BONE

Bone is used in its own right but has for a very long time also been used to simulate the more expensive ivory (which is, of course, no longer available). These have been carved with a fairly simple pattern and slightly darkened, more so in the dips, for an antiqued look.

Hole: *Large*
Stringing: *Medium tiger tail or heavy thread*
Weight: *1.5g*
Other sizes: *None*
Color range: *Small*
Length: *11mm*
Width: *12.5mm*
Depth: *12.5mm*

Actual size

Mix and match
25
448

542 BLACK BONE

These have been made as plain, slightly uneven, round beads, dyed black on the surface, and then carved to reveal the natural white. This gives a very sharp edge to the color, which would be impossible to achieve by painting the surface after cutting. These need to be stored carefully because dirt can get into the deep cuts and stain the bone.

Hole: *Large*
Stringing: *Medium tiger tail or heavy thread*
Weight: *1.5g*
Other sizes: *8mm*
Color range: *None*

Length: *10mm*
Width: *12mm*
Depth: *12mm*

Actual size

543 FLOWER CARVING BONE

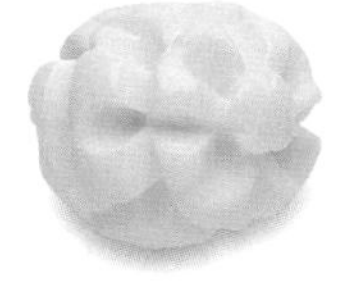

Probably the most deeply carved bone in this chapter, these have a three-layer flower on the front and back, but do tend to lie on their sides in wear and so do not look quite as attractive as they could. The high raised parts tend to catch on fabric so take care when wearing.

Hole: *Large*
Stringing: *Medium tiger tail or heavy thread*
Weight: *1.3g*
Other sizes: *None*
Color range: *Small*

Length: *10mm*
Width: *12mm*
Depth: *12mm*

Actual size

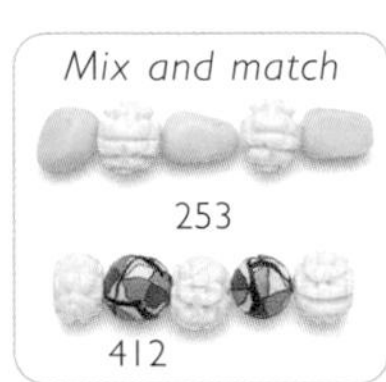

544 FILIGREE BONE

Filigree is the most delicate type of carving: the whole of the inside of the bead is removed to leave only the cut work of the thin surface as a network of lines. These are very light and look fragile but are actually quite strong. Take care not to damage them when using with very hard, heavy beads.

Hole: *Large*
Stringing: *Heavy thread or fine cord*
Weight: *0.5g*
Other sizes: *None*
Color range: *None*

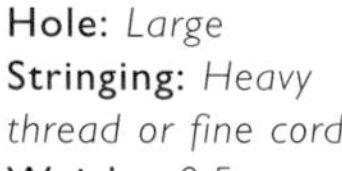

Length: *10mm*
Width: *12mm*
Depth: *12mm*

Actual size

545 BLACK BLEACHED BONE

In contrast to the carving of 542, these have been dyed black but then painted with a substance that bleaches out the color and is then removed. The marks are much less crisp, and the surface is left almost flat. From a short distance, these look as though the lighter parts are inlaid into the darker bead.

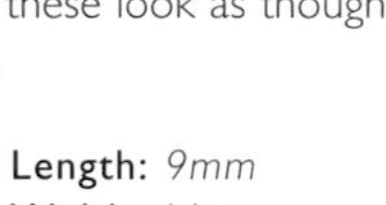

Hole: *Large*
Stringing: *Medium tiger tail or heavy thread*
Weight: *0.8g*
Other sizes: *None*
Color range: *None*
Length: *9mm*
Width: *11mm*
Depth: *11mm*

Actual size

546 BLUE CUT DOT HORN

Horn is usually found in cream, brown, and black, but the maker has dyed these beads a bright blue before shaving off small sections from the round shape to leave flat areas showing the natural color. They are rather uneven but would make a fun addition to light summer jewelry such as necklaces.

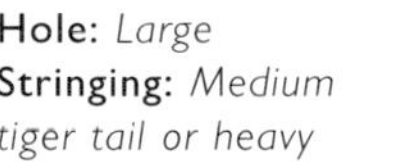

Hole: *Large*
Stringing: *Medium tiger tail or heavy thread*
Weight: *0.8g*
Other sizes: *None*
Color range: *Medium*
Length: *8mm*
Width: *10mm*
Depth: *10mm*

Actual size

547 RIDGED BONE

An ancient bead design, these have been made deliberately rough and darkened to look old, too. These beads would work well as spacers with heavily antiqued metals, aged unglazed or crackle-glazed ceramic, or frosted glass that could look sea-worn. They could also be used as a main bead with an eclectic mix of found objects.

Hole: *Large*
Stringing: *Medium tiger tail or heavy thread*
Weight: *0.5g*
Other sizes: *8mm, 10mm*
Color range: *Small*
Length: *6mm*
Width: *9mm*
Depth: *9mm*

Actual size

548 LAMINATED SHELL

Handmade and covered with tiny sections of pastel dyed shell, these are slightly irregular in size, shape, and color, which only adds to their charm. A whole strand of these could be too overwhelming but a few used as focal beads would be attractive for summer wear or in decorations for a light room.

Actual size

Hole: *Large*
Stringing: *Medium tiger tail or heavy thread*
Weight: *2.6g*
Other sizes: *9mm, 20mm*
Color range: *Medium*
Length: *14.5mm*
Width: *15mm*
Depth: *15mm*

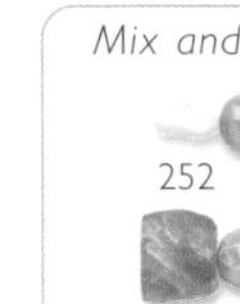

Mix and match

252

250

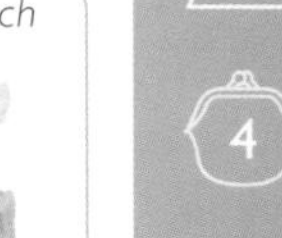

549 ROUND HORN

Horn is often naturally lighter on the surface and darker beneath (see 562), and this has been taken advantage of here by carving deeply into the beads to expose the underlayer. The horn may have been heated and pressed to form the rounded shape before carving. The surface color is attractively uneven.

Actual size

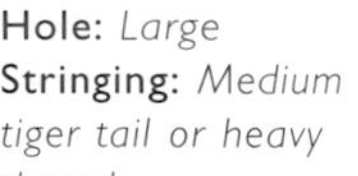

Hole: *Large*
Stringing: *Medium tiger tail or heavy thread*
Weight: *2.8g*
Other sizes: *None*
Color range: *None*
Length: *15mm*
Width: *16mm*
Depth: *16mm*

Mix and match

555

223

550 SEED RUDRAKSHA

Rudraksha are seeds grown in the Nepal region (although they may originally be from Indonesia), and they have been drilled and used as beads for centuries. They are said to have healing properties, especially good for stress relief and circulatory problems, as well as being very beautiful.

Hole: *Large*
Stringing: *Medium tiger tail or heavy thread*
Weight: *1.1g*
Other sizes: *Variable*
Color range: *None*
Length: *14mm*
Width: *14mm*
Depth: *14mm*

Actual size

Mix and match

271

461

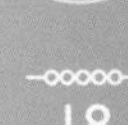

551 CARVED CINNABAR

Cinnabar is actually a mineral, and varies in tone from bright scarlet to deep brick red, but most beads called "cinnabar," mainly made in China, are made of layers of lacquer derived from tree sap. This can be dyed many colors, but black and red (see 571) are the most common. These are carved with good luck symbols.

Actual size

Hole: *Medium*
Stringing: *Medium tiger tail or heavy thread*
Weight: *2.3g*
Other sizes: *None*
Color range: *Small*

Length: *15mm*
Width: *15mm*
Depth: *15mm*

Mix and match

591
418

552 NATURAL BETEL NUT

Betel nuts are more commonly known for their slight stimulant effect, and are often chewed (along with the leaves) by those who live in the parts of Asia where the tree is grown. Because the stimulant is addictive and has side effects, using the nut to make beads seems far preferable.

Hole: *Medium*
Stringing: *Medium tiger tail or heavy thread*
Weight: *0.2g*
Other sizes: *8mm*
Color range: *None*

Length: *6mm*
Width: *7mm*
Depth: *7mm*

Actual size

Mix and match

456
19

553 MOSAIC SHELL

Little barrel shapes with rounded ends are useful as spacers, or at the back of a necklace to add length without too much distraction from the main beads. These are shaped from mosaic shells, and have attractive patches of creams and browns to break up the plain color, making them suitable for use with most natural materials.

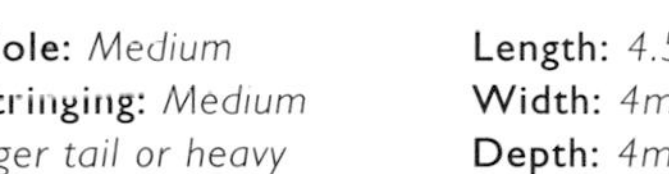

Hole: *Medium*
Stringing: *Medium tiger tail or heavy thread*
Weight: *0.2g*
Other sizes: *None*
Color range: *None*

Length: *4.5mm*
Width: *4mm*
Depth: *4mm*

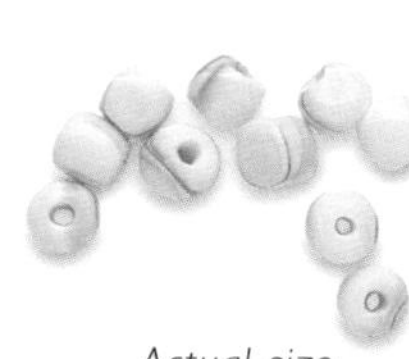
Actual size

Mix and match

593

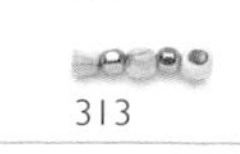
313

554 OVAL BONE

Plain or dyed bone is available in many simple shapes, and this is one of the most useful. Ovals are suitable for almost any style of jewelry and can be employed as spacers because they allow most types of beads strung on either side to move easily.

Hole: *Large*
Stringing: *Medium tiger tail or heavy thread*
Weight: *0.3g*
Other sizes: *9mm, 12mm*
Color range: *Small*

Length: *8mm*
Width: *6mm*
Depth: *6mm*

Actual size

Mix and match

200

459

32

555 RIDGED OVAL HORN

The colors on these beads are natural, the dark inside of the horn showing where the lighter surface color has been carved away by turning on a simple lathe. The shape is suitable for all kinds of projects from jewelry to home decor, and the texture makes it easy to hold, so one would make an excellent zipper pull.

Hole: *Large*
Stringing: *Medium tiger tail or heavy thread*
Weight: *1.0g*
Other sizes: *None*
Color range: *None*

Length: *15.5mm*
Width: *10mm*
Depth: *10mm*

Actual size

Mix and match

374

508

17

556 BLACKENED BONE

Actual size

Almost the opposite to 542, these bone beads have been carved and then dipped into black dye or paint that has been quickly wiped off the surface so that it only remains in the engraved pattern. Some smearing and darkening remains on the exterior, though, so the color change is not as crisp as for 542.

Hole: *Large*
Stringing: *Medium tiger tail or heavy thread*
Weight: *2.2g*
Other sizes: *12mm*
Color range: *None*

Length: *25mm*
Width: *9mm*
Depth: *9mm*

Mix and match

369

542

10

10

557 HAIR PIPE HORN

This shape is known as a hair pipe and is popular in Native American-style beadwork. These are made of naturally dark horn but may have been dyed to make them absolutely black and even in color. Small round beads between these will help the movement of the piece.

Actual size

Hole: *Large*
Stringing: *Heavy thread or fine cord*
Weight: *1.1g*
Other sizes: *Many*
Color range: *Small*

Length: *25mm*
Width: *8mm*
Depth: *8mm*

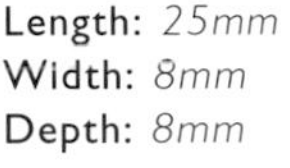

Mix and match
375
434

11

558 HAIR PIPE BONE

As for 557 but this time made of natural-colored bone, possibly slightly darkened to look aged. These are good for fringes on leather or suede clothing, bags, and other items, as well as in jewelry. The creamy matte surface works well with opaque semiprecious stones such as turquoise, rhodochrosite, and jasper.

Actual size

Hole: *Large*
Stringing: *Medium tiger tail or heavy thread*
Weight: *1.0g*
Other sizes: *Many*
Color range: *Small*

Length: *24mm*
Width: *6mm*
Depth: *6mm*

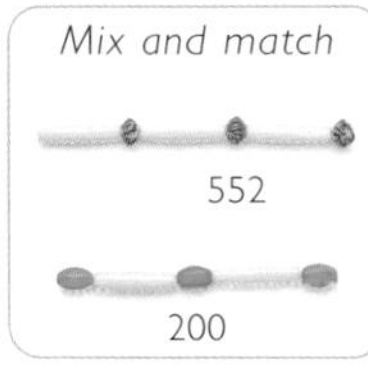
Mix and match
552
200

16

559 TUBE BAMBOO

A very simple type of bead, each bead is merely a section of a slim bamboo cane with the soft center removed to make the hole. These have been drawn on using a basic pyrography technique: a heated tool is used to burn the bamboo leaving lines and dots of charred color.

Hole: *Large*
Stringing: *Heavy thread or fine cord*
Weight: *0.2g*
Other sizes: *None*
Color range: *None*

Length: *16mm*
Width: *6mm*
Depth: *6mm*

Actual size

Mix and match
520
547

560 TUBE BONE

The very deep black polish on these tubes is probably intended to simulate ebony, a wood that is very hard and slow to grow and is worth avoiding for environmental reasons as well as because of the very high price. Plain tubes make good spacers for round beads but do not move well with other flat-ended shapes.

Hole: *Large*
Stringing: *Medium tiger tail or heavy thread*
Weight: *0.7g*
Other sizes: *None*
Color range: *Small*

Length: *13mm*
Width: *7mm*
Depth: *7mm*

Actual size

561 TUBE BURI NUT

The dark ends of these tubes are the outer surface of the buri nut, and the pale translucent color of the main tube is the inside, so these have been cut straight through the whole nut. The ends of the tubes are thus a little irregular and slightly rounded, which makes a strand of these move well.

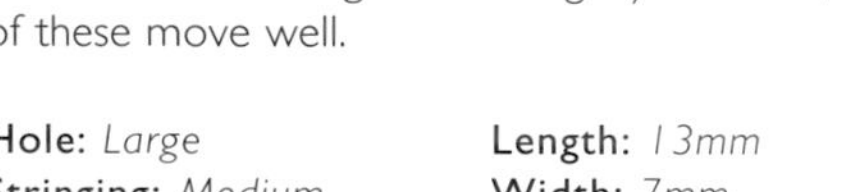

Hole: *Large*
Stringing: *Medium tiger tail or heavy thread*
Weight: *0.7g*
Other sizes: *None*
Color range: *Small*

Length: *13mm*
Width: *7mm*
Depth: *7mm*

Actual size

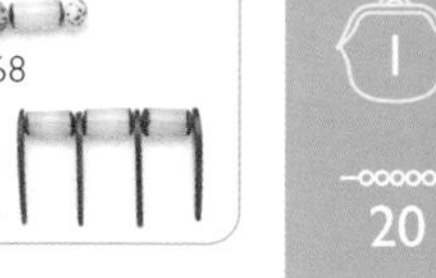

562 TUBE HORN

Perhaps one of the most simple beads available, each of these is a slice taken through a narrow section of horn, and the inside color shows at the ends, which have been smoothed and drilled. The naturally irregular shape and color on the outside of the horn only add to the appeal.

Hole: *Large*
Stringing: *Heavy thread or fine cord*
Weight: *0.9g*
Other sizes: *None*
Color range: *None*

Length: *11mm*
Width: *10mm*
Depth: *10mm*

Actual size

563 CRACKLED TUBE HORN

The crackle pattern in these horn pieces is natural but may have been enhanced. Because the cracks look rather like the matrix often seen in turquoise this type of horn is often dyed to simulate the stone. These thick short tubes will require fairly wide rounded spacers to allow a strand to drape properly.

Hole: *Large*
Stringing: *Medium tiger tail or heavy thread*
Weight: *2.9g*
Other sizes: *8mm*
Color range: *Small*

Length: *15.5mm*
Width: *14mm*
Depth: *14mm*

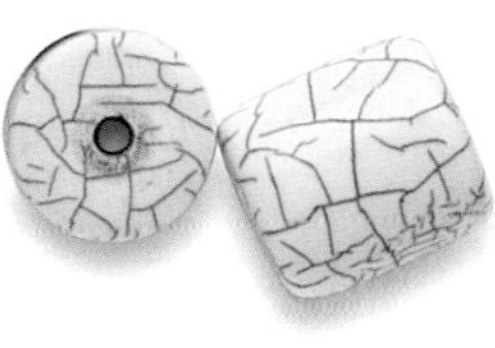

Actual size

Mix and match

19

275

17

564 MULTIHOLE HORN

These tubes, oval in cross section, have more holes through them than any other bead in this book. They can be strung along their length, across the width, or through the middle in the narrowest direction. Use these to create a complex network, or choose a direction and add small beads from other holes for extra decoration.

Actual size

Hole: *Medium*
Stringing: *Medium tiger tail or heavy thread*
Weight: *3.9g*
Other sizes: *None*
Color range: *None*

Length: *31mm*
Width: *12mm*
Depth: *7mm*

Mix and match

522

31

9

565 SCRIMSHAW WORK TUBE BONE

This oval tube has been lightly engraved with a flower on one side and a sprig of leaves on the other; the engraving was then darkened with ink or paint, which takes well in the lines but wipes off the polished surface. This technique is called scrimshaw work, traditionally done on ivory but now mainly seen on bone.

Hole: *Large*
Stringing: *Medium tiger tail or heavy thread*
Weight: *1.7g*
Other sizes: *None*
Color range: *None*

Length: *15mm*
Width: *10mm*
Depth: *6.5mm*

Actual size

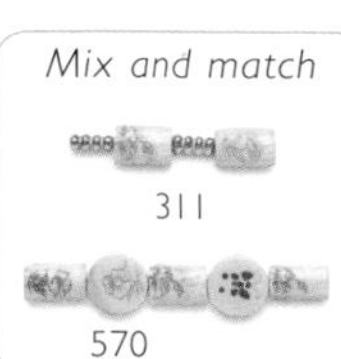

Mix and match

311

570

17

566 OVAL TIGER COWRIE

Made from four pieces of tiger cowrie shell, these are not a natural shape, although they do look very like a flattened seashell. The flat ovals are more regular and more comfortable to wear than a simple drilled shell, such as 567 or 568, without the loss of much of the beauty of the material.

Actual size

Hole: *Medium*
Stringing: *Medium tiger tail or heavy thread*
Weight: *3.9g*
Other sizes: *Variable*
Color range: *None*

Length: *25mm*
Width: *17mm*
Depth: *7mm*

Mix and match

294

448

567 VARNISHED KAPOT SHELL

The two halves of shell have been cleaned out and then fixed together and varnished to give them a wet look, as though they have just come out of the sea. Shells that have been deliberately drilled to wear as decoration technically count as beads, and the earliest beads known at the time of writing are pierced shells 75,000 years old.

Actual size

Hole: *Medium*
Stringing: *Medium tiger tail or heavy thread*
Weight: *5.0g*
Other sizes: *Variable*
Color range: *None*

Length: *25mm*
Width: *20mm*
Depth: *18mm*

Mix and match

539

420

568 NATURAL COCKLES

Prepared like 567, these cockle shells are hard to string because the rather small holes are far apart across a hollow shape, so it can be difficult to get the threading material through to other side. A long fine needle would help, but if it is too flexible, it could get caught inside the shell.

Actual size

Hole: *Small*
Stringing: *Fine tiger tail*
Weight: *3.7g*
Other sizes: *Variable*
Color range: *None*

Length: *23mm*
Width: *14.5mm*
Depth: *14mm*

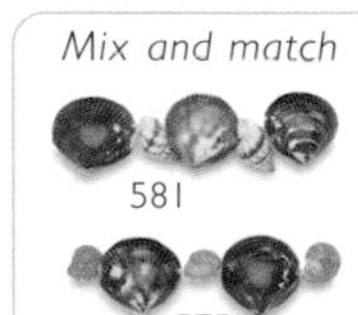

Mix and match

581

575

569 OWL FACE BONE

Both sides of this disk have been carved into the face of an owl with dark spots added in the eyes. Due to the direction of the hole, these would look best strung vertically, perhaps at the sides of a necklace, or it could be dangled on a head pin (629) as part of an earring or descending from a strand.

Actual size

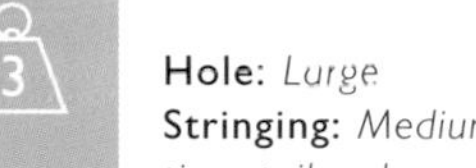

Hole: *Large*
Stringing: *Medium tiger tail or heavy thread*
Weight: *2.3g*
Other sizes: *None*
Color range: *Small*

Length: *17mm*
Width: *17mm*
Depth: *6.5mm*

Mix and match

500

549

15

570 INLAID BONE

One side of these thick disks is engraved with a scrimshaw flower (see 565) but the other has been more deeply carved to leave open spaces, which were then filled with resin with tiny multicolored grains of shell or stone. The hole is drilled at a slight angle to the butterfly image.

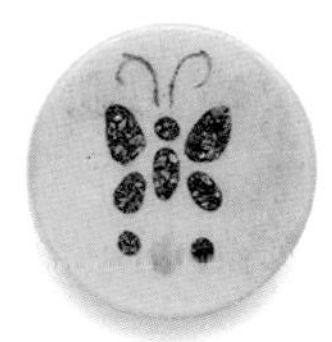

Hole: *Medium*
Stringing: *Medium tiger tail or heavy thread*
Weight: *2.1g*
Other sizes: *None*
Color range: *None*

Length: *15.5mm*
Width: *15.5mm*
Depth: *5.5mm*

Actual size

Mix and match

213

137

17

571 DISK CINNABAR

One of the standard cinnabar colors (see 551) simulating the original mineral. These have been cast or pressed rather than hand carved, so the pattern is a little less crisp, particularly at the edges of some of these beads. The main, central symbol means "good luck" in Chinese.

Hole: *Medium*
Stringing: *Medium tiger tail or heavy thread*
Weight: *1.7g*
Other sizes: *None*
Color range: *Small*

Length: *15mm*
Width: *15mm*
Depth: *10mm*

Actual size

Mix and match

551

513

17

572 LENTIL HORN

This type of horn is naturally amber in color and translucent, unlike the horn used for 579 (for example). It is also rather more fragile. Lentil shapes are excellent spacers because their curved surfaces allow even beads with flat ends the same width as themselves to move easily.

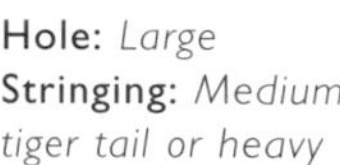

Hole: *Large*
Stringing: *Medium tiger tail or heavy thread*
Weight: *0.3g*
Other sizes: *None*
Color range: *Small*

Length: *4mm*
Width: *11.5mm*
Depth: *11.5mm*

Actual size

63

573 HEISHE SHELL

Heishe are made by cutting disks out of shell, usually using the whole thickness of whatever shell is in use, and drilling a hole at the center of the circle. It can be done with very basic tools, and so these are some of the earliest beads known. Ostrich egg shells and nut shells can also be used.

Hole: *Medium*
Stringing: *Fine tiger tail*
Weight: *0.1g*
Other sizes: *Many*
Color range: *Large*

Length: *2.5mm*
Width: *5mm*
Depth: *5mm*

Actual size

100

574 LAMINATED PAUA SHELL

Thin layers of paua shell (from a species of abalone found near New Zealand) have been added to both sides of these flat disks. Although a rainbow of color can sometimes be seen in this shell, greens and blues with fine black lines are most common. The edges of the beads show black, which is probably a resin.

Hole: *Medium*
Stringing: *Medium tiger tail or heavy thread*
Weight: *0.2g*
Other sizes: *None*
Color range: *None*

Length: *8mm*
Width: *8mm*
Depth: *3mm*

Actual size

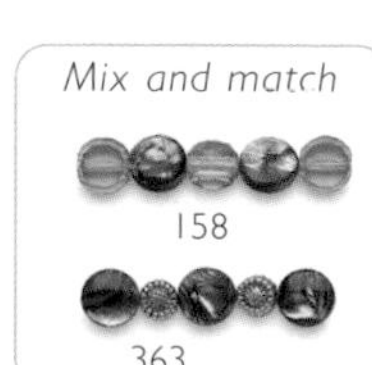

32

1
2
25

575 NATURAL EBONIUM SHELL

Fairly flat, these have been drilled through the natural opening in the same direction as that opening: this makes them easy to string and allows them to lie flat in use showing the spiral on their sides. The disadvantage is that small beads can go inside the shell, through the natural opening, so extras may be needed for the length required.

Hole: *Medium*
Stringing: *Fine tiger tail*
Weight: *0.4g*
Other sizes: *Variable*
Color range: *None*

Length: *10mm*
Width: *11mm*
Depth: *6mm*

Actual size

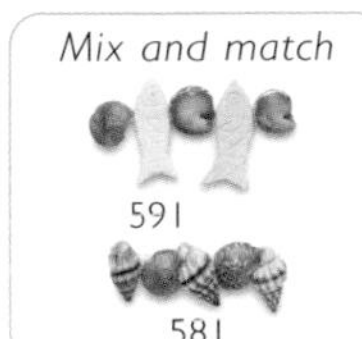

Mix and match
591
581

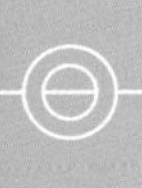

2
3
21

576 DONUT HORN

The same horn as 572, these can also be dyed or even lightened to a yellow color. These small donuts are drilled through both sides, so they could be used through the large hole as a ring bead, dangled from one hole on a head pin (629), or strung with a small bead to fit into the middle.

Hole: *Medium*
Stringing: *Fine tiger tail or medium thread*
Weight: *0.3g*
Other sizes: *None*
Color range: *Small*

Length: *12mm*
Width: *12mm*
Depth: *3mm*

Actual size

Mix and match
219
8

2
3
25

577 SQUARE LAMINATED PAUA SHELL

The same construction as 574, these are thin and so would make a magnificent choker or bracelet, either on their own or with small spacers. If they are to show their flat decorative sides rather than the black edges along the curve at the bottom of a necklace, they will need more distance between them.

Hole: *Medium*
Stringing: *Medium tiger tail or heavy thread*
Weight: *0.4g*
Other sizes: *None*
Color range: *None*

Length: *10mm*
Width: *10mm*
Depth: *4mm*

Actual size

Mix and match
392
487

578 BLACK LIP RECTANGLES SHELL

Cut from the flat parts of large shells and polished on the edges, these have been drilled across the top so that they will dangle from a strand. With small rounded beads between them and used at the bottom curve of a necklace these will fan out, or they would drop elegantly from a choker worn on a long slim neck.

Actual size

Hole: *Medium*
Stringing: *Medium tiger tail or heavy thread*
Weight: *1.3g*
Other sizes: *None*
Color range: *None*

Length: *8mm*
Width: *25mm*
Depth: *2.5mm*

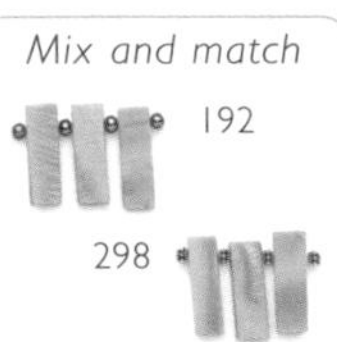

Mix and match

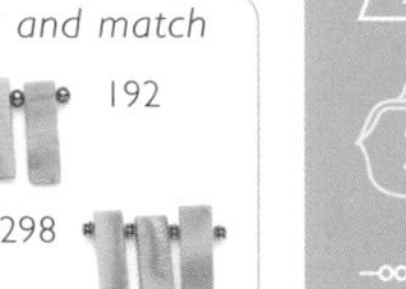

2
3
32

579 POLYGON HORN

To make these beads, the horn has been heated and pressed into a square tube shape. This has then been cut into cubes, and the corners of the cubes cut at an angle; this leaves the outer, lighter horn layer showing as a diamond shape on the flat faces, while the darker inside of the horn shows elsewhere.

Hole: *Large*
Stringing: *Medium tiger tail or heavy thread*
Weight: *1.0g*
Other sizes: *None*
Color range: *None*

Length: *11mm*
Width: *10mm*
Depth: *10mm*

Actual size

Mix and match

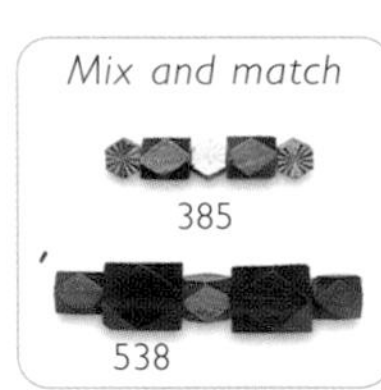

23

580 DOUBLE PYRAMID CINNABAR

Because bicone beads are two cones that meet in the middle, this shape could be called a bipyramid. The beads are carved from cinnabar resin (see 551) and would make a fine strand on their own. They are also very useful spacers where a larger shape with some texture is needed without distracting from the focal beads.

Actual size

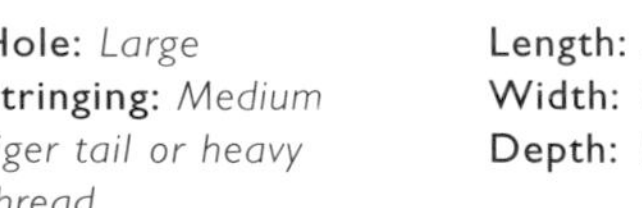

Hole: *Large*
Stringing: *Medium tiger tail or heavy thread*
Weight: *1.0g*
Other sizes: *None*
Color range: *Small*

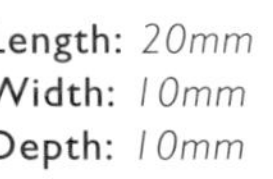

Length: *20mm*
Width: *10mm*
Depth: *10mm*

Mix and match

13

581 NATURAL NASA SHELL

There are a number of similar spiral shells to be found, and they may be drilled through the edge by the opening like these so they dangle or through the tip so that they lie along the string. The latter are usually difficult to string, depending on the drilling, because the thread may have to follow the spiral inside the shell.

Hole: *Large*
Stringing: *Fine tiger tail*
Weight: *0.4g*
Other sizes: *Variable*
Color range: *None*
Length: *7.5mm*
Width: *15mm*
Depth: *10mm*

Actual size

Mix and match

34

582 NATURAL CEBU LILY SHELL

Unlikely as it seems, the color of these shell pieces is natural. Used together in a strand these will point in all directions making a mass of curves and spirals that looks wonderful yet simple. Alternatively, space them out between toning beads to add texture and color.

Hole: *Medium*
Stringing: *Medium tiger tail or heavy thread*
Weight: *0.2g*
Other sizes: *None*
Color range: *None*
Length: *5mm*
Width: *5.5mm*
Depth: *4.5mm*

Actual size

Mix and match

50

583 EVERLASTING SHELL

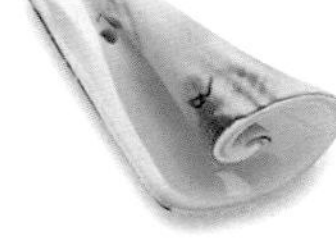

Actual size

Shells cut, polished, and drilled across the narrow end, these look just like some kind of exotic flower. Used together in a strand they will point in all directions and might be rather overwhelming. They are perhaps better used with a long spacer so that they can hang neatly or with a long triangle bail (626) to make earrings.

Hole: *Large*
Stringing: *Medium tiger tail or heavy thread*
Weight: *2.5g*
Other sizes: *5mm, 7mm*
Color range: *None*
Length: *15mm*
Width: *24mm*
Depth: *13mm*

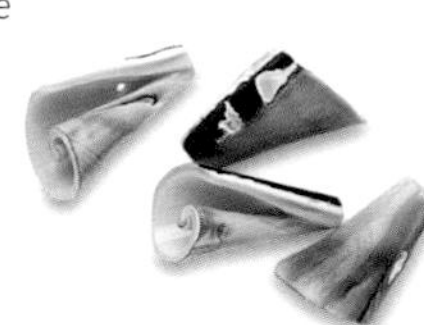

Mix and match

17

584 JOB'S TEARS SEED

These seeds, known as Job's tears, are the most easily available ready-drilled seeds sold for use as beads, but many other dried seeds and pulses could also be used, pierced or drilled at home if necessary. Store the beads, and jewelry made of such items, in a dry place since damp could cause them to spoil.

Hole: *Small*
Stringing: *Fine tiger tail or medium thread*
Weight: *0.1g*
Other sizes: *Variable*
Color range: *None*

Length: *10mm*
Width: *6mm*
Depth: *6mm*

Actual size

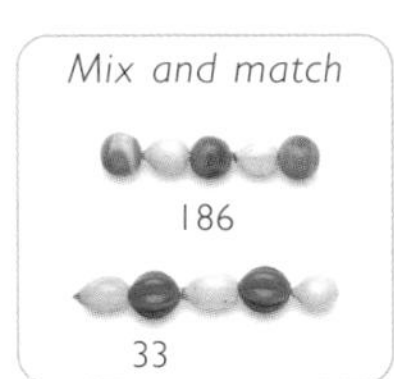

585 CHIP RED LIP SHELL

Drilled chips with smoothed edges, sometimes done in a tumble polisher, are made from almost all kinds of shell used for jewelry. These have an attractive color rather like red coral, and are from a shell called "red lip." Try such random chips alternated with smaller heishe (573), for an unusually textured strand.

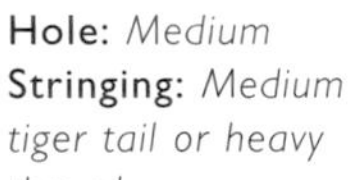

Hole: *Medium*
Stringing: *Medium tiger tail or heavy thread*
Weight: *0.2g*
Other sizes: *None*
Color range: *None*

Length: *2.5mm*
Width: *6mm*
Depth: *5mm*

Actual size

100

586 SECTION PEN SHELL

These are sections cut from a pen shell, which is a fan-shaped mussel. The hole is at the wide end and this, along with the flat back, allows the curved top of these beads to hang and lie neatly. Because they are so thin, they can move fairly well alone but may look more eye-catching if separated slightly.

Actual size

Hole: *Small*
Stringing: *Fine tiger tail or medium thread*
Weight: *0.4g*
Other sizes: *None*
Color range: *None*

Length: *2mm*
Width: *30mm*
Depth: *4.5mm*

125

587 **POINTS** ABALONE SHELL

Although they look rather like teeth, these are pieces cut from a shell, smoothed, then drilled. They are somewhat irregular and will stick up in all directions if strung together without spacers. Even with small spacers care must be taken not to string them too tightly or they will not lie down.

Actual size

Hole: *Medium*
Stringing: *Medium tiger tail or heavy thread*
Weight: *1.6g*
Other sizes: *Variable*
Color range: *None*

Length: *6mm*
Width: *30mm*
Depth: *6mm*

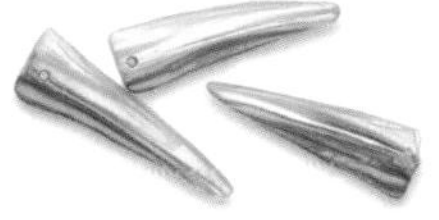

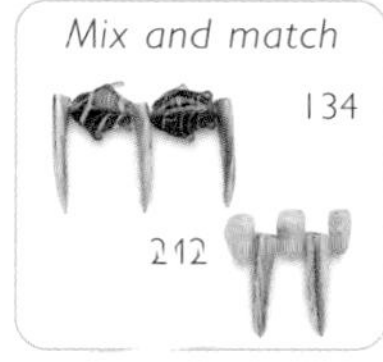

588 **DRUMSTICK** BONES

This bone has been shaped, dyed, and then not only carved but also hollowed out to leave quite a thin shell in the area of the spiral, although the ends are more solid. The middle section is so open that any stringing material can be seen, and with care, seed beads could be used on the thread inside these beads.

Actual size

Hole: *Large*
Stringing: *Heavy thread or fine cord*
Weight: *1.8g*
Other sizes: *None*
Color range: *Small*

Length: *38.5mm*
Width: *7mm*
Depth: *7mm*

589 **SHAPED** BAMBOO WITH PAUA INLAY

These shapes have been cut from thick bamboo and a circular section has been removed from the front of each one and replaced with a disk of paua shell (see 574) after varnishing. They will only lie neatly together if the curve is very sharp so use separators if a gentler curve is required.

Actual size

Hole: *Medium*
Stringing: *Medium tiger tail or heavy thread*
Weight: *7.6g total*
Other sizes: *None*
Color range: *None*

Length: *50mm total*
Width: *39mm longest*
Depth: *5.5mm*

590 LEAF BONE

A large slice of bone shaped into a leaf, this is intended to hang from the stalk, and the weight and length will prevent any turning, so it is decorated with veins on one side only. Rather large for most jewelry applications, these would work well stitched around the neck of a summer T-shirt or in home decor projects.

Actual size

Hole: *Medium*
Stringing: *Medium tiger tail or heavy thread*
Weight: *4.4g*
Other sizes: *None*
Color range: *Small*

Length: *19mm*
Width: *47mm*
Depth: *4mm*

Mix and match

555

349

14

591 FISH BONE

Cut from a flat section of bone, these fish shapes are decorated on both sides. Unusually for fish beads, they are drilled across the widest point, not along the length or through the mouth end, so they hang with the heads above the strand. Spacers are needed for even hanging because the tail is slightly wider than the hole.

Actual size

Hole: *Medium*
Stringing: *Medium tiger tail or heavy thread*
Weight: *1.4g*
Other sizes: *None*
Color range: *Small*

Length: *12.5mm*
Width: *28mm*
Depth: *4mm*

20

592 OWL BONE

Many creatures are carved from bone and drilled for beads in this way. This fully three-dimensional little owl has no thin parts, but some animals can have quite fragile legs and other features and so need to be stored carefully. These are often antiqued or dyed before carving, like 542.

Hole: *Medium*
Stringing: *Medium tiger tail or heavy thread*
Weight: *2.5g*
Other sizes: *None*
Color range: *Small*

Length: *19mm*
Width: *14mm*
Depth: *8mm*

Actual size

14

CHAPTER 10

Other materials

This chapter covers the beads that do not fit into any of the other categories. There are probably other unusual materials in use, but these are the ones commonly available for purchase. Items with holes in them that are used for jewelry, but were not intended for that purpose (generally known as "found items"), are not included.

Some of these beads, such as the rolled paper and felt beads, can be made in the home with very little equipment (as of course can polymer clay beads, see page 158). The elastic cord elaborately worked over the wooden bead could be homemade, too, by those experienced in Chinese knotting. Others, such as the rubber-spiked beads, rely on modern machinery.

The candy beads are, of course, not intended to be kept or worn for long, but they do seem to last pretty well if varnished carefully (hang them to dry). They should, however, be kept away from small children and anyone who may not realize they have been coated, since it could be dangerous to swallow varnish.

Soft, puffy ball beads contrast with spiky rolled paper in this bracelet. It is very light to wear.

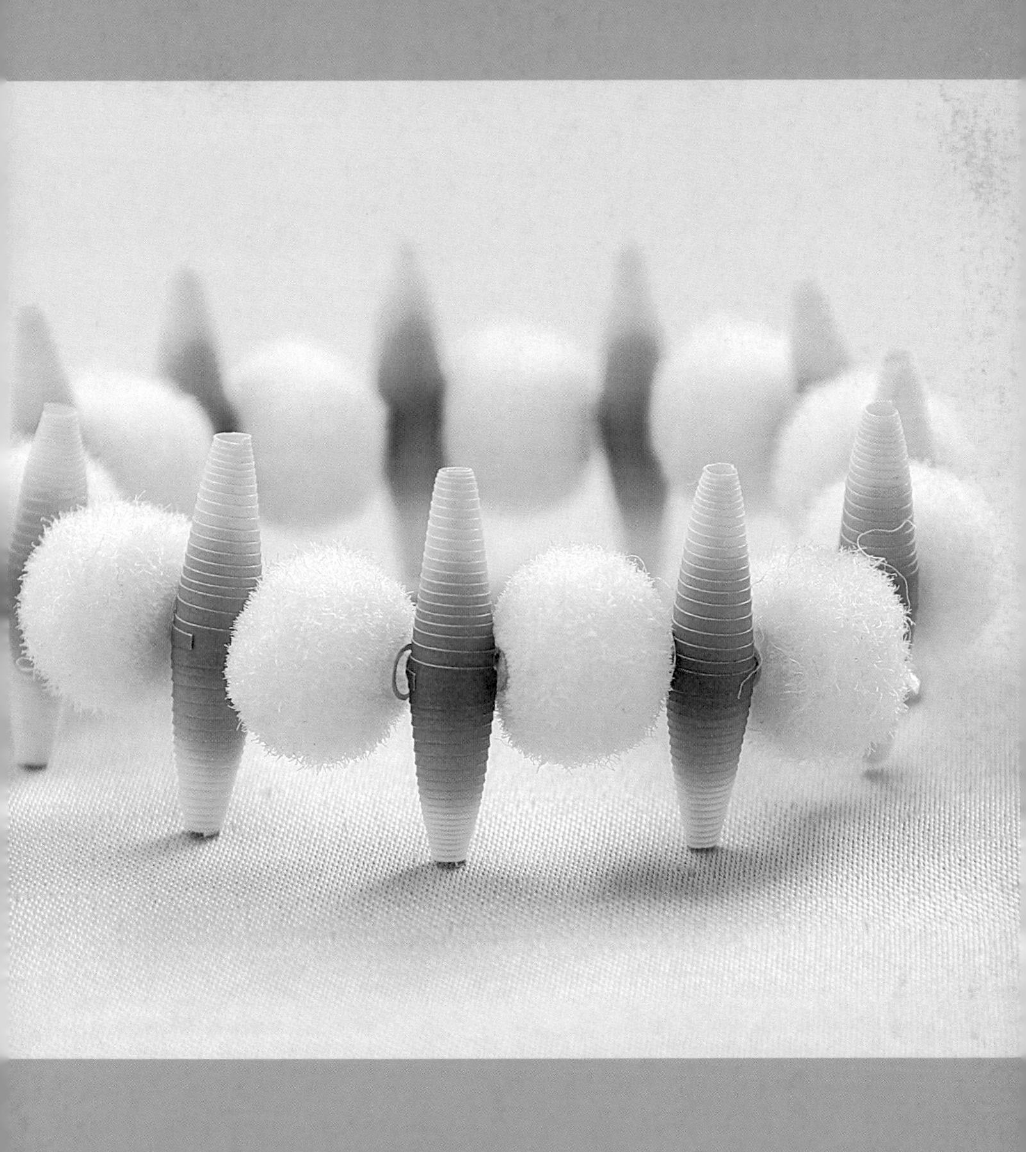

2

25

593 COVERED SILK

This is a plastic bead completely covered with strands of silk glued in neatly at the holes. Silk shimmers in the light, so these have a lovely, soft look. Unfortunately, the seam line of the underbead can just be seen. Avoid using these with rough beads because the individual strands of silk could be cut or frayed.

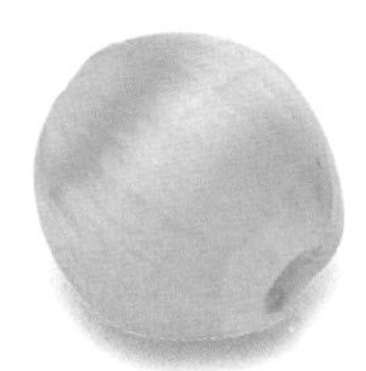

Hole: *Large*
Stringing: *Medium tiger tail or heavy thread*
Weight: *0.5g*
Other sizes: *None*
Color range: *Medium*

Length: *10mm*
Width: *10mm*
Depth: *10mm*

Actual size

Mix and match

543

124

1

13

594 POM-POM SYNTHETIC FIBERS

A ball of synthetic fuzzy fibers, this uses what appears to be a narrow transparent drinking straw to form the hole. These beads glow in the dark after exposure to light, so they could be useful for a decoration near a light switch or in a fun bracelet to wear at a dark club.

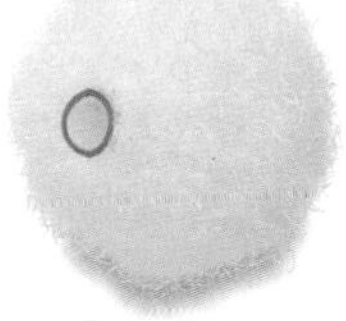

Actual size

Hole: *Large*
Stringing: *Fine tiger tail or medium thread*
Weight: *0.5g*
Other sizes: *10mm, 15mm*
Color range: *Small*

Length: *20mm*
Width: *20mm*
Depth: *20mm*

Mix and match

475

481

1

20

595 PRESSED PAPER

Pressed paper shapes are made for crafters to use as a base, and these beads could be covered with scraps of glued paper, stitched or woven seed beads, paint, glitter, ink and embossing powder, thread, ribbon, and coiled cord, among other things. Some pressed paper beads are only half pierced, so it may be necessary to finish the hole with a thick needle.

Actual size

Hole: *Large*
Stringing: *Fine tiger tail or medium thread*
Weight: *0.5g*
Other sizes: *Many*
Color range: *None*

Length: *13mm*
Width: *16mm*
Depth: *16mm*

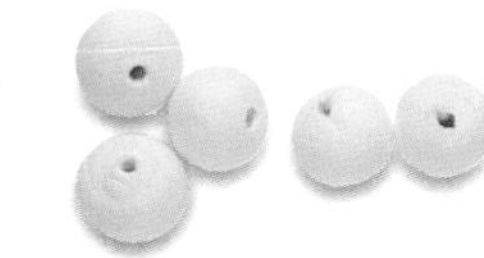

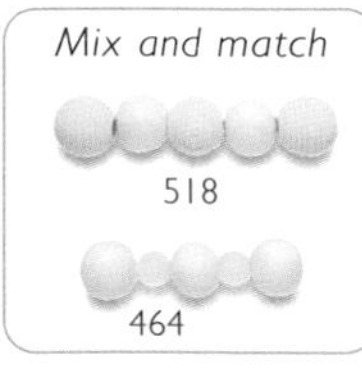

Mix and match

518

464

596 ROUND FELT

These beads are made from cleaned, combed, dyed sheep's wool, wetted with hot soapy water and rubbed and rolled in the hand until felt is formed. They were pierced with a needle and hung on a thick thread to dry. Felt beads tend to be rather irregular but are soft and warm to wear.

Hole: *Medium*
Stringing: *Medium thread*
Weight: *8.0g*
Other sizes: *None*
Color range: *Small*

Length: *16mm*
Width: *16mm*
Depth: *16mm*

Actual size

16

597 CHINESE KNOT ELASTIC CORD

Thick elastic cord has been worked around a large, round, wooden bead in a six-layer Chinese ball knot. The start and end of the cord are hidden under one of the wraps. This is an excellent bead to use in home decor projects but is perhaps a little bulky for most jewelry applications.

Hole: *Large*
Stringing: *Cord*
Weight: *18.0g*
Other sizes: *None*
Color range: *Small*

Length: *32mm*
Width: *37mm*
Depth: *37mm*

Actual size

8

598 SPIKES RUBBER

Round, black, solid silicon rubber base beads have had many tiny dots of molten rubber added to their surfaces; each dot was pulled away as it set to form a spike. These spikes look sharp and very uncomfortable to wear, but they are actually soft and feel almost fluffy against the skin.

Hole: *Medium*
Stringing: *Medium tiger tail or heavy thread*
Weight: *0.5g*
Other sizes: *12mm*
Color range: *Medium*

Length: *10mm*
Width: *14mm*
Depth: *14mm*

Actual size

25

599 CLASSIC ROLLED PAPER

Rolled paper beads have been made almost since the first creation of paper. The strip used to create this shape is an isosceles triangle rolled from base to tip. The longer the triangle is in relation to its base the rounder the bead will appear. This paper is shaded from dark to light along the strip, so the bead is shaded too.

Actual size

1

2

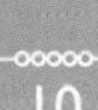

10

Hole: *Medium*
Stringing: *Fine tiger tail or medium thread*
Weight: *0.3g*
Other sizes: *None*
Color range: *Medium*

Length: *25mm*
Width: *7mm*
Depth: *7mm*

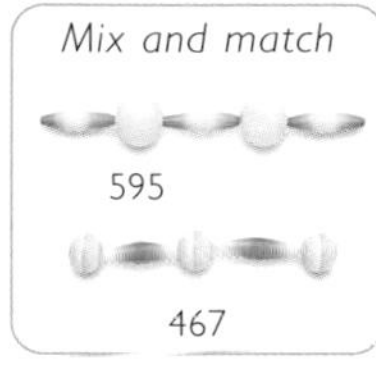

Mix and match

595

467

600 TUBE PAPER

Paper tubes are rolled from straight strips: the thicker the paper and longer the strip, the wider the bead. The pattern on these has been printed so that the glued end of the paper exactly overlaps the same point on the layer underneath, so there is no break in the design around the bead.

Actual size

1

2

10

Hole: *Medium*
Stringing: *Fine tiger tail or medium thread*
Weight: *0.8g*
Other sizes: *None*
Color range: *Small*

Length: *25mm*
Width: *8mm*
Depth: *8mm*

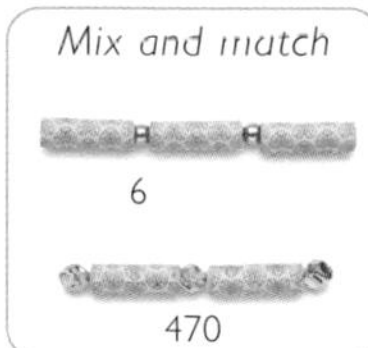

Mix and match

6

470

601 SPACER PAPER

Disk spacers can easily be made from the ready-cut strips of paper used for quilling (paper filigree), and the split tip of a quilling tool is helpful to roll them tightly. This paper is silver faced, but many colors are available, some with silver or gold edges that will show on the flat sides of the disk.

1

2

84

Hole: *Medium*
Stringing: *Fine tiger tail or medium thread*
Weight: *0.1g*
Other sizes: *None*
Color range: *Small*

Length: *3mm*
Width: *7mm*
Depth: *7mm*

Actual size

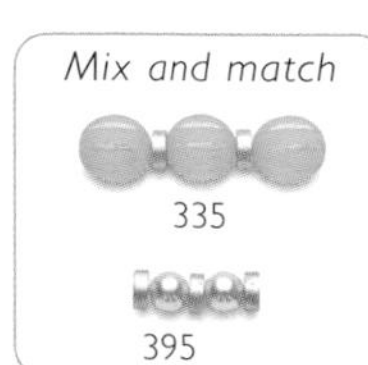

Mix and match

335

395

602 FLOWER CANDY

Edible candy beads, bracelets, and necklaces have been around for a very long time and are still available, mostly in the shape of 603. Do not introduce children to these too young, or they may not understand that most beads cannot be eaten and may choke on ordinary ones.

Hole: *Large*
Stringing: *Elastic*
Weight: *0.5g*
Other sizes: *None*
Color range: *Mixed*

Length: *5mm*
Width: *11mm*
Depth: *11mm*

Actual size

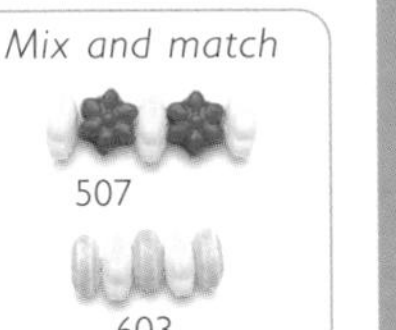

Mix and match

50

603 RING CHEWING GUM

The same shape as most candy beads but fractionally larger, these are, amazingly, made from chewing gum. A child old enough to chew gum may be old enough to recognize that these are special, but check to be sure they will not break teeth or choke through trying to chew other beads.

Hole: *Large*
Stringing: *Elastic*
Weight: *0.4g*
Other sizes: *None*
Color range: *Mixed*

Length: *5mm*
Width: *10mm*
Depth: *10mm*

Actual size

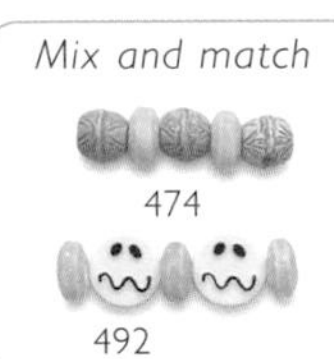

Mix and match

1

50

604 POLISHED STONE AND RESIN SET

Fragments of stone, not semiprecious, have been set into resin, and these beads have then been cut and shaped from the resulting block and finally polished. These could be used together in the middle of a necklace or spread out along the piece.

Mix and match

554

461

Hole: *Medium*
Stringing: *Medium tiger tail or heavy thread*
Weight: *27g total*
Other sizes: *None*
Color range: *Small*

Length: *90mm*
Width: *43mm*
Depth: *7mm*

One third of actual size

3

3

CHAPTER 11

Findings

Findings are the little parts, usually metal, used to attach parts of jewelry pieces together, to add decorative features, to space rows of beads, and as fastenings.

One alternative to using a clasp or catch on a necklace is to make the strand continuous (knotting the thread ends together), and large enough to go over the head. For bracelets, elastic cord can be used so that the piece can be pulled over the hand. In most other types of jewelry, findings will be necessary.

Clasps and catches are attached in different ways, depending on the stringing material in use. Two types of ends for thick cords, including leather cord are shown, and medium to heavy thread can be finished in a knot cup to give a neat, safe end. Fine thread is often finished by working it several times around a loop of small beads, sometimes with the findings in the middle of the loop, then taking it back into the beadwork. Tiger tail and similar materials are usually used with round or tube crimps, with the finding added before the material is looped back into the crimp.

Simple findings can be made from stiff wire, as long as it is strong enough to ensure that the shape will not pull out in wear.

Findings can improve or spoil a beaded piece. They should be chosen to blend well with the beadwork, as does the hook and loop clasp shown here.

167

605 JUMP RING

Jump rings are so called because they are used to connect sections of jewelry, jumping the gap between one and the other. They are available soldered closed or with a cut and should be twisted open (like a door) rather than pulled open (like a book) so as not to strain the metal, which would make it difficult to close them fully again.

Weight: *0.2g*
Other sizes: *Many*
Color range: *Small*

Length: *1.5mm*
Width: *7mm*
Depth: *7mm*

Actual size

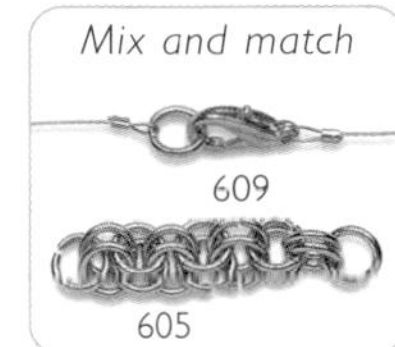
Mix and match
609
605

250

606 OVAL JUMP RING

Oval jump rings can be neater with flatter pieces of beadwork because they give enough space to attach two sections of jewelry but do not sit as high as would a round jump ring of similar length. The cut being on the side also helps to prevent either part of the jewelry rubbing on it and perhaps opening the gap in wear.

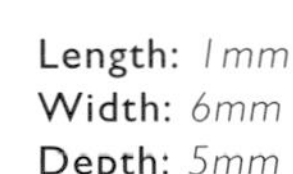

Weight: *1.0g*
Other sizes: *Many*
Color range: *Small*

Length: *1mm*
Width: *6mm*
Depth: *5mm*

Actual size

Mix and match
608
606

250

607 SPLIT RING

A double ring of wire makes up a split ring. Much larger split rings are often used as key ring parts. To hang something with a closed loop on to a split ring, slide it under one end and twist the ring until the top of the loop reaches the middle.

Weight: *1.0g*
Other sizes: *Many*
Color range: *Small*

Length: *1mm*
Width: *6mm*
Depth: *5mm*

Actual size

Mix and match
607
609

608 BOLT RING

A common catch for inexpensive jewelry and cheap chains, the bolt ring has a sprung sliding section, which allows it to be held open and then hitched onto a ring or loop at the other end of a necklace or similar, then released to close. Always check that the slide works before adding these to your work.

Hole: *Medium*
Weight: *0.1g*
Other sizes: *Many*
Color range: *Small*

Length: *9mm*
Width: *6mm*
Depth: *1.5mm*

Actual size

609 LOBSTER CLAW OR TRIGGER CLASP

Several shapes of lobster claw catch are available. Instead of the slide of a bolt ring, these have a hinged section with a spring to keep it in place. They are generally more robust than a bolt ring, look more interesting, and are easier to use, especially on bracelets. Check the spring before using each one.

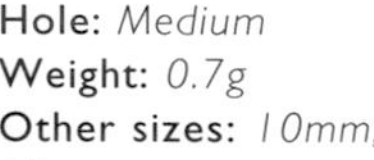

Hole: *Medium*
Weight: *0.7g*
Other sizes: *10mm, 15mm*
Color range: *Small*

Length: *13mm*
Width: *7mm*
Depth: *3mm*

Actual size

610 TOGGLE OR RING AND BAR CLASP

These are fairly simple, but this kind of catch is available in many forms. The bar must be able to pass through the ring and turn to hold the ends in place, so it must be able to lie flat. Large beads next to the catch can prevent this so check before finishing and add small beads if necessary.

Hole: *Medium*
Weight: *1.3g*
Other sizes: *None*
Color range: *Small*

Length: *15mm*
Width: *10mm*
Depth: *3.5mm*

Actual size

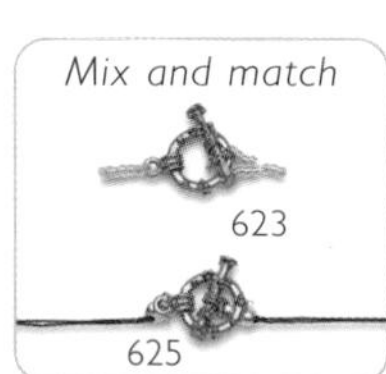

611 BARREL CLASP

The ends of a barrel clasp screw together. This makes a very neat finish with nothing that can catch on clothing and pull open. In this case the loops are loose and need not turn when the clasp is screwed closed or open but check that this is the case when you use them because some are fixed.

Hole: *Medium*
Weight: *0.6g*
Other sizes: *20mm*
Color range: *Small*

Length: *15mm*
Width: *3.5mm*
Depth: *3.5mm*

Actual size

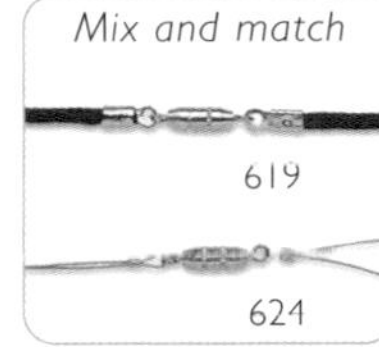

612 THREE-HOLE SLIDE CATCH

Slide catches are usually fairly flat, and they rely on the springiness of the folded metal slider to catch on the inside of the main piece and hold the catch closed. These are made for three-strand necklaces of fairly small beads (for larger beads, the loops need to be farther apart). As they age some sliders break at the fold.

Hole: *Medium*
Weight: *0.7g*
Other sizes: *None*
Color range: *Small*

Length: *15mm*
Width: *10mm*
Depth: *2.5mm*

Actual size

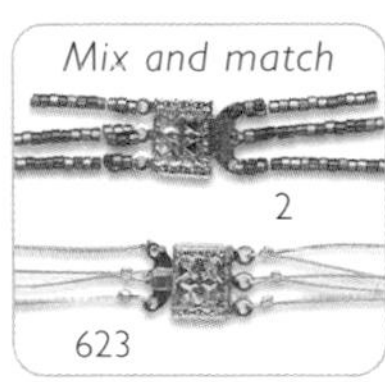

613 HOOK AND DOUBLE LOOP

One end of the double loop (or 8 ring) is intended to be attached to the piece and the other is for the hook to go into in use. Since the hook is not closed these catches can come undone fairly easily, but they are suitable for pieces where the weight of the beads holds the ends taut.

Hole: *Large*
Weight: *0.4g*
Other sizes: *None*
Color range: *Small*

Length: *24mm*
Width: *8mm*
Depth: *1mm*

Actual size

614 BEAD SLIDE

This catch works on the same principle as 612, but the main section is shaped into a ridged, round bead so that the fastening of the jewelry piece is less noticeable and can be incorporated into the design, perhaps by using several similar beads elsewhere. Some screw clasps are made inside semiprecious beads.

Hole: *Medium*
Weight: *0.6g*
Other sizes: *None*
Color range: *Small*

Length: *15mm*
Width: *8mm*
Depth: *8mm*

Actual size

Mix and match

623

625

615 MAGNETIC CLASP

The only thing that holds the two sides of this clasp together is magnetism. This makes it very easy to use but does mean that a sharp tug can open the clasp even when the wearer does not mean it to. It is also not suitable for bracelets if the wearer is working with magnetic media such as computer disks.

Hole: *Medium*
Weight: *1.2g*
Other sizes: *None*
Color range: *Small*

Length: *15mm*
Width: *5mm*
Depth: *5mm*

Actual size

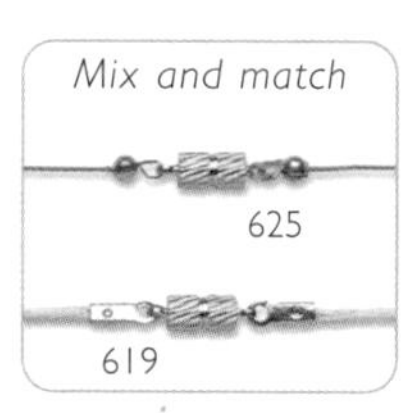

Mix and match

625

619

616 EYEGLASS HOLDERS

These can be added to both ends of a strand of beads; the other side of each loop slides over one arm of a pair of eyeglasses, so that they can be worn around the neck for easy access. Holders are very useful for reading glasses, ensuring that they can always be found when needed.

Hole: *Large*
Weight: *0.4g*
Other sizes: *None*
Color range: *Small*

Length: *18mm*
Width: *6mm*
Depth: *5mm*

Actual size

Mix and match

1

30, 624

617 DOMES FOR MULTISTRAND ENDS

When many strands of small beads are used together, they may not need to lie separately (see 621) at the ends and can instead be attached onto an eye pin (630) and pulled into a dome for a neat finish, making a loop on the outer side to attach to a clasp. Cones and other similar shapes are also available.

Hole: *Medium*
Weight: *0.4g*
Other sizes: *None*
Color range: *Small*

Length: *8mm*
Width: *8mm*
Depth: *8mm*

Actual size

Mix and match

605, 609, 629

2, 629

618 COIL CORD END

A coil of stiff wire, this has one loop standing up that can be attached to either side of a clasp in order to connect the ends of cord or leather thong. Soft or slippery materials can be glued into these, but a cord or thong can usually be held in place simply by squashing flat the first loop of wire, using pliers.

Hole: *Large*
Stringing: *Cord*
Weight: *0.4g*
Other sizes: *None*
Color range: *Small*

Length: *11mm*
Width: *4mm*
Depth: *4mm*

Actual size

Mix and match

610

608, 606

619 FOLDING CORD END

Place the cord into the channel of these flatter ends and use pliers to fold the two sides in to grasp it. This is best used with flatter cords where the sides can be made to overlap on to each other; otherwise a little glue may be necessary to keep these ends in place.

Hole: *Medium*
Stringing: *Cord*
Weight: *0.2g*
Other sizes: *None*
Color range: *Small*

Length: *9mm*
Width: *3.5mm*
Depth: *3.5mm*

Actual size

Mix and match

611

613

620 BEAD CAPS

These are simple filigree metal caps made to fit on to round beads of about ½ inch (12mm) or oval beads with similar sized ends, as additional decoration. Very much more elaborate bead caps are available and those are probably best used with single-color, simply shaped beads to avoid confusing the eye.

Hole: *Medium*
Stringing: *Tiger tail or thick thread*
Weight: *0.5g*
Other sizes: *None*
Color range: *Small*

Length: *1mm*
Width: *10mm*
Depth: *10mm*

Actual size

Mix and match

63

471

621 THREE-STRAND END

Findings like this, sometimes plain or with even more decoration than shown here, are used to allow the strands of multistrand pieces to lie neatly separated rather than bunching together on to one loop at the ends of the piece. The loops should be far enough apart to allow for the width of the beads used.

Actual size

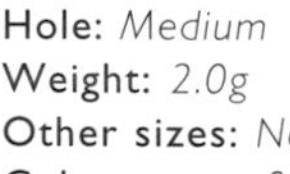

Hole: *Medium*
Weight: *2.0g*
Other sizes: *None*
Color range: *Small*

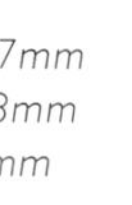

Length: *17mm*
Width: *23mm*
Depth: *3mm*

Mix and match

1

613, 80

622 PLAIN STRAND SPACER

These spacers are used to hold strands separate along the length of a bracelet or at the sides of a necklace. These are thin and plain so they blend in, but wide elaborate versions are also available. Holes must be far enough apart to allow for the width of the beads, unless bunching is an intended part of the design.

Hole: *Medium*
Stringing: *Tiger tail or thick thread*
Weight: *0.1g*
Other sizes: *None*
Color range: *Small*

Length: *1mm*
Width: *18mm*
Depth: *2mm*

Actual size

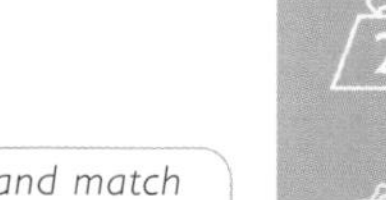

Mix and match

2

1

623 ROUND CRIMP

Crimps are used to hold the two ends of a loop of tiger tail or any other stiff stringing material at the ends of a strand of beads. They should be crushed with crimping pliers to create a dip in one side, then folded over neatly with the other section of these pliers. See also 624.

Hole: *Medium*
Stringing: *Tiger tail*
Weight: *0.1g*
Other sizes: *3mm*
Color range: *Small*

Length: *2mm*
Width: *2mm*
Depth: *2mm*

Actual size

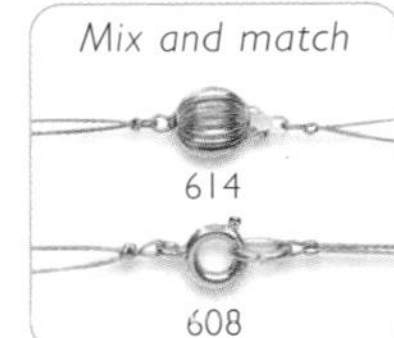

125

624 TUBE CRIMP

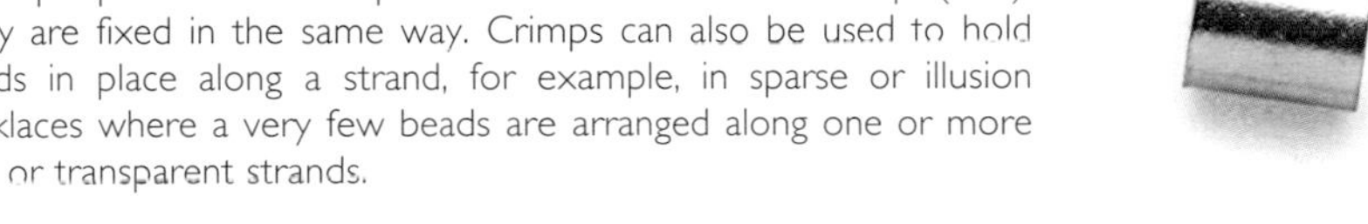

Some people find tube crimps neater to use than round crimps (623). They are fixed in the same way. Crimps can also be used to hold beads in place along a strand, for example, in sparse or illusion necklaces where a very few beads are arranged along one or more thin or transparent strands.

Hole: *Medium*
Stringing: *Tiger tail*
Weight: *0.1g*
Other sizes: *1mm, 3mm*
Color range: *Small*

Length: *2mm*
Width: *2mm*
Depth: *2mm*

Actual size

125

625 KNOT CUP

Knot cups can be used at the ends of pieces made using soft stringing materials. The thread is knotted, glued if necessary, and trimmed, and then the sides of the crimp are closed over the knot. The tongue is then made into a loop. Some knot cups are arranged so that the thread must be passed through a hole before knotting.

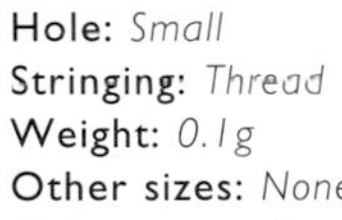

Hole: *Small*
Stringing: *Thread*
Weight: *0.1g*
Other sizes: *None*
Color range: *Small*

Length: *6.5mm*
Width: *3mm*
Depth: *3mm*

Actual size

626 TRIANGLE BAIL

These can be used by pushing the two spikes at the opening into either side of a bead with a fairly short hole, to add findings at the end of a piece where the beads are held horizontally (such as right-angle weave), or by threading it on a strand so that it lies perpendicular to its hole direction.

Weight: *0.1g*
Other sizes: *None*
Color range: *Small*

Length: *8mm*
Width: *4mm*
Depth: *3mm*

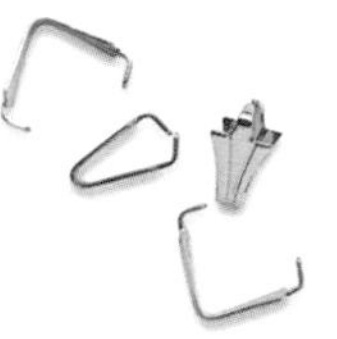

Actual size

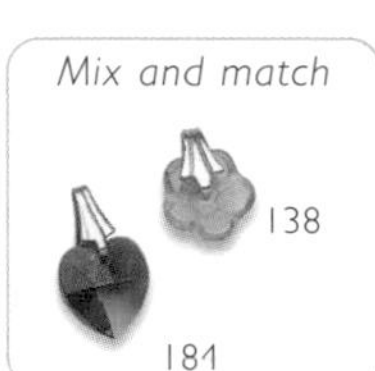

627 ICE PICK BAIL

So called because of the shape, the spikes of this bail can go into the holes of a fairly flat bead, drilled front to back, so that it hangs facing outward from a strand of beads or at the ends or bottom of a piece.

Weight: *0.1g*
Other sizes: *Many*
Color range: *Small*

Length: *7mm*
Width: *5mm*
Depth: *1mm*

Actual size

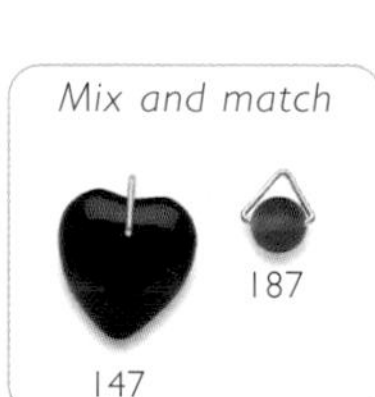

628 BEAD HOLDER

These are made to hang and display very special beads, which can be changed easily. The bottom section unscrews so that any bead that will fit into the space and has a large enough hole can be added without removing the top part from its chain or strand of beads.

Actual size

Hole: *Medium*
Stringing: *Tiger tail or thread*

Weight: *0.7g*
Other sizes: *None*
Color range: *Small*

Length: *3mm*
Width: *36mm*
Depth: *3mm*

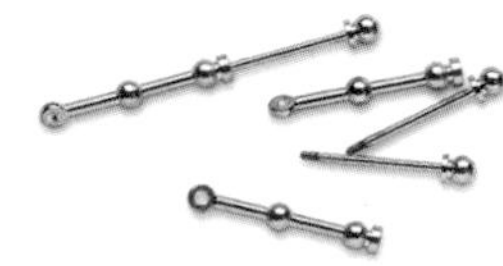

629 HEAD PIN

Head pins are merely long pieces of wire with a head, like the head of a sewing pin, to stop small beads from sliding off the end. They are used to hang single or multiple beads for earrings or down from strands such as necklaces. Cut the top to length and make a loop to finish the pin for hanging.

50% of actual size

Weight: *0.2g*
Other sizes: *Many*
Color range: *Small*

Length: *54mm*
Width: *3mm*
Depth: *3mm*

Mix and match
96
145

630 EYE PINS

Like head pins, these are finished with a loop for hanging, but they also have a loop at the bottom for hanging more pieces. Other variations on the head pin have flat wide paddles at one end, decorated metal shapes, fixed half-drilled beads, or even set stones.

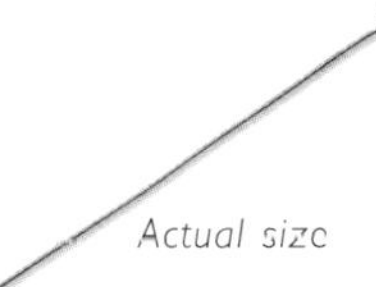
Actual size

Hole: *Medium*
Weight: *0.1g*
Other sizes: *Many*
Color range: *Small*

Length: *35mm*
Width: *2mm*
Depth: *2mm*

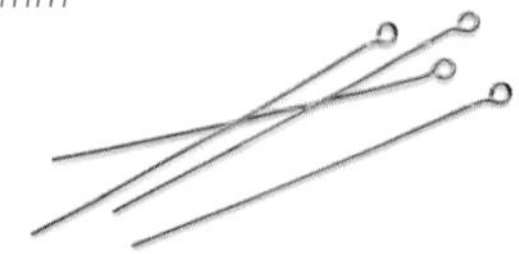

Mix and match
476
145

631 EAR STUD

These studs for pierced ears have a butterfly fixing at the back to hold them in place and a loop to add the beads, perhaps using head or eye pins (629 and 630). Studs with flat pads on to which decorations can be glued are also widely available. The ball is not required but adds to the look of the finished earring.

Hole: *Large*
Weight: *0.3g*
Other sizes: *None*
Color range: *Small*

Length: *14mm*
Width: *7mm*
Depth: *3mm*

Actual size

Mix and match

629, 268
630, 142

632 FISH HOOK EAR WIRE

Also for pierced ears, these are known as fish hooks because of the shape. The ball and coil are decorative and cheaper versions without these are also available. Open the loop as for jump rings (605) to hang the beadwork so as not to stress the metal and hold upside down when closing to avoid the ball slipping into the loop.

Actual size

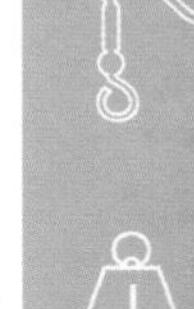

Hole: *Large*
Weight: *0.2g*
Other sizes: *None*
Color range: *Small*

Length: *20mm*
Width: *8mm*
Depth: *1mm*

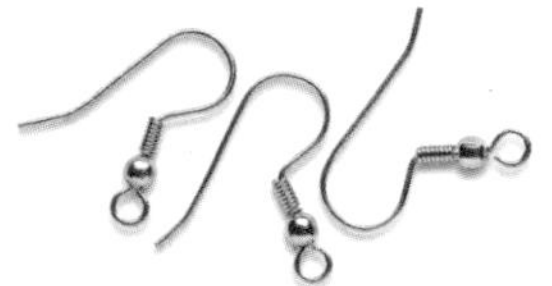

Mix and match
626, 147
629, 144

633 SCREW EARRINGS

Perhaps a little old-fashioned but still available and quite widely used for unpierced ears because they pinch less than clips (634). The loop is cut and can be opened as for 632, but because it is a little fragile it may be preferable to open the loop on the hanging part, if possible.

Actual size

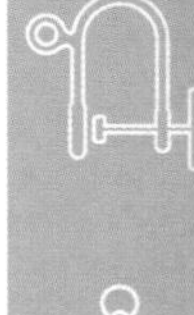

Hole: *Large*
Weight: *0.7g*
Other sizes: *None*
Color range: *Small*

Length: *15mm*
Width: *10mm*
Depth: *1.5mm*

Mix and match
630, 131
630, 256

634 CLIP EARRINGS

Easier to put on and take off than 633, these are probably the most common findings in use for beaded earrings for those without pierced ears. Again the loops are split but fragile, so if possible, open the loops on the hanging part or put wires or threads directly through and finish underneath.

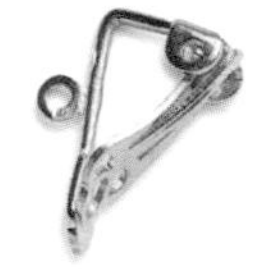

Actual size

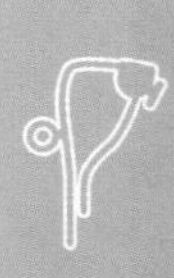

Hole: *Large*
Weight: *0.7g*
Other sizes: *None*
Color range: *Small*

Length: *16mm*
Width: *10mm*
Depth: *7mm*

Mix and match
629, 496
626, 174

How to buy beads

Buying beads can be a very simple operation: go to a store or Internet site or mail-order catalog, choose something you like and can afford, hand over your money, and get your beads.

But there are things you may want to consider in order to make the most of your money and not end up with a lot of beads you cannot use in a proposed project—although for many beadworkers unused beads can spark a whole new set of projects!

MAKING SELECTIONS

When following a design from a book or magazine, it is usually best to use the recommended beads, especially if the sizes and shapes have been carefully chosen so that they fit together well. Weight must also be taken into account—substituting heavier beads might require a stronger stringing material, much lighter ones might prevent the piece from hanging properly. If you intend to adapt a pattern design, use this book to compare the types of beads suggested with the ones you propose to use. Don't feel too restricted, though—if only one size and shape of bead is used in a pattern, you can probably substitute smaller or larger beads in that shape, adjust

the stringing material if necessary, and make a different sized item.

For original designs, consider the method you are using and bear in mind the advice about stringing materials for different types of beads. Complex stitches may require beads that fit together in a certain way—for example, bicones and fairly small round beads work well for right-angle weave, whereas cube beads might not sit well in the pattern and could be more suitable for peyote, brick stitch, or weaving.

In many cases, a single or multistranded design is inspired by some particularly appealing beads, and it is then a matter of finding others to complement them. Consider the combinations of materials—a light, soft material will not last well if the beads to either side are rough and heavy, but a few heavier beads may be needed to give a necklace a good feel and hang. Different shapes can work well together, especially if they are the same width, such as cubes with rounds, or ovals or crystals with disk spacers.

Having said all that, do not be afraid of random, eclectic mixes of beads—just be sure that the stringing materials can cope with the wear from the roughest and heaviest beads.

FINDING SOURCES

Your local bead store, if you are lucky enough to have one, should be your first port of call. There is no doubt that the best way to choose beads

and make combinations is to actually have them in your hands. That way there is no doubt about colors, relative weights, widths (most beads are cataloged by length), and so forth.

Beads are also available by mail order, either from catalogs or from the Internet. Good color catalogs are often expensive, but many companies will refund the price on a first order. The problem with catalogs is that photographs don't always reproduce the exact colors of the beads, and in most cases the beads are shown from one angle only. Moreover, not all pictures are actual size, although most are in modern catalogs. Do not be afraid to write or call to ask for more details—a good supplier will want to help.

Online catalogs often give more information, but the colors may be less accurate. If color is critical, order a small amount to begin with or confirm that beads may be returned if they do not match (accept the fact that you will lose the cost of postage). Sizes may also look wrong on-screen, so it is important to check that the description of the beads matches your requirements.

In both mail-order cases, sample cards with actual beads sewn on to them are often available for beads that come in large color ranges—such as seed beads, tube beads, and bugles—so that you can choose colors with confidence. Because these are usually handmade they are expensive but worth it if you are concerned about accuracy.

SAVING MONEY

Most beads are cheaper in bulk. This does not necessarily mean a huge number of beads—sometimes a pack of ten beads is far better value than buying them singly, and often a pack of fifty or a temporarily strung whole strand is actually cheaper than buying just the required number. A lot of bead stores will tell you if, for example, you could have a bulk bag for only a little more than the handful of individual beads you have selected, but some places require the customer to ask about discounts for larger quantities. When using mail order, however, be sure the beads are exactly what you want before buying in bulk (unless they can be returned). Buy one or two as a sample, then buy the rest in bulk when you have seen and felt the items.

KEEPING AN INVENTORY

It is always worth having some basic beads on hand for experimental purposes. A good selection would include small metal beads in gold and silver colors, disk spacers, round beads in various sizes of clear glass, a few crystal shapes, cubes and ovals, and a range of seed beads in various colors. These can be used to compare how different colors and sizes look with focal beads, or what shapes work well together, and thus help to plan out what to buy next.

Index

A

abalone shell 228
agate 93
  blue lace 98, 104
  crazy lace 93
  moss 82, 99, 105
aluminum 142
amber: barrel 86
  rough oval 87
  simulated 188
amethyst 82, 90, 100
ancient gem shape, glass 44
ancient symbols, plastic 191
angel, ceramic 177
animal beads: ceramic 162, 177, 178
  fluorite 105
  glass 60, 61
  plastic 195
  wood 206
aquamarine 90
arch, two-hole plastic 191
arrowhead bead, hematite 96
axe head bead, agate 97

B

bails: ice pick 245
  triangle 245
bamboo 218
  with paua inlay 228
banana bead, glass 45
banded bead: ceramic 167
  glass 42
barrel beads: amber 86
  silver 123
  wood 204, 205
base metal: antiqued 140, 141, 143, 146
  bicone 141
  bow 150
  butterfly 157
  and copper 143
  cube 155
  cushion 153
  dangle 157
  disk 147
  donut 146
  drop 143
  face 157
  filigree 140
  hexagon 152
  lentil 147
  oval 141
  rhinestone set 139
  rice 142
  ring 147
  round 136–137, 139
  spacer 148, 153
  spiral 146
  square 154, 155
  tube 142, 150, 151, 152, 156
  wave edge 140
  wheel 149
bead caps 243
bead holder 245
betel nuts 216
bicone beads: base metal 141
  ceramic 164
  crystal 73, 75, 77
  glass 40, 41, 43
  gold 118
  silver 119
blobs: cracked clay 164
  silver 133
block, flat glass 44
bone: disk 222
  drumstick 228
  fish 229
  hair pipe 218
  inlaid 222
  leaf 229
  oval 217
  owl 222, 229
  round 212, 213, 214
  tube 219
brass spacer 148
bugles, glass 16
buri nuts 212, 219
butterfly beads: cloisonné 157
  plastic 195
button beads: glass 62
  pearl 90

C

candy bead 235
cane slice bead 161, 168, 173, 179
carnelian 93, 94, 101
carved beads: bone 213
  cinnabar 216
  wood 202, 203
cat head bead, glass 61
cathedral bead, glass 42
cebu lily shell 226
Celtic knotwork pattern 153, 170
ceramic: angel 177
  animals 162, 177, 178
  banded 167
  bean 167
  bicone 164
  Buddha face 178
  cane slice 173
  cube 175
  donut 174
  drop 175, 176
  flower 179
  heart 178
  impressed 167
  molded diamond 164
  multibead 172
  oval 165, 166
  pillow 174
  ring 170, 173
  round 160, 161, 162, 163
  scarab 173
  simulated 186
  spindle 172
  triangle 179
  tube 168, 169, 170, 171, 172
  vase 176
chewing gum beads 235
Chinese knot: elastic cord 233
  pewter 137
chips: peridot 103
  shell 227
chunk beads: fluorite 103
  glass 59
cinnabar 216, 222, 225
circle bead, silver 131
citrine 101
clasps: barrel 240
  lobster claw (trigger) 239
  magnetic 241
  toggle (ring and bar) 239
clay: cracked 164
  impressed 167
cloisonné: base metal 146, 151, 153, 157
  copper 138
cockle shells 221
coil beads: base metal and copper 143

spacer 148
copper: 138, 140, 146
antiqued 140, 146, 148
cloisonné 138
spacer 148, 149
coral 102
crimps: round 244
tube 244
cross, glass 45
cross-hole bead, silver 131
cube beads: agate 93
base metal 155
carnelian 93
ceramic 175
enameled 155
glass 57–59, 74–75
hematite 93
plastic 189, 190
silver 127
wood 209
curved beads: base metal 151
plastic 189
silver 128
cushion beads: base metal cloisonné 153
copper 146
crystal 70
glass 32, 52
jasper 94
plastic 189
cut glass 33, 39
cut hogans 33
cylinders, glass 15

D

dagger beads, glass 46
dangle, two-stone 157
diamond beads: lapis 95
molded ceramic 164
pewter 153
silver 119
diamond-cut, wood 209
dice, plastic 190
dichroic glass 32, 37, 50, 54, 56, 59
disk beads: base metal 147
bone 222
cinnabar 222
crystal 70–71, 72
glass 34
hematite 91
jade 89
mother-of-pearl 88
plastic 192
pyrite 91
shell 223
silver-plated 117
dog beads, ceramic 177
domes for multi-strand ends 242
donut beads: base metal cloisonné 146
ceramic 174
glass 34, 35
horn 224
jade 96
jasper 97
sodalite 96
drops: amethyst 100
base metal 143
ceramic 175, 176
citrine 101
crystal 77–79
garnet 100
glass 45, 46–49
gold-filled 129
graduated 102
howlite 102
plastic 193
quartz 100
druks 19
drum beads: aluminum 142
base metal 144, 145
drumstick bead, bone 228
duck foot bead, glass 50
dyeable bead 183
dyed glass 57

E

earrings: clip 247
screw 247
earstuds 246
earwires, fish hook 247
ebonium shell 224
elastic cord bead 233
ends: coil cord 242
folding cord 242
three-strand 243
exotic wood 201
eyeglass holders 241

F

face beads: base metal 157
ceramic Buddha 178
glass Chinese 60
plastic 192
faceted glass 33, 39, 40, 42, 43, 44, 46, 47
fan bead, glass 44
felt bead 233
filigree beads: base metal 136, 137
bone 213
gold-plated 110
silver 113, 114
vermeil 112
fish beads: bone 229
glass 61
silver 133
flamework 32
simulated 183
flower beads: base metal 145
candy 235
carnelian 99
ceramic 179
crystal 72
glass 62
jade 98
plastic 197
silver 132
flower-garden beads 161, 179
fluorite 103, 105
frog beads: glass 60
wood 206

G

garnet 84, 87, 91, 100
glass: cut 33, 39
dichroic 32, 37, 50, 54, 56, 59
dyed 57
faceted 33, 39, 40, 42, 43, 44, 46, 47
luster 36, 49, 61
metallic 55, 65
moonstone 36
oil slick 33
silk 58
glow tube 188
gold: bicones 118
rondelles 116
round beads 108
trumpet 129
gold-filled metal: drops 129
lentils 115
oval 123
round 108, 109, 126
tube 124
gold-plated beads 110
goldstone 92

H

hair pipes 218
half-disk, two-hole tiger eye 95
half donut, jasper 97
heart beads: agate 98
  ceramic 178
  crystal 79
  glass 64–65
  plastic 194
  polymer clay 179
  rodonite 98
  silver 132
heishe bead 223
hematite 91, 92, 93, 96
hook and double loop 240
horn: crackled 220
  hair pipe 218
  lentil 223
  oval 217
  polygon 225
  round 214, 215
  tube 219, 220
howlite 102

J

jade 89, 96, 104
  Chinese 98
jasper 97
  leopard-skin 82, 97
  ocean 94

K

kapot shells 221
knot cup 244

L

labradorite 94
lace maker's beads 58
laminated plastic 184, 190
laminated shell 215, 224
lapis lazuli 88, 95
leaf beads: agate 99
  bone 229
  glass 63
  silver 130
lentil beads: base metal 147
  gold-filled 115
letter beads: plastic 192
  polymer clay 174
  silver 132
luck symbols 160, 165, 201
luster glass 36, 49, 61

M

magatama 46
malachite 92
melon shape, plastic 185
metallic glass 55, 65
millefiori bead 35, 53
miracle bead 182
moonstone glass 36
mosaic beads: glass 51
  shell 216
mother-of-pearl 88, 104
mouse bead, plastic 195
multibead shape, ceramic 172
multi-hole, horn 220
multisection, wood 202

N

nasa shell 226
nugget, pewter 156
nuts: betel 216
  buri 212, 219

O

off-center bead 46, 186
oil slick: glass 33
  pearl 85
onyx 83
oval beads: amber 87
  aventurine 86
  base metal 141, 144
  ceramic 165, 166
  crystal 76
  flat 144, 165
  glass 36–40, 42, 53
  pearl 86
  plastic 187
  rhodochrosite 88
  silver 120, 121, 122
  turquoise 87
  wood 205, 206, 207
owl beads: bone 222, 229
  glass 60
  plastic 195

P

paper: pressed 232
  rolled 234
  spacers 234
paua shell 223, 224
  inlay 228
pearls: black 84
  cultured 83
  freshwater 83, 84, 85, 86, 89, 90, 99, 103
  glass simulated 38, 49
  plastic simulated 193
  potato 84
pen shell 227
peridot 103
pewter: antiqued 137
  colored 151, 156
  diamond 153
  nugget 156
  round 136, 137
pillow shape, ceramic 174
pins: eye 246
  head 246
points: abalone 228
  plastic 185
  quartz 101
polygon beads: glass 59
  horn 225
  silver 127
  silver and brass 128
polymer clay: cane slice 161, 168, 173, 179
  heart 179
  letters 174
  round 161, 162, 163
  tube 168, 169
pompom bead 232
pony shape, plastic 186
porcelain 160
  simulated 183
pyramid beads: cinnabar
double 225
  glass 50
pyrite 91

Q

quartz: rose 89, 105
  smoky 101
  strawberry 40
  tourmalinated 100

R

rabbit bead, ceramic 178
rectangle beads: jasper 94
  labradorite 94
  plastic 190, 191
  shell 225
red lip shell 227
redwood 203
resin, stone-set 235
rhodochrosite 88
rice beads: base metal 142
  garnet 87
ring beads: base metal 147
  ceramic 170, 173
  chewing gum 235
  glass 33
rings: bolt 239

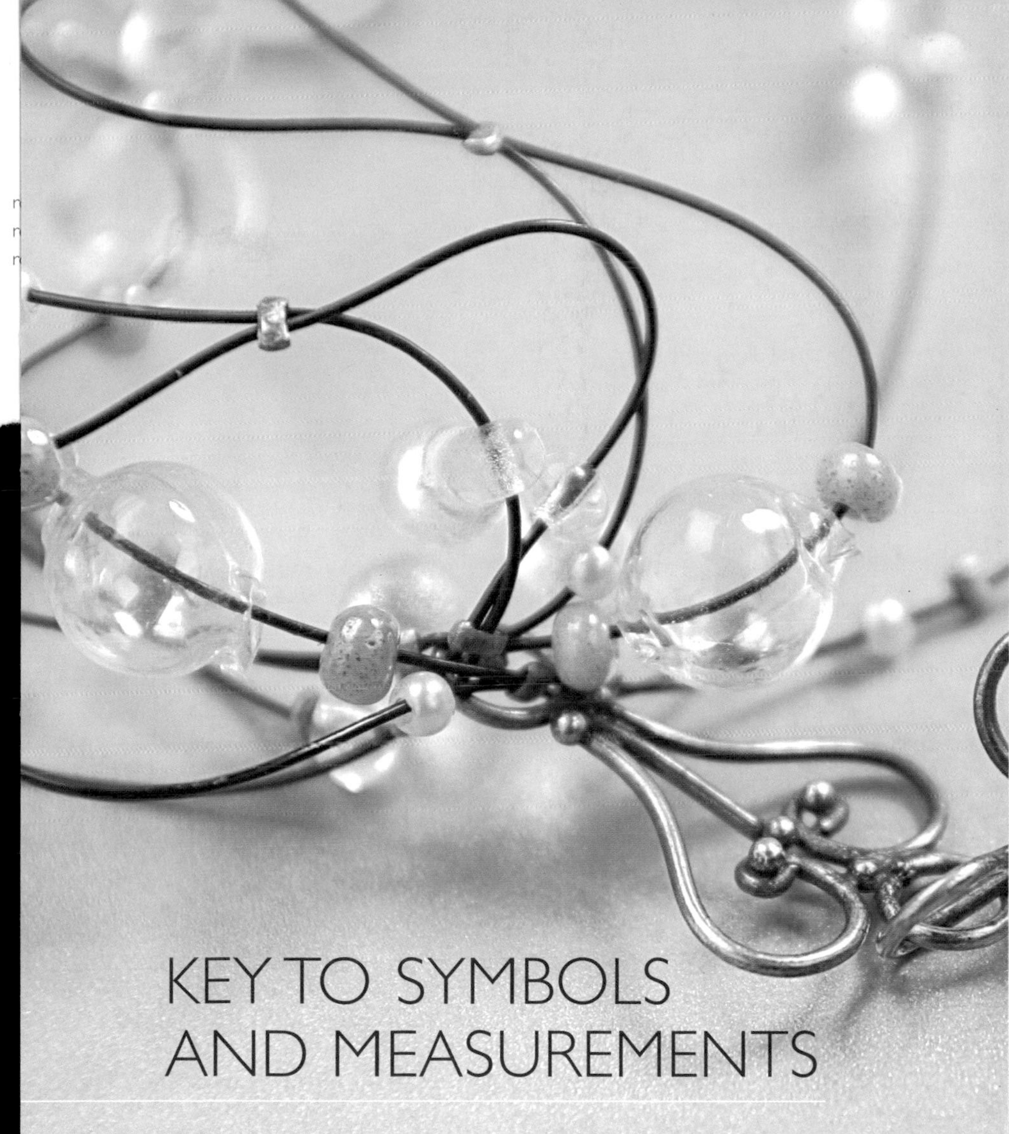

KEY TO SYMBOLS AND MEASUREMENTS

Fold out this flap to find an at-a-glance key explaining all the symbols and measurements used throughout the book.

Resources

The beads and supplies used in this book are widely available through local and online bead shops, bead shows, and mail-order catalogs. Some of the supplies used are from well-known brands. The contact information is listed even though some of these companies do not sell directly to the public.

BUTTONS:
JHB International*
www.buttons.com

BOROSILICATE GLASS BEADS:
Nancy Tobey Glass Beads
www.nancytobey.com

CAST PEWTER BEADS:
Green Girl Studios
www.greengirlstudios.com

DICHROIC GLASS BEADS AND COMPONENTS:
Paula Radke Dichroic Glass Beads*
www.pauluradke.com

ETCHED SHELL PENDANTS AND BEADS:
Lillypilly Designs
www.lillypillydesigns.com

HAND-PAINTED SILK BEADS:
Kristal Wick Creations
www.KristalWick.com

PRESSED GLASS AND GENERAL BEADING SUPPLIES:
Beadcats
www.beadcats.com

SEED BEADS AND GENERAL BEADING SUPPLIES:
Beadalon*
www.beadalon.com

Halcraft USA, Inc.*
www.halcraft.com

Out on a Whim
www.whimbeads.com

Rio Grande
www.riogrande.com

Shipwreck Beads
www.shipwreckbeads.com

Stormcloud Trading Co.
www.beadstorm.com

Thunderbird Supply Company
www.thunderbirdsupply.com

SEMIPRECIOUS STONES AND GENERAL BEADING SUPPLIES:
Fire Mountain Gems
www.firemountaingems.com

SEQUINS AND BUTTONS:
Cartwright's Sequins & Vintage Buttons
www.ccartwright.com

SPECIALTY BEADS AND FINDINGS:
Blue Moon Beads*
www.bluemoonbeads.com

STERLING SILVER CHARMS AND BRACELETS:
Charm Factory, Inc.
www.charmfactory.com

SWAROVSKI CRYSTALS AND PEARLS:
Crystal Beads of Boston
www.crystalbeadsofboston.com

*Wholesale or distributor only

Credits

Quarto would like to thank and acknowledge the following for supplying beads and beaded pieces shown in this book:

Handmade Beads
Roy Ayre T/A GallowGlass
gallowglassbead@aol.com

Pauline Holt
Jazzy Lily Hot Glass
www.jazzylily.com

The Crafty Owl
CraftyUK@aol.com

Leigh Ross
sincereleigh@polymerclaycentral.con

Beaded Pieces
Page 107: Ann Biederman, www.anni22k.com
Pages 81, 211: Monica Boxley, www.monicaboxley.co.uk
Page 199: Stephanie Burnham, www.thebeadscene.com
Pages 12, 67: Gillian Lamb, www.gillianlamb.co.uk
Pages 135, 181, 231: Elise Mann
Pages 159, 236: Kati Torda, www.katitordadagadu.hu
All other photographs and illustrations are the copyright of Quarto Publishing plc. While every effort has been mad to credit contributors, Quarto would like to apologize should there have been any omissions or errors—and would be pleased to make the appropriate correction for future editions of the book.

Author Dedication
This book is dedicated to my husband Ken, without whom my life would hav no shape and no color.